Edited by
Philip Hammond and Edward S. Herman

Degraded Capability: The Media and the Kosovo Crisis

Pluto Press

LONDON • STERLING, VIRGINIA

First published 2000 by Pluto Press
345 Archway Road, London N6 5AA
and 22883 Quicksilver Drive,
Sterling, VA 20166–2012, USA

British Library Cataloguing in Publication Data
A catalogue record for this book is available from
the British Library

ISBN 0 7453 1632 8 hbk

Library of Congress Cataloging in Publication Data
Degraded capability : the media and the Kosovo crisis / edited by
Philip Hammond and Edward S. Herman.
    p. cm.
Includes bibliographical references and index.
   ISBN 0–7453–1632–8
  1. Kosovo (Serbia)—History—Civil War, 1998– 2. Kosovo
(Serbia)—History—Civil War, 1998—Press coverage. 3. Kosovo
(Serbia)—History—Civil War, 1998—Mass media and the war. 4.
Kosovo (Serbia)—History—Civil War, 1998—Propaganda. I.
Hammond, Phil. II. Herman, Edward S.
  DR2087 .D44 2000
  949.703—dc21

00–008500

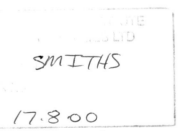
Designed and produced for Pluto Press by
Chase Production Services, Chadlington, OX7 3LN
Typeset from disk by Stanford DTP Services, Northampton
Printed in the European Union by TJ International, Padstow

bility

'This extraordinary volume provides a comprehensive analysis of the role of the media in advancing Nato's Kosovo war. It brings together the world's leading authorities on the subject and the combination makes for an overpowering volume. For those who wish to understand just how flawed the media are in our democracies, this is necessary reading. For those who wish to make our media and our governments serve more democratic aims, this is mandatory reading.' Robert W. McChesney, Associate Professor, Institute of Communications Research, University of Illinois at Urbana-Champaign

'A shocking exposé of the war crime of our times and its uncritical media coverage. Its description of how Nato's war was fought and reported around the world is essential reading for students, scholars, and citizens concerned about democracy in our country and the world.' George Gerbner, Dean Emeritus, The Annenberg School for Communications, University of Pennsylvania

'In these penetrating and well-informed essays the simplifications, demonology, obfuscation, passivity, and partisanship of much of the Western media are all exposed and comprehensively explored. This is a critical and illuminating volume which offers provocative insights into one of the key episodes of recent history.' Professor Peter Golding, Head of the Department of Social Sciences, Loughborough University

'In this important book a distinguished cast of contributors correct the many media myths of the war in Kosovo. Unless we realise that news coverage of international crises is now dictated by Western governments with their spin doctors and propagandists, then we are doomed to become puppets, manipulated in the deadly service of the new world order.' Phillip Knightley, author of *The First Casualty: The War Correspondent as Hero* and *Myth Maker from the Crimea to Kosovo*

Contents

Harold Pinter

Foreword

Nato has claimed that the bombings of civilians in Serbia were accidents. I suggest that the bombing of civilians was part of a deliberate attempt to terrorise the population. Nato's supreme commander, General Wesley K. Clark, declared as the bombing began: 'We are going to systematically and progressively attack, disrupt, degrade, devastate and ultimately – unless President Milosevic complies with the demands of the international community – we are going to destroy these forces and their facilities and support.' Milosevic's 'forces', as we now know, included television stations, schools, hospitals, theatres, old people's homes. The Geneva Convention states that no civilian can be targeted unless he is taking a direct part in the hostilities, which I take to mean firing guns or throwing hand grenades. These civilian deaths were therefore acts of murder.

A body of lawyers and law professors based in Toronto in association with the American Association of Jurists, a non-government organisation with consultative status before the United Nations, has laid a complaint before the War Crimes Tribunal charging all the Nato leaders (headed by President Clinton and Prime Minister Blair) with war crimes committed in its campaign against Yugoslavia. The list of crimes includes: 'wilful killing, wilfully causing great suffering or serious injury to body or health, extensive destruction of property, not justified by military necessity and carried out unlawfully and wantonly, employment of poisonous weapons or other weapons to cause unnecessary suffering, wanton destruction of cities, towns or villages, devastation not justified by military necessity, bombardment of undefended towns, villages, dwellings or buildings, destruction or wilful damage done to institutions dedicated to religion, charity and education, the arts and sciences, historic monuments'. The charge also alleges 'open violation of the United Nations Charter, the Nato Treaty itself, the Geneva Conventions and the principles of International Law'.

It is worth remarking here that the enormous quantities of high explosives dropped on Serbia have done substantial damage to irreplaceable treasures of Byzantine religious art. Precious mosaics and frescos have been destroyed. The thirteenth-century city of Pec has been flattened. The sixteenth-century Hadum mosque in Djakovica, the Byzantine Basilica in Nis and the ninth-century church in Prokuplje have been badly damaged. The fifteenth-century rampart in the Belgrade fort has collapsed. The Banovina palace in Novi Sad, the finest work of art deco architecture in the Balkans, has been blown up. This is psychotic vandalism.

Why were cluster bombs used to kill civilians in Serbian marketplaces? The Nato high command can hardly have been ignorant of the effect of these weapons. They quite simply tear people to pieces. The effect of depleted uranium in the nose of missile shells cannot be precisely measured. Jamie Shea, our distinguished Nato spokesman, would probably say, 'Oh come on lads, a little piece of depleted uranium never did anyone any harm.' It can be said, however, that Iraqi citizens are still suffering serious effects from depleted uranium after nine years, not to mention the Gulf War syndrome experienced by British and American soldiers. What is known is that depleted uranium leaves toxic and radioactive particles of uranium oxide that endanger human beings and pollute the environment. Nato also targeted chemical and pharmaceutical plants, plastics factories and oil refineries, causing substantial environmental damage. The Worldwide Fund for Nature warned of an environmental crisis looming in the lower Danube, due mainly to oil slicks. The river is a source of drinking water for ten million people.

Tony Blair said that 'Milosevic has devastated his own country.' This statement reminds me of the story of the English actress and the Japanese actor. The Japanese actor couldn't understand why the English actress was so cold towards him, so unfriendly. Finally he appealed to the director. He said, 'We have a love scene to do tomorrow but she simply won't smile at me, she never looks at me, she won't speak to me. How can we play the love scene?' The director said to the actress 'Now what's the trouble, darling? Kobo is really an extremely nice man.' The actress looked at the Japanese actor and said 'He may be – but some of us haven't forgotten Hiroshima.'

This is standing language – and the world – on its head. There is indeed a breathtaking discrepancy between, let us say, US government language and US government action. The United States has exercised a sustained, systematic and clinical manipulation of power worldwide since the end of the last World War, while masquerading as a force for universal good. Or to put it another way, pretending to be the world's Dad. It's a brilliant – even witty – stratagem and in fact has been remarkably successful. But in 1948 George Kennan, head of the US State Department set out the ground rules for US foreign policy in a 'top secret' internal document. He said:

> We will have to dispense with all sentimentality and day dreaming and our attention will have to be concentrated everywhere on our immediate national objectives. We should cease to talk about vague and unreal objectives such as human rights, the raising of living standards and democratisation. The day is not far off when we will have to deal in straight power concepts. The less we are hampered by idealistic slogans the better.

Kennan was a very unusual man. He told the truth.

I believe that the United States, so often described – mostly by itself – as the bastion of democracy, freedom and Christian values, for so long accepted as leader of the 'free world', is in fact and has in fact been for a very long time a profoundly dangerous and aggressive force, contemptuous of international law, indifferent to the fate of millions of people who suffer from its actions, dismissive of dissent or criticism, concerned only to maintain its economic power, ready at the drop of a hat to protect that power by military means, hypocritical, brutal, ruthless and unswerving.

But US foreign policy has always been remarkably consistent and entirely logical. It's also extremely simple. 'The free market must prevail, big business must be free to do business and nobody, but nobody can get in the way of that.' A banker I know addressed a meeting of potential US investors on the complex political and economic structure of Mexican society, attempting to place this in an historical context. An American investor stood up and said 'Listen, we don't give a damn about any of that, all we want to know is what do we get for our dollar?'

Nato is America's missile. I found nothing intrinsically surprising in what was essentially an American action. There are plenty of precedents. The US did tremendous damage to Iraq in the Gulf War, did it again in December 1998, and is still doing it. In 1998 it destroyed a pharmaceutical factory in Khartoum, declaring that chemical weapons were made there. They were not. Baby powder was. Sudan asked the United Nations to set up an international inquiry into the bombing. The United States prevented this inquiry from taking place. All this goes back a very long way. The US invaded Panama in 1990, Grenada in 1983, the Dominican Republic in 1965. It destabilised and brought down democratically elected governments in Guatemala, Chile, Greece and Haiti, all acts entirely outside the parameters of international law. It has supported, subsidised and in a number of cases engendered every right-wing dictatorship in the world since 1945. I refer again to Guatemala, Chile, Greece and Haiti. Add to these Indonesia, Uruguay, the Philippines, Brazil, Paraguay, Turkey, El Salvador, for example. Hundreds upon hundreds of thousands of people have been murdered by these regimes but the money, the resources, the equipment (all kinds), the advice, the moral support as it were, has come from successive US administrations. The devastation the US inflicted upon Vietnam, Laos and Cambodia, the use of napalm, agent orange, was a remorseless, savage, systematic course of destruction, which however failed to destroy the spirit of the Vietnamese people. When the US was defeated it at once set out to starve the country by way of trade embargo. Its covert action against Nicaragua was declared by the International Court of Justice in The Hague in 1986 to be in clear breach of international law. The US dismissed this judgment, saying it regarded its actions as outside the jurisdiction of any international court. Over the last six years the United Nations has passed six resolutions with overwhelming majorities (at the last one only Israel voting with the US) demanding that the US stop its embargo on Cuba. The US has ignored all of them.

Milosevic is brutal. Saddam Hussein is brutal. But the brutality of Clinton (and of course Blair) is insidious, since it hides behind sanctimony and the rhetoric of moral outrage.

Philip Hammond and Edward S. Herman

Introduction

When the North Atlantic Treaty Organisation launched a bombing campaign against the Federal Republic of Yugoslavia on the evening of 24 March 1999, we were told it was for the best possible motives. Politicians in the Nato bloc maintained that, reluctantly, they had taken military action because diplomacy had failed; because there was an impending 'humanitarian catastrophe'; because Yugoslav forces were committing 'genocidal' acts; because the foreign policy of the leading Nato powers is driven by the highest moral concerns. With very few exceptions, Western journalists uncritically framed the conflict in these terms: Nato was trying to help. This volume aims to challenge the received wisdom, subjecting both the war, and the media coverage it received, to critical scrutiny. The book is organised in three parts: the first deals with the background of Western intervention in the former Yugoslavia; the second with key issues in media coverage; the third with the way the conflict was reported in a number of countries around the world.

Part I: The West's Destruction of Yugoslavia

The concept of 'humanitarian war' is surely one of the strangest ever coined. Yet today the language of Western foreign policy – now 'ethical foreign policy' – is littered with such oxymoronic phrases. Soldiers are called 'peace-keepers', deliberately destroyed infrastructure and dead civilians are called 'collateral damage', and the occupation of part of a sovereign state by Nato troops and United Nations administrators is referred to as 'liberation'. In her chapter on 'Nato and the New World Order', Diana Johnstone looks at the *realpolitik* behind the rhetoric, arguing that proclaimed Western ideals have been the window-dressing for geostrategic interests. Kosovo provided Nato with a new *raison d'être*, facilitating US global dominance and undermining the old international order based on the premise of state sovereignty.

This calculated disregard for sovereignty in the name of 'human rights' is also taken up by David Chandler, who sets the Kosovo war in the context of Great Power interference in the Balkans throughout the 1990s. Assessing the record, he demonstrates how outside intervention – far from helping the people of the former Yugoslavia – has only fuelled conflict and sharpened

1

divisions. Chandler also notes the elitist and anti-democratic character of Western policy, whereby the people of the region are assumed to be incapable of self-government. Mirjana Skoco and William Woodger focus on one aspect of this – the assumption that belligerent parties in the West have the right to sit in judgment through the International Criminal Tribunal for Former Yugoslavia. Skoco and Woodger indicate how The Hague Tribunal, although feted by journalists as an independent court, has consistently served as a political tool of the dominant Nato powers.

Finally in this first part of the book, Peter Gowan examines the conduct and aftermath of the Kosovo war itself, looking in detail at how manoeuvring by Western powers affected both the way the war was waged and how it was brought to an end. Contrasting Nato's declared goals with the operational aims of the war, Gowan uncovers the diplomatic context – of US relations with other Nato countries, and with Russia – which is indispensable for an understanding of why the war was really fought. He argues that the bombing campaign was a significant, though not unqualified, success for post-Cold War US expansionist aims.

Part II: Seeing the Enemy

As Johnstone notes, the 'humanitarian war' concept is promoted through the media, which play a vital role in preparing public opinion and acting as cheerleaders and advocates of war. Opening the second part of the book, Richard Keeble develops this point with a review of what he terms the 'new militarist' wars fought in the 1980s and 1990s. Nato's bombing of Yugoslavia was not really 'war' in the conventional sense, Keeble argues, but the devastation and slaughter, by an overwhelmingly superior military alliance, of an enemy demonised by Western officials and journalists. Such 'wars' are media spectacles, manufactured for the militarised societies of Britain and America.

The demonisation of enemies is also examined by Mick Hume, who focuses on the way the Serbs were portrayed as the 'new Nazis', led by a 'new Hitler', committing 'genocide' in both Bosnia and Kosovo. This manipulative process of 'Nazification' not only led to gross distortion of the Bosnian and Kosovo conflicts, it also belittled the Nazi Holocaust by implying it was the equivalent of these local civil wars. While Nato politicians were eager to push the Second World War comparison regarding Kosovo, in doing so they drew on a ready-made image of the Serbs developed by crusading journalists in Bosnia. The 'anti-Nazi' campaigning of Western reporters is driven more by their own search for moral certainties than by the reality of the conflicts themselves, argues Hume.

Though relentlessly denouncing Yugoslav propaganda, Nato politicians maintained that their own countries' media were models of independence and accuracy. Skoco and Woodger look at the evolution of US military strategies of news management, whereby direct control and censorship have given way to a new emphasis on 'working with' the media. The end result is similar, since the new doctrine of 'security at source' means that, though providing an avalanche of 'information', the military themselves control the flow of news, while journalists develop an ever cosier relationship with the Pentagon's Public Affairs Officers.

The Nato attacks on the Yugoslav media provide the starting point for Goran Gocic's chapter, which reflects on the information war fought on TV and the Internet. Gocic, a Yugoslav journalist, describes the significance of the symbolic victories won by Serbian television and the 'wired elite' on the Internet, though he argues that these have to be set against US dominance in the field of global communications.

Part III: Reporting the War around the World

The series of studies which make up this part of the book begins with the core Nato countries. Seth Ackerman and Jim Naureckas survey US media coverage of the build-up to the bombing and the conflict itself, and Edward S. Herman and David Peterson examine the role of the 24-hour news channel CNN. Both chapters reveal the extraordinary degree to which the mainstream media accepted Nato's language, frames of reference, selections of fact, and rewriting of history in supporting the war. Philip Hammond summarises key issues in the similar propaganda framework developed by the British media, and John Pilger provides specially edited extracts from articles he wrote during and after the bombing. Diana Johnstone traces the contribution of French intellectuals and media commentators in promoting the ideology of 'humanitarian intervention', both during the Bosnian war and the Kosovo air campaign. Thomas Deichmann reveals how German journalists swept democratic debate aside in their eagerness to embrace the 'ethical foreign policy' of bombing.

A similar lack of debate was evident in Norwegian politics and press reporting, argues Karin Trandheim Røn. Although Norway played a negligible military role, many Norwegian reporters were enthusiastic supporters of war, uncritically reproducing Nato propaganda and going out of their way to adopt a patriotic angle in their coverage. For journalists in Greece, a peripheral Nato ally, there were contradictory pressures: politicians toed the US line while the overwhelming majority of the country's population vigorously demonstrated their opposition to the bombing. Nikos Raptis draws on interviews with correspondents who reported from Belgrade and Kosovo during the war to show how most Greek journalists sided with popular opinion rather than media owners and government.

As the example of Greece suggests, the notion that the whole 'international community' supported the war is a fiction. Coverage in non-Nato countries which opposed the bombing offers a markedly different picture. Analysing Russian press reporting, Philip Hammond, Lilia Nizamova and Irina Savelieva describe how, despite political divisions between privately owned, pro-market newspapers and nationalist or communist titles, there was nevertheless a consensus against the war across all sections of the media. Like Russia, India also felt itself threatened by Nato's attack on Yugoslavia, and coverage in the country's English-language press combined reports reproduced from Western news agencies with highly critical commentaries and editorials. Raju Thomas provides an overall analysis of the coverage, while *Times of India* correspondent Siddharth Varadarajan gives an insider's perspective. Drawing on his experience of reporting from Yugoslavia and other war zones, Varadarajan recounts how news coverage of international crises is dominated by the official Western world view.

The Manichean Struggle

The media have played a key role in sustaining the idea of 'humanitarian' intervention since the end of the Cold War. Complex conflicts have been simplified into epic battles between Good and Evil; enemies have been demonised; and the Western powers have been lionised as heroic saviours of the world. The price exacted by such 'humanitarianism' has been a heavy one. From Iraq, Somalia and Haiti, to Yugoslavia, the death toll now runs into the hundreds of thousands. In 1999, Nato killed at least as many civilians in its 78 days of 'humanitarian' bombing as the total number of people who died in Kosovo in the twelve months preceding the air war. Unfortunately, we can predict with a great deal of confidence that there will be a 'next time'. But the evidence presented here suggests that whenever we hear talk of the 'ethical' concerns of the 'international community', some critical questions must be asked.

Part I

The West's Destruction of Yugoslavia

1

Diana Johnstone

Nato and the New World Order: Ideals and Self-Interest

The relationship between media and official war propaganda is more obscure in 'open' than in 'closed' societies. In the latter, it is taken for granted that the same government which wages war controls information, and directs the press and other media to select, distort and occasionally invent news reports in order to contribute to public support and enthusiasm for the war effort. In such societies, many people are aware of government censorship of the news and distrust whatever they are told by state-controlled media.

The United States, in contrast, is generally considered the 'open' society *par excellence*. With the exception of Turkey, all the Nato countries engaged in the 1999 war against Yugoslavia enjoyed freedom of the press. In such countries, the overwhelming media support for Nato's Kosovo war cannot be explained by government censorship, control or intimidation. Indeed, throughout the Yugoslav crises of the 1990s, it often seemed that the media were dictating policy to Western governments, rather than the other way around.

Both civilian officials and military officers have complained from time to time of the influence of the media on Western policy toward the Balkans. A 1999 survey of a thousand United Nations officials with experience in the Yugoslav area found that three out of four believed the media had influenced the course of the war itself. The influence of the media in preparing public opinion to accept and applaud the war was even more crucial. For years, numerous editorialists and columnists had publicly nagged apparently reluctant governments into military action in Yugoslavia. It was the conspicuous performance of the media as moralising chorus that enabled Nato governments to claim that Kosovo was the scene of history's first purely unselfish war, devoid of geostrategic purpose or economic interest, waged solely in response to the proddings of the conscience of the 'international community'.

The Problem and the Solution

According to the official version, Kosovo had a problem, and Nato provided the solution. In reality, Nato had a problem, and Kosovo provided the solution.

Nato's problem was to find a new *raison d'être* in the absence of the 'Soviet threat'. After the collapse of communism, the disbanding of the Warsaw Pact and the break-up of the Soviet Union itself, the official reason for the existence of Nato no longer existed.

The Kosovo problem was essentially merely one of many disputes over the status of a territory inhabited and claimed by different peoples. It was far from being the most violent or intractable conflict of that type. Fair, impartial and patient outside mediation would have been appropriate. Instead, military intervention on behalf of an armed rebel group turned a problem into a catastrophe.

The sudden insistence of the Clinton administration in early 1999 that this century-old problem must be solved now, immediately, by force, was motivated quite simply by the desire to demonstrate Nato's new mission in time for its fiftieth anniversary. The Kosovo crisis had to be grasped and used as a unique opportunity to impose the US vision of the alliance's new 'strategic concept' by a major *fait accompli*.

Only a decade earlier, it had seemed to many that the end of the Cold War would bring an era of peace. There was talk of a 'peace dividend' in the form of a shift of resources from the arms race to social programmes. Ten years later, US military spending has resumed its upward spiral, Washington is pressuring its allies to spend more on armaments, Nato is expanding eastwards and its 'partnership for peace' is solidifying United States influence all across the southernmost tier of the former Soviet Union. Quite predictably, this has been perceived in Russia as a threat and has in turn strengthened the most belligerent factions in Moscow. The short-term Russian response to Nato's war in Kosovo has been war in Chechnya. The long-term response is most likely to be a new worldwide arms race, more dangerous than that of the Cold War.[1]

Nato's purpose in Europe was succinctly described in its early days as 'keeping the Americans in, the Russians out, and the Germans down'. Such a geopolitical role could survive the demise of 'the Soviet threat', but was never suitable for persuading public opinion. The collapse of the Soviet Union presented United States strategists with a double challenge: an unprecedented opportunity to pursue worldwide domination, and the need to define a new ideological pretext for this pursuit that could win public support.

Happy Birthday Dear Nato

Nato's fiftieth birthday celebration was held in Washington on 23–25 April 1999. The bombing of Yugoslavia had been going on for a month. The outcome was still uncertain, but dissension was muted and triumphalism was the prescribed tone. Thanks to Kosovo, Nato had asserted its new role as a 'humanitarian' strike force unlimited by geographical boundaries or provisions of international law.

No humanitarian mission had been necessary to persuade major US private corporations to put up the $8 million to pay for the birthday party, or to incite a dozen chief executive officers of major Pentagon contractors to pay $250,000 each to serve as official sponsors.[2] Corporate America was well aware of the importance of Nato as a source of long-term, guaranteed profits. US Congressmen had been heavily lobbied by a special 'US Committee to Expand Nato', presided over by Lockheed's chief executive. No wonder: Nato's expansion will require the Central Eastern European countries to strain their budgets in order to procure US military equipment. Poland, for instance, is expected to buy 100–150 new fighter planes, which could be either the Lockheed F-16 ($20 million each) or the Boeing F-18 ($40–$60 million each).[3]

Such prospects are certainly sufficient to justify the expansion of Nato from the standpoint of the arms merchants. But public opinion calls for a more uplifting rationale.

Changing the Rules

Vaguely announced by US President George Bush on the occasion of the Gulf War,[4] the 'New World Order' is the world as ordered by the United States since it emerged as sole superpower, following the collapse of the Soviet Union, with an overwhelming advantage in three key areas:

- *Economic*: in addition to the wealth of its own economy, the United States exercises overwhelming institutionalised economic power through its guiding role in establishing and running global economic regulatory bodies such as the International Monetary Fund and the World Trade Organisation.
- *Military*: the United States possesses a quantitative and qualitative superiority in weapons and surveillance systems which can be used selectively to further its economic hegemony.
- *Ideological*: the United States entertainment and media industries interpret reality and popularise attitudes favourable to the hegemony of US capitalism.

These three levels of power are tightly interrelated and strongly reinforce each other.

It has taken the Kosovo war to reveal just what is 'new' about this world order, insofar as the Nato bombing of Yugoslavia amounted to an assault on the previous construction of an international order undertaken at the end of the Second World War, centring on the United Nations organisation. That essentially political order of sovereign states was based on the principle that aggressive war should be outlawed. The 'crime against peace' was set at the Nuremberg trials as the primary war crime committed by the Third Reich. The Nato bombing quite consciously violated the United Nations Charter and virtually all the relevant treaties and conventions of the post-1945 international order. As the founding event of a 'world order', the Kosovo war, although extremely minor compared to the Second World War, was verbally inflated into its moral equivalent (with its own 'Hitler' and even its own 'holocaust') sufficient to usher out the old order and bring in the new.

This 'new' order is essentially an *economic* order with a military arm. War has been rehabilitated as a morally justifiable option, to be decided over the heads of the UN Security Council by a vague entity called the 'international community' whose decisions are taken at Nato meetings.

Throughout the 1990s, the mass media and political leaders together have vigorously promoted the belief that 'privatisation' is the only proper way to improve economic performance, that 'globalisation' is the next inevitable phase of human development and that this essentially economic world process is guided by a contemporary secular version of divine providence: the 'international community' endowed with an unerring moral sense applicable to all situations everywhere.

As sole superpower, the United States is less willing than ever to let the United Nations interfere with Washington's own unilateral decision-making. Moreover, the very composition of the United Nations as an organisation of sovereign states is becoming irrelevant to a 'New World Order' in which nation states – with the immediate exception of the United States itself – are slated to lose their sovereignty in key areas. First and foremost, national sovereignty must not be allowed to obstruct the worldwide *privatisation* of economic wealth and decision-making that is the heart of 'globalisation'.

The new powers, already asserting themselves, are the international financial institutions, investment houses, banks, transnational corporations, commodity dealers and so on – themselves totally undemocratic in their operations, outside the control or even knowledge of the vast majority of the populations affected by them. While the state's power over the economy declines, the necessary co-ordination, mediation, arbitration, and rule setting between these new economic powers is bestowed on such global institutions as the World Trade Organisation, which severely limit the power of governments to protect public interests, whether citizens' welfare or the environment, from the demands of private business. The stalled Multilateral Agreement on Investment (MAI) would go even further in shifting vital political decision-making power to the private sector, acting in co-optive, non-elected bureaucratic tribunals.[5]

As the ability of nation states to protect the interests of their citizens diminishes, the importance of citizenship itself diminishes in turn. In compensation, group identities of all kinds offer the prospect of mutual assistance, protection or at least comfort to populations struggling to cope with changes beyond their control. These conditions of ruthlessly competitive 'struggle for life' underlie the growing tendency for people to turn to identity groups – national, religious, 'ethnic', and so on – for protection. In the post-communist era, the most successful form of socio-economic organisation has been the ethnic-based cross-border mafia.

This new world *economic* order causes great social disorder. US-led globalisation is a violent process, bringing huge benefits to some but wiping out traditional means of sustenance, uprooting millions of people, destroying natural and cultural environments. As participants in and beneficiaries of economic globalisation, the mass media quite naturally portray it as a natural planetary unification flowing happily from the peaceful expansion of free trade. Globalisation is presented not as the result of specific government policies of privatisation and deregulation enacted in the interests of financial capital, but rather as their cause, an inevitable and irreversible movement which must be followed, to which resistance is both perverse and vain. 'Globalisation' has stepped into the empty shoes of 'progress'. Because it is unstoppable, politics and policy must adapt or be left behind.

However, the very liberals who champion this natural process are apparently convinced that it cannot occur naturally. 'For globalism to work, America can't be afraid to act like the almighty superpower that it is', announced the *New York Times* as the bombs began to fall on Belgrade. In the authoritative opinion of the paper's foreign policy analyst, Thomas Friedman: 'The hidden hand of the market will never work without a hidden fist – McDonald's cannot flourish without McDonnell Douglas, the designer of the F-15, and the hidden fist that keeps the world safe for Silicon Valley's technologies is called the United States Army, Air Force, Navy and Marine Corps.'[6]

In reality, the 'fist' is not hidden. It is merely cloaked in moral purpose, as it is brandished conspicuously for the world at large. The 'fist' was boastfully displayed throughout the bombing of Yugoslavia.

What was hidden was almost everything on the receiving end of the 'fist': the hatred it inflamed in Kosovo, the fear and trauma of the civilians in Serbian cities and towns, the despair and confusion, the destruction of people's jobs, hopes and future.

Ideals and Self-Interest

'American ideals and self-interest merge when the United States supports the spread of democracy around the globe – or what we prefer to call "limited" constitutional democracy, meaning rule by a government that has been legitimised by free elections', according to a 1992 publication of the Carnegie Endowment for International Peace entitled *Self-Determination in the New World Order* (Halperin et al., 1992). The merging of American ideals and self-interest is a constant feature of US policy, facilitated by an unshakable conviction in the minds of its leaders that the worldwide extension of the American economic system is an end of such benefit to mankind as to justify whatever means may be employed.

The vision of a 'new world order' since 1990 has been a world with one superpower – the United States – in which the rule of law supplants the rule of the jungle, disputes are settled peacefully, aggression is firmly met by collective resistance, and all people are justly treated. (ibid.:1)

This utopian vision rests on a 'rule of law' that has not yet been written. The rest of the world may mistakenly still believe the rules are those in existing international law, but they will learn better. 'International law – as it always has done – will respond and adjust to the behaviour of nations and the actions of multilateral institutions' (ibid.:3). The Nato war against Yugoslavia, in flagrant violation of existing international law, announced the new dispensation.

A major feature of the 'New World Order' is the demolition of national sovereignty, the basis of existing international law. A world with a single superpower is a world where only that superpower has a sure claim to 'national sovereignty' – an outdated concept for the rest. The sovereign nation is to be broken down not only from the outside, by the pressures of economic globalisation, but also and more acceptably from the inside.

In the post-Cold War world, the Carnegie Endowment study noted, 'groups within states are staking claims to independence, greater autonomy, or the overthrow of an existing government, all in the name of self-determination'. In regard to these conflicts, 'American interests and ideals compel a more active role.' This may go so far as military intervention when self-determination claims or internal repression of such claims lead to 'humanitarian calamities' (ibid.:108). In the future, the authors announced in 1992, 'humanitarian interventions will become increasingly unavoidable'. The United States will have the final word as to when and how to intervene. 'The United States should seek to build a consensus within regional and international organisations for its position, but should not sacrifice its own judgment and principles if such a consensus fails to materialise.'

This 1992 text is significant because it expresses the vision of precisely the people who later led the United States and Nato into the Kosovo war. It was the product of a Carnegie Endowment project in the early 1990s to develop a new US foreign policy for the post-Cold War era. The selected experts included Richard Holbrooke and Madeleine Albright, among others who were to become senior officials in the Clinton administration. The co-author of *Self-Determination in the New World Order*, David Scheffer, became Albright's special ambassador for war crimes issues. The Carnegie president who organised the studies, Morton Abramowitz, went on to become a champion of ethnic Albanian rebels in Kosovo and an adviser to their delegation at the Rambouillet talks whose programmed breakdown provided the pretext for Nato bombing.

Meanwhile, the principle of 'humanitarian intervention' had been promoted by both media and non-governmental organisations. A broad consensus emerged that such intervention could be necessary – without, however, any clear method for determining what sort of intervention might be appropriate for what sort of 'humanitarian crisis'. The importance or nature of any given crisis was left to the fickle spotlight of mass media. This provided broad opportunities for manipulation of public opinion, in particular by manufacture of 'incidents' (an age-old practice on the eve of wars) and distortion or invention of 'facts'. And the uncertainty over appropriate means of intervention provided the opportunity to use humanitarian concern to justify military aggression.

The Free Marketplace of Ideas

The United States is a 'free market democracy' with emphasis on 'market'. Everyone is allowed and encouraged to trade on that market, which includes a 'free marketplace of ideas'. The freedom to sell ideas – any ideas – is not the same thing as freedom to pursue the truth. It can be very different indeed. For on the 'free marketplace of ideas', notions which are trivial or false may outsell serious and important facts, especially when the 'free' marketplace is dominated by huge conglomerates and monopolies governed by a consensus among the profit-taking class.

In a free marketplace, there is no 'official ideology'. There is, instead, a sum total of best-selling ideas – which have been actively promoted by opinion-making institutions. This shifting best-seller list of ideas makes up the ideology, and the public opinion, of the moment.

Foreign policies also need to sell themselves on the marketplace. There is the 'up market' of the professional geostrategists, the 'foreign policy community' with its think tanks, elite clubs and sober publications. And there is the 'down market' that goes all the way down to the British tabloids. A successful policy will be one that can sell itself both to the up market, as being in line with dominant interests, and to the down market, as appealing to ready stereotypes and gratifying emotions.

For the 'up market', there is Zbigniew Brzezinski and his *realpolitik* objective: 'to perpetuate America's own dominant position for at least a generation and preferably longer still' (Brzezinski, 1997:215). This involves creating a 'geopolitical framework' around Nato that will initially include Ukraine and exclude Russia. This will establish the geostrategic basis for controlling conflict in what Brzezinski calls 'the Eurasian Balkans', the huge area between the Eastern shore of the Black Sea to China, which includes the Caspian Sea and its petroleum resources, a top priority for US foreign policy.

Transforming Yugoslavia from a medium-sized independent state, with a unique reputation in the region for resistance to foreign empires, into a series of ethnic statelets whose economic assets can be easily expropriated and whose territory can be used for Nato bases on the way to Ukraine and the Caspian certainly fits in generally to the Brzezinski scheme of things. But this sort of geostrategic chess game is not at all suitable to the mass market of Western public opinion. (In Russia, however, Brzezinski's theories are both taken seriously by policy-makers and cited to the public to justify defensive measures, including the war to wipe out Chechen rebels.)

While geostrategists saw the Yugoslav disintegration as a case study in preparation for more dangerous conflicts in Ukraine or the Caspian region, throughout the 1990s the ongoing Yugoslav crisis was interpreted in more emotional terms by the media and the opportunistic Clinton administration, combining 'ideals and interests' to further the establishment of the 'New World Order'.

The Yugoslav crisis was in reality dauntingly complex, morally ambiguous, factually hard to follow, ridden with historic complexities, genuine fears and deception on all sides. In the world of mass media, such complicated foreign news stories do not 'sell'. The only way to sell that story was to reduce it to a moral tale, with a villain to revile and victims to inspire pity. This effect was most rapidly produced by analogy with highly charged contemporary historical symbols: Hitler, Auschwitz, the Holocaust. The marketplace, helped along by professional public relations firms and active lobbies in Washington, soon settled on Serbia as the single villain and everybody else as the victims. This became the easy standard media approach, occasionally contradicted by details of a report from the scene, but vigorously upheld on the editorial pages.

The Manichean approach is particularly appropriate for television, which can 'tell a story' in a few seconds simply with pictures of victims. The story need not be accurate, complete or enlightening: the pathos of tears in the eyes of women and children is enough to ensure emotional impact. The pathos is intensified if the impression is given, one way or another, that the blond, blue-eyed children are victims of a diabolical campaign of extermination by the latest 'Hitler' – a proper name which is rapidly being transformed into the generic term for the latest adversary selected by the United States in its policy of creating regional pariah or 'rogue' states.[7]

The version most appropriate to the media market proved useful on the policy marketplace as well. The Clinton administration, groping for a way to preserve Nato as the essential instrument of its dominance over its European trade rivals, grasped the potential of the Yugoslav mess. The Manichean interpretations in the media, coupled with the inevitable cry of 'Munich!' at any attempt to work out a compromise, could and did serve to scuttle any attempt at negotiated settlement. Diplomacy was discredited. Thus, eventually, the United States could and did provide 'the only solution': application of bombs and missiles to the problem. The European allies were finally led sheepishly into military aggression in a new Nato without legal or geographic limits.

The New Crusade

The great strength of 'humanitarian intervention' is its appeal to American liberal and European social democratic leaders who find themselves without effective economic policies to promote the social justice they claim to serve, but still need a virtuous cause to distinguish themselves from 'the right', presumed to be indifferent to human suffering. Obliged to accept tax breaks for big investors, mass dismissals of factory workers and cutbacks in social programmes, in terms of domestic policy the 'third way' retains its position on the left primarily by a receptiveness to cultural diversity. The enemy can no longer be capitalism, accepted as the best and only socio-economic system. The enemy now is *nationalism*, portrayed as the source of all modern evil. This new generation of centre-left politicians recoil in horror from such archaic notions as 'imperialism'. For the 'third way' of the left, we are living in a world where economic forces are innocent, even benevolent. All evil comes from bad people who adopt wrong ideas, such as nationalism. In this way, those who today occupy the left side of Western parliaments are the successful heirs and rivals to the traditional right.

Anti-nationalism has been indispensable in the promotion of European unification. The more the European Union has been reduced to an instrument of transnational business and finance, the more it has been necessary, in public rhetoric, to stress its noble mission of putting an end to the national antagonisms that led to major European wars. The nation state has been stigmatised as the cause of war, oppression and violation of human rights. This interpretation overlooks both the persistence of war in the absence of strong states and the historic function of the nation state as the most effective existing framework for the social pact enabling citizens to build structures of social protection and cultural development, as well as to develop legal systems able to provide equality before the law and to defend citizens' rights. Demonising as 'nationalism' the only existing context for functioning institutionalised democracy obviously facilitates the dictates of 'the markets', which are innocent of nationalist prejudice.

As political parties have declined, the creative centre of the old liberal left has shifted to single-issue and humanitarian non-governmental organisations. This is part of the privatisation trend. Social problems are removed from the domain of the state, including its democratically elected parliaments, to become the concern of private volunteer organisations. NGOs are not all strictly 'non-governmental'. Many depend on contracts from governments. But their growth represents a shift from the notion of social welfare as a human right to its status as one of many contenders for support on the 'free marketplace of ideas', as Médecins Sans Frontières, animal rights groups, denouncers of human rights violations, defenders of the rain forest and funds to feed starving children all compete for the cheques of donors and the grants of governments and foundations.

Some NGOs are even set up by governments to intervene in the political affairs of other countries, such as the National Endowment for Democracy, an instrument of the US government. A number of NGOs serve as indirect aids to economic globalisation, by providing some of the public services which poor states are obliged to eliminate under the dictates of International Monetary Fund 'structural adjustment' policies.

The NGOs provide the flesh and bones as well as the moral identity of the otherwise amorphous 'international community'. Internationally active NGOs have been in the forefront of the demand for humanitarian intervention. Operating across borders, such NGOs as Médecins Sans Frontières tend to see national sovereignty as a mere obstacle to their own operations. Based in the rich Nato countries, operating in poorer countries, the direction of their intervention is the same as that of Nato acting as policeman of the New

World Order. Such NGOs risk playing a role similar to that of Christian missionaries as pretext and justification for military expeditions in earlier imperialist conquests. When, as in Bosnia-Herzegovina, a military protectorate is established, much of the foreign aid actually goes to Western NGOs.

The humanitarian NGOs have become a primary source of media coverage of poor countries and trouble spots. The plight of victims always provides a story for television, without any need to go into the obscure causes of their misfortune. Urged on by humanitarian NGOs, the media and popular entertainers, the Bush administration undertook the United States' first 'humanitarian intervention' in Somalia in 1992. Ostensibly dispatched to save children from starving, the foreign troops ended up in a losing fight with local warlords. The expedition turned into a grisly farce, which risked discrediting the entire concept.

In 1999, the United Nations was left aside, and the United States led Nato not into a mere 'humanitarian intervention' but into a 'humanitarian war'.

The Fruits of Humanitarian War

From any distance in time, space, or allegiance, aggressive wars are generally judged not in terms of declared purpose – usually noble – but in terms of results. The 'humanitarian' war for Kosovo produced human catastrophe. Judged by its declared purpose, it was a ghastly failure. On the other hand, in terms of *realpolitik*, it served to achieve a number of important objectives:

- Assert the United States' authority in deciding when and where to carry out 'humanitarian intervention'.
- Rehabilitate aggressive war as a morally acceptable and even necessary extension of politics, in the pursuit of self-proclaimed 'humanitarian' aims.
- Put military action by the United States and its Nato allies above existing international law, thanks to the concept of 'humanitarian war', the latest avatar of the 'white man's burden' and other such noble pretexts, which had been inhibited for half a century by the international order set up after the Second World War designed to outlaw aggressive imperialist war such as waged by the Third Reich and the Empire of Japan.
- Clearly demonstrate the technological superiority of US weaponry to the whole world – both to Nato allies, who must buy it, and to others, who must fear it.
- Establish, on its fiftieth anniversary, the vitality of a new, more aggressive Nato, endowed with a new post-Cold War mission unrestricted by Treaty or geographical limits.
- Assert United States domination over the still embryonic 'Foreign and Security Policy' of the European Union – confirmed by the choice of Nato's wartime Secretary-General, Javier Solana, to take charge of the 'FaSP'.

- Establish Nato's primacy over the European Union in integrating the countries of Central Eastern Europe, with decisive economic and political implications.
- Demonstrate to United States public opinion the feasibility of the concept of 'zero casualties' air war (zero US casualties, that is), the better to eliminate serious domestic opposition to future aggressive wars.
- Pursue to the end the destruction of Yugoslavia, considered – rightly or wrongly – by US policy-makers to be a dangerous centre of potential resistance to the American New World Order for several reasons: the Serb tradition of resistance to empires; the ongoing attachment of a significant part of the population to the benefits of a socialist system differing from the Soviet model; the role of multinational Yugoslavia in the now defunct Non-Aligned Movement, in practice capable of offering a cut-rate technological modernisation to a certain number of developing countries; the possibility that Orthodox Christian Southern Slavs might provide a regional foothold for Russia.
- Take economic control of Yugoslavia, starting with the important mines and transport routes of Kosovo.
- Set up Nato bases in a region considered strategic both by its position as a crossroads for trade routes – including the hypothetical future East–West oil pipeline to bring Caspian Sea oil from the Black Sea, avoiding the traffic-clogged Bosporus – and for its proximity to future war zones where the United States strategists intend to bring US military superiority into play, that is, in Ukraine and the Caspian region.
- Prevent Europe alone – especially Germany alone – from becoming the single hegemonic power in the Balkans, thus blocking a much 'Greater Europe' extending Eastward into Slavic lands and Central Asia, to the exclusion of the United States.

So many useful results suggest that the New World Order demonstrated by the Kosovo war is nothing but the old world disorder of power politics where might makes right, transformed into a popular entertainment spectacle for well-intentioned Western audiences by the 'virtual reality' of modern media.

Notes

1. Analyst Pavel Felgenhauer wrote in the *Moscow Times*, 18 November 1999, 'Defence Dossier', that:

   > Western protestations against the killings in Chechnya sound hollow to most Russian ears. During the latest war in the Balkans the West violated many international agreements: The UN Charter, the Nato Charter, the OSCE Final Act as well as the CFE treaty by concentrating more than a thousand warplanes in Italy to attack Yugoslavia. In Nato's Balkan war – as today in Chechnya – the innocent suffered more than the fighters. Nato bombs actually killed more civilians than Serbs in uniform. There is evidence that Nato overestimated Serbian atrocities in Kosovo. In Pusto Selo, Albanian villagers said 106 civilians had been killed by the Serbs and Nato rushed out satellite photos of mass graves. It seems these photos were deliberately forged,

since an on-site inspection revealed no graves at that location after Nato troops occupied Kosovo. Western political and military leaders committed war crimes during the Balkan war by authorising attacks against civilian targets like the television station in Belgrade or the bridges in Novi Sad in northern Serbia. Nato forces in Kosovo have presided over a massive ethnic cleansing of the Serbian and Gypsy population. Hundreds of thousands have been cleansed and the West has done virtually nothing to reverse this cleansing or to adequately protect the ethnic minorities. Nato's recent war in the Balkans has forced down overall standards of public morality in Europe to an all-time low. Privately, many Russian military officers acknowledge that innocent civilians are being killed today in Chechnya, but they also claim that 'we are just doing what Nato was doing in the Balkans – no more, no less.' ... Today suspicion and hatred have again divided Europe.

More cautiously, as befits Moscow's chief diplomat, Russian foreign minister Igor Ivanov wrote in *Military Parade* (Russia), Issue 36, November–December 1999, on 'The Kosovo Crisis and Its Possible Consequences', that 'Nato's operation was an example of implementing the policy of countries that would like to endorse in the 21st century a unipolar world order which would enable them to decide, at their own discretion, the fate of other nations', and that as a result, 'The relations of trust and cooperation between Russia and Nato countries, which were painstakingly built after the Cold War, have been undermined. It has taken a great deal of effort to preserve even prerequisites for normalizing of affairs.'

2. Tim Smart, 'Count Corporate America Among Nato's Staunchest Allies', *Washington Post*, 13 April 1999, pE1.
3. Katharine Q. Seelye, 'Arms Lobby Investing Heavily in Nato Growth', *New York Times/International Herald Tribune*, 2 April 1999.
4. In his State of the Union message on 29 January 1991, President Bush spoke of a 'New World Order' under US leadership for 'the next American century'.
5. The Yale-educated US Deputy Secretary of State, Nelson Strobridge ('Strobe') Talbott the Third, perfectly reflects current American ruling class attitudes when he writes: 'I'll bet that within the next hundred years ... nationhood as we know it will be obsolete; all states will recognise a single, global authority.' The origin of that authority is implicit in the title of this essay, 'America Abroad; The Birth of the Global Nation', published in the 20 July 1992 edition of *Time* magazine. He adds the observation that such multilateral financial institutions as the International Monetary Fund and the General Agreement on Tariffs and Trade 'can be seen as the protoministries of trade, finance and development for a united world'.
6. Thomas Friedman, 'A Manifesto For a Fast World', *New York Times Magazine*, 28 March 1999. The surprising frankness of this article is not matched by its veracity. Friedman declares complacently: 'It's true that no two countries that both have a McDonald's have ever fought a war since they each got their McDonald's. (I call this the Golden Arches Theory of Conflict Prevention.)' This is not only silly. It is untrue. The McDonald's restaurant in Belgrade did not deter the United States from bombing Belgrade.
7. The designation and punishment of 'rogue states' is a constant feature of US policy, similar at world level to the pitiless treatment dealt to delinquents at home. German CDU parliamentarian Willy Wimmer, in a 6 September 1999 interview with the *Berliner Zeitung*, observed that for the United States, as a great power in the field of world trade, 'claiming unhindered access to markets the world over, identifying and denouncing "rogue states" in regions of economic interest offers the opportunity to ensure control over the markets of the rest of the region concerned, with help from security guarantees'. The war against Serbia has served to precipitate subservience to Nato even among countries that do not yet belong, notably Bulgaria and Romania, against the feelings of much of their own populations. The message is clear that Nato members, such as Turkey, need not fear being the scene of a 'humanitarian catastrophe' calling for Nato bombing, whereas non-members are vulnerable. The message is similar to the one delivered by gangsters who smash one shop on the block.

2

David Chandler

Western Intervention and the Disintegration of Yugoslavia, 1989–1999

Introduction

In 1989, Yugoslavia was a federal state consisting of six republics, Slovenia, Croatia, Bosnia-Herzegovina, Macedonia, Montenegro and Serbia. By the end of 1999 only two republics, Serbia and Montenegro, remained within the rump of the federation which was undergoing further disintegration with Montenegro seeking greater autonomy and Serbia having lost control of the province of Kosovo. The disintegration of Yugoslavia over the last decade has been a bloody and protracted one. In 1991, Slovenian and Croatian independence was marked by armed conflict, in the next four years the war in Bosnia-Herzegovina took central stage and then, in the late 1990s, armed conflict in Kosovo, culminating in the Nato bombing of Serbia and Montenegro.

The causes of Yugoslavia's disintegration are often located within former Yugoslavia itself – either in long-standing ethnic differences, in the territorial ambitions of Serb President Slobodan Milosevic, or a potent mixture of the two. The search for domestic or internal explanations for the turmoil within the region has produced a dominant view that considers the elected governments as unable to deal safely with their own political problems and poses international intervention as necessary to safeguard democracy and human rights. In the view of many commentators, bloodshed could have been avoided or minimised had the international community assumed a more proactive relationship to the situation and acted decisively to prevent elected leaders from stirring the ethnic caldron in the Balkans.

According to this perspective, the Western powers stood by and did little to stop the conflict spreading from Slovenia to Croatia and then to Bosnia and Kosovo. It was only the Nato actions against Serb forces in Bosnia in the summer of 1995, after nearly four years of war, and further Nato action against Serbia and Montenegro in the spring of 1999, after the breakdown of the Rambouillet talks on Kosovo, which demonstrated the will of the international community to take action to help the peoples of former Yugoslavia achieve some level of peace and democracy (Hartmann, 1999; Robertson, 1999).

This chapter seeks to question the above assumptions about the process of Yugoslav disintegration and, in turn, the lessons drawn about the need for further intervention in the Balkan region. In tracing the process of fragmentation over the last decade, this study highlights the frailty of the federal state, caught in the dual processes of international and domestic social and political realignments after the Cold War. These weaknesses were fully exposed, and regional and ethnic divisions consolidated, as a variety of external diplomatic, economic, political and military interventions by major Western powers and international institutions undermined regional mechanisms of conflict resolution. International intervention, it will be suggested, was a determining factor in the process of disintegration from 1989 onwards. Far from contributing to peace and stability, the policy and actions of Western powers undermined the federal institutions that held Yugoslavia together and then prevented compromise solutions, between and within republics, that could have minimised the conflict.

1989–1991: The End of Federal Yugoslavia

The problem of Yugoslav fragmentation had been a subject of concern since the mid-1960s, as economic reform and increasing exposure to the world market highlighted the uneven economic development within the federation. More industrialised republics which had greater financial contacts with the West, such as Slovenia and Croatia, came to resent the subsidies and cross-payments to the less developed regions, such as Montenegro, Macedonia and Kosovo. They wanted more control over their foreign earnings and less federal say over the state budget. Once the early attempt to overcome economic differentials by state-management had failed, Tito attempted to minimise the political fall-out over budgetary policy by a mixture of repression and liberalisation, sacking regional bureaucrats who were too outspoken while giving republics greater autonomy and veto powers at the federal level. In the 1980s federal life ossified further under the toll of rising foreign debt, the imposition of IMF austerity packages under emergency legislation and the autarchic economic policies pursued in the republics as a response to the economic crisis. The weakened federal state had trouble collecting tax and custom revenues from the wealthier republics and, without funding for subsidies, maintaining order in the poorer provinces such as Kosovo.

Although under strain, until 1989 there was little possibility of these economic disagreements leading to the collapse of the federal state. The key factor that meant the richer republics had little choice but to negotiate a solution at federal level was the international situation. A bulwark of Western policy during the Cold War was United States' support for Yugoslavia's unity, independence and territorial integrity. For the West, Yugoslavia's brand of market communism was an example to the rest of the Soviet Bloc to leave the constraints of the Soviet Union and open up to Western influence. Yugoslavia had special access to Western credits to keep the economy afloat in exchange for Yugoslav neutrality and rejection of the Warsaw Pact. In the late 1980s the IMF attempted to reinforce the federal institutions and weaken the republics' veto powers in order to push economic reform against those regional elites who sought greater control over local economic resources. Without international support, no separatist development strategy was possible for Slovenia and Croatia.

In 1989, Yugoslavia's international position changed dramatically with the end of the Cold War. The federal state was no longer of vital geostrategic importance to the United States. The weakness of the federal state and its inability to restore order in Kosovo was now portrayed as an issue of human rights by US officials keen to reshape their links in the region (Zimmermann, 1995). The federal government failed to receive economic assistance from the US for its radical market reform programme, and its bid to join the Council of Europe was blocked. The threat of exclusion from avenues of essential international support was heightened by the newly independent states in Central Europe defining themselves, and appealing for inclusion in Western institutions, on the basis of historical and cultural criteria. This historical and cultural division ran through Yugoslavia and reinforced the separatist arguments being made by Croatia and Slovenia, keen to become integrated into the new pan-European political structures and eager not to be dragged down by the parlous economic condition of the rest of the federal state.[1] In this context, the already weakened federal government was under new pressure both from within and without.

In 1989 the disagreements over economic reform became re-presented as a struggle between state sovereignty and human rights. Even before the US had raised the issue of human rights in Kosovo, the Slovene president had linked the promotion of human rights with greater autonomy for his republic. The US focus on the human rights issue, as justification for de-prioritising assistance for Yugoslavia, fed into and encouraged Slovene and Croat demands for greater autonomy and linked the separatist demands with a pro-human rights position. The Slovenes played on the Kosovo issue as a way of legitimising their own position and weakening federal constraints. The US stated its support for federal unity but at the same time undermined the legitimacy of the federal state by asserting that this unity could not be 'imposed or preserved by force' (Zimmermann, 1995:3).

The federal Communist Party collapsed in 1990 and free elections were held at republic level. In all the republics nationalist parties and politicians came to the fore although none of them contested the elections on the grounds of complete separation from the federation. Talks over the federal budget continued as the Slovene and Croat elites declared their right to sovereign powers and argued for a looser federal arrangement. The US and European states publicly declared their support for the federation and opinion surveys, as late as the summer of 1991, showed that in Slovenia and Croatia the publics were strongly divided on the question of separation while in the rest of Yugoslavia there was strong support for the maintenance of the federation.

Despite the public show of international unity, leading politicians in Austria and Germany were sympathetic to the claims of Slovenia and Croatia, encouraging them to hold back from accepting a new deal at federal level. At the end of June 1991, negotiations broke down and the two republics unilaterally declared their independence. The Yugoslav Peoples' Army (JNA) acted to secure the federal state's borders with Italy and Austria, clashing with Slovene defence forces. The European Community (EC) insisted on a peaceful settlement of the dispute and only the defensive use of force. The actions of the JNA in securing the federal borders were judged to be aggressive and the EC applied sanctions to the federal government. The EC mediated a cease-fire, at the Brioni peace conference, in early July, which, in effect, recognised Slovene claims to territorial separation.

While the withdrawal of the JNA from Slovenia was unproblematic, the situation in Croatia was more contested as the 600,000 Serb minority wished to remain part of Yugoslavia and had proclaimed their right to secede. In August, the European Community declared the use of force by the federal army 'illegal' and stated that the Serb minority could not receive JNA support for their claims. The EC established the Badinter Commission of international jurists, to arbitrate on the question of secession, and opened a peace conference in The Hague, in September, to organise a new confederal framework, with republics, which desired it, having the right to seek independence. Before the Badinter Commission could make its rulings, Germany forcefully argued for 'preventive recognition' of Slovenian and Croatian sovereignty to enable international forces to intervene on the ground without the assent of the Yugoslav government. Germany unilaterally recognised the independence of the two separatist republics in December and the European Community states followed, keen to preserve unity ahead of the Maastricht talks.

The international recognition of Slovenia and Croatia prior to any settlement on the situation of the Serb minority, which had declared their autonomy in the Croatian regions of Krajina and Slavonia, was to prove disastrous. Conflict within Croatia flared up as the emboldened Croatian state felt little need to compromise with its Serb minority which, in turn, became more desperate to remain within the federation. The possibilities of a negotiated solution with the federal state, involving border changes or regional autonomy, were further undermined by the Badinter Commission's ruling that republic borders were inviolate. This decision made little sense in the Yugoslav context where borders were drawn largely for administrative purposes and deliberately designed to prevent larger national groups establishing separate republics. For this reason 30 per cent of the Serbs and 20 per cent of the Croats were left out of 'their' respective republics, Serbia and Croatia (Pavkovic, 1997:50). The artificial nature of the borders of the Croatian republic was demonstrated by the fact that the new state could not impose its rule in nearly a third of its claimed territory. The six-month Croatian conflict over the status of the Serb-controlled areas was brought to a temporary halt by the establishment of four UN Protected Areas.

Germany's campaign for Croatian and Slovenian recognition was opposed by leading international mediators from the European Community and the United States, Lord Carrington and Cyrus Vance, as well as Bosnia's President Alija Izetbegovic and the United Nations Secretary-General Perez de Cuellar, on the grounds that the premature break-up of the federation would lead to regional conflicts and 'the most terrible war in Bosnia' (Glenny, 1996:163). Germany's prime concern, however, was not Yugoslavia but matters closer to home. The campaign's focus was the international rehabilitation of the newly united Germany. Bonn claimed a new legitimacy to take a lead on the international stage, and intervene in Yugoslav affairs, on the basis of anti-militarism and human rights, in direct contrast to the discredited language of German expansionism in the past (Woodward, 1995:186). In order to rehabilitate German power it was necessary to moralise the conflict in Yugoslavia and represent it not as a civil war with economic causes but as an ethnic conflict and war of external aggression. Germany therefore led the campaign to recognise Croatia and, in the process, began the Western demonisation of the Serbs and Serb President Slobodan Milosevic, now deemed to be the aggressors.

The European Community-negotiated Brioni agreement, of July 1991, and acceptance, in December 1991, of the German policy of 'preventive recognition' together ended the effective sovereignty of the Yugoslav state. The European Community had abandoned its previous support for the federal government and decisively weakened the federal regime by prejudging the actions of the federal army, in attempting to restore order in the republics, as acts of aggression and therefore illegitimate. Taking over from the Yugoslav people and their elected representatives the EC established the framework for the disintegration of the federal state, calling into existence new states along the lines of largely artificial republic boundaries.

Instead of offering economic and diplomatic support for the federal state's attempt to push through IMF market reforms and integrate into new pan-European institutions, Western policy-makers attempted to 'mediate' in a political stand-off between the state and the separatist republics. This process of mediation legitimated separatist claims and weakened the legitimacy of the state, further encouraging the process of fragmentation. In the context of greater instability and armed clashes, the Western powers then intervened more directly to impose a settlement on the separatists' terms, fatally undermining the federal mechanisms of regulation. The federal state, with its system of checks and balances, to protect the rights both of republics and national groupings, was no longer able to play a cohesive role at either the federal or republic level. This meant the region fragmented further as the new states, with the exception of Slovenia, had little political consensus binding society together.

1992–1995: The Disintegration of Bosnia

Prior to the breakdown of the federal order, Bosnia had been recognised internationally as a model of multicultural co-existence and symbolic of federal Yugoslavia's progressive minority policies. Only six months before the first free elections in the republic, 74 per cent of the population had been in favour of a ban on nationally or confessionally based parties, later overturned by the Bosnian constitutional court. The November 1990 elections were held against the background of uncertainty as to constitutional reform and new federal arrangements, and the results reflected these concerns as nationalist parties took the majority of the votes among all three groups. The Serbian and Croatian minorities, roughly half the population (31 per cent and 17 per cent, respectively), previously guaranteed protections through the federal framework, were concerned for their future, and the larger Muslim community (43 per cent of the population) feared the consequences of the republic disintegrating.

Public opinion polls in May and June 1990 and in November 1991 had shown overwhelming majorities (in the range of 70–90 per cent) against separation from Yugoslavia and an ethnically divided republic. However, with the recognition of Slovenian and Croatian independence, Bosnia was facing sharp division over the question of whether to leave the federation and seek independence. The failure to agree on a new federal framework, before dismantling the institutions of the Yugoslav state, put to question the guarantees of security and equal treatment, for the three main ethnic groups. Without the guarantees provided by the counterbalancing mechanisms of the federal state, questions of security became even more closely tied up with those of ethnic or nationalist orientation. Bosnian Croats and Serbs threatened moves towards autonomy to guarantee their security.

The breakdown of inter-ethnic co-operation in Bosnia was a direct consequence of external pressures on the political mechanisms holding the republic together within a federal framework, as opposed to the product of external invasion or a resurgence of ancient ethnic hatreds. With US encouragement, the Muslim-led government decided to seek international recognition for independence despite the wishes of the Serb community, bringing to an end the government of national unity. The Bosnian republic had little to hold it together in the absence of elite consensus and fragmented on ethnic and regional lines as the state institutions began to collapse. The Muslim leadership believed that, with international support, UN troops would be able to secure their control over the republic.

The European powers were reluctant to provide this support, by recognising Bosnian independence without a consensus between the three major ethnic groupings. This was also the opinion of the Badinter arbitration commission. The EC-led negotiations at Lisbon, in March 1992, led to an agreement on independence with minority groups protected by regional cantonisation and a high level of autonomy. A week later the Muslim leader, Alija Izetbegovic, rejected the agreement after US encouragement to hold out for a greater say (Cohen, 1995:243). The US then moved the process of disintegration further by recognising Bosnian independence in the face of European opposition. As in Croatia, recognition directly led to a higher level of conflict as negotiations between the republic and the rest of the federation broke down and all sides tried to strengthen their positions on the ground. This led to a rising casualty toll and refugee flows, 'ethnic cleansing', as Serb and Croatian separatists carved out areas under their own control.

Recognising the Bosnian state on the grounds that this would enable international troops to protect its sovereignty was a circular argument. More to the point, it was a fiction. Any new settlement in Bosnia would have relied on the republic and federal representatives negotiating a compromise settlement that satisfied minority demands and avoided conflict. US pressure encouraged the Muslim leadership to refrain from reaching such a compromise and fed Bosnian Croat and Serb fears that only autonomy and closer links with Croatia and Serbia would safeguard their interests. In this context, international recognition did not stabilise the situation in the divided republic, in fact, it destroyed the possibility of it, ensuring that conflict was inevitable.

Once independence had been recognised by the international community there was no longer an equitable basis for negotiations. The Muslim government claimed the mantle of international legitimacy and portrayed the Serb and Croatian autonomists as belligerents trying to undermine Bosnian independence and claim ethnic territory. The United States publicly shared this view, arguing that the Europeans were wrong to try to negotiate a political solution between the representatives of the three main ethnic constituencies, and encouraging Izetbegovic to hold out against successive European and UN deals (Petras and Vieux, 1996:16–17). While the Europeans looked to mediate a settlement between the Bosnian parties and contain the conflict, Washington called for a war crimes tribunal for Serb leaders, threatened to lift arms sanctions to supply Muslim forces and to launch Nato strikes against Serb positions. For the Americans, this was a low-risk strategy – the Europeans could be accused of compromise while the US demonstrated leadership and coherence at home, defending moral absolutes and international norms, although at the cost of continuation of the war. As Woodward (1995:323) notes, moralising the war was given priority over the European goal of a political solution.

The international politicisation of the Bosnian war meant the moral language of human rights shaped the course and conduct of the war itself. The war was no longer seen as the predicted result of the collapse of state authority, leading to ethnic and regional fragmentation, but as an assault on multi-ethnic democracy by Serb and Croat extremists. As campaigning journalist and author David Rieff (1995:11) explained:

I and many other foreign writers, photographers, and television journalists kept choosing ... to spend time on the Bosnian [government] side. We did not just think that what was going on was tragic – all wars are tragic – but the values that the Republic of Bosnia-Herzegovina exemplified were worth preserving.

For the beleaguered Sarajevo government, with few resources to fall back on, fighting the war soon became of secondary importance to winning support for international intervention. Weakness became an asset as the war became increasingly staged for international media crews with the government attempting to provoke incidents around Sarajevo and UN-declared safe areas to encourage military intervention. This strategy included exaggerating numbers of war casualties, preventing the reconnection of water supplies to Sarajevo, halting the evacuation of civilians from war zones and government shelling of their own territory (Boyd, 1995:26–9). These were rational responses to US human rights rhetoric which encouraged the Muslim government to play the victim card and refuse to negotiate a settlement in the belief that international aid was around the corner.

The more the Bosnian war became seen as a morality play of good against evil the less relationship the rhetoric had to the reality on the ground. In fact, it would be an exaggeration to see the war as primarily driven by the separatist desire for ethnic and religious division. Once the state institutions collapsed, the struggle for some form of security took on a regional as much as an ethnic shape. People searched for security in different ways according to locality. In the northern Bihac pocket, Muslim leader Fikret Abdic made alliances with local Serbs and Croats in a direct challenge to government policy; this split in the Muslim camp resulted in fierce fighting between two Muslim-led armies. Around Vares and Kiseljak, Serbs and Croats allied against Muslim militias, and around Mostar, Serbs and Muslims allied against Croat-led forces. The breakdown of the mechanisms of government authority resulted in increasingly localised, and criminalised, military configurations. Territories under nominal Croat, Serb or Muslim control fragmented into disparate enclaves as the process of political and social fragmentation continued (Bougarel, 1996:105). Ignoring the reality on the ground, the international community continued to support the Sarajevo government, which had become a small coterie around Alija Izetbegovic (whose elected term as state president expired in December 1991), despite the fact that the government's writ extended to no more than 12 per cent of the territory claimed (Owen, 1996:52).

In a repeat of the process of disintegration at federal level, Western powers' intrusion into negotiations between the Bosnian parties resulted in a breakdown of co-operation, as the side favoured by external powers had less incentive to compromise. This led to the institutionalisation of ethnic and regional divisions on the ground, and an increase in the levels of conflict. Failed intervention then led to greater international involvement and, finally, direct Western intervention to impose a settlement. In March 1994, the United States established a cease-fire between the Croat and Muslim forces, creating a Muslim-Croat Federation, offered military support and economic assistance. The Bosnian Croats were encouraged to sign up by the Croatian government, which was promised US diplomatic and tactical support for retaking the Serb-held areas of Krajina and Slavonia (Silber and Little, 1996:320).

The following year, the tide of war and diplomacy turned fully against the Bosnian Serbs, who suffered military defeats at the hands of the Federation forces and US-led Nato air strikes in August, 1995. The Serbs had little choice but to accept the US peace plan, in the face of military defeat and international sanctions. The Dayton Peace Agreement divided Bosnia between two separate entities, the Muslim-Croat Federation, which held 51 per cent of the territory, and the Serb-held region, Republika Srpska (RS), which held 49 per cent: a settlement little different from the Lisbon proposals rejected by the US, prior to the war, back in 1992. What had changed over the intervening years was the rising toll of death and destruction within Bosnia and, internationally, the discrediting of UN principles of neutrality and respect for state sovereignty.

1996–1999: The Protectorate Solution

The US and Nato claimed the credit for ending the Bosnian war and the peace was signed at the US Air Force base in Dayton, Ohio. The detailed agreement laying out Bosnia's constitutional structure was drawn up by US government advisers and imposed on the parties separately (Bildt, 1998:120–61). The fact that elected representatives from the new state had little input into the agreement was to be par for the course for the region, and repeated in the Rambouillet, Paris, 'talks' on Kosovo in 1999. There was little international hesitation in taking over the management of the political process. The lesson drawn, from the Bosnian experience, by most leading policymakers, was that UN neutrality and cautious diplomacy had given too much credibility to Yugoslav political leaders and impeded the decisive international actions necessary to regulate conflict in the region.[2] As leading liberal academic Bogdan Denitch (1996:210) noted: 'The sad but important fact is this: the meddling "Western outsiders" ... are far better representatives of the genuine interests of the Bosnian peoples.' Dayton marked a new phase of direct Western intervention in the region with growing mandates for the UN, Nato and OSCE (Organisation for Security and Co-operation in Europe) replacing government authority with regulation by international appointees. To this end, the UN appointed a colonial-style governor for Bosnia, given the Office of the High Representative (OHR).[3]

At the level of the Bosnian state, the High Representative viewed democratic consensus-building, in bodies such as the tripartite Presidency, Council of Ministers and State Parliament, as an unnecessary delay to imposing international plans.[4] In December 1997, the 'cumbersome' need for elected Bosnian representatives to assent to international edicts was removed and the High Representative was empowered both to dismiss elected representatives who obstructed policy and to impose legislation directly. The international community thereby assumed complete legislative and executive power over the formally independent state. In the Muslim-Croat Federation, policy has since been devised and enforced by the OHR in close co-operation with US state officials. In Republika Srpska, the international community supported the dissolution of the RS Parliamentary Assembly and overruled the RS constitutional court, to force new elections, and then organised the selection of a governing coalition which excluded the largest party, the SDS (Serb Democratic Party). In March 1999, before the Nato military campaign over Kosovo, the High Representative took international interference in entity politics further by dismissing the newly elected RS President Nikola Poplasen.

At city and local levels the international community has similarly had a free hand to overrule elected representatives and impose policy against the wishes of all three ethnic constituencies. In the divided city of Mostar, for example, council seats are allocated in advance on the basis of ethnicity and then, under international guidance, 'consensus' politics are enforced against the Croat representatives from West Mostar and Muslim representatives from East Mostar. In the disputed region of Brcko, under a Supervisory Order on Multi-Ethnic Administration, an international administrator regulates the composition of the consultative assembly and issues binding regulations. As the *Washington Post* described, his 'kingly powers' extend 'right down to determining who will live in which house, the list of required attendees at meetings of the local police chiefs, the ethnic composition of the local municipal council and the pace at which privatisation will proceed'.[5] At municipal level, representatives of the international community can enforce policy by imposing economic sanctions, dismissing local Mayors who are judged to be obstructive, and disregarding municipal election results, to impose power-sharing administrations or executive boards run by international appointees.[6]

Under direct international regulation, the institutions of Bosnian government at every level became hollow structures, not designed to operate autonomously, or enable elected representatives to negotiate their own solutions. For example, the Bosnian state Council of Ministers, with the nominal role of assenting to pre-prepared policy, has few staff or resources and is aptly described by the OHR as 'effectively, little more than an extended working group'.[7] Muslim, Croat and Serb representatives have all argued for greater autonomy in policy-making. As an adviser to Bosnian President Izetbegovic noted, there is a contradiction between the stated aims of the international administration and its consequences: 'A protectorate solution is not good, because the international community would bring all the decisions which would decrease all the functions of Bosnia-Herzegovina institutions. The High Representative's mandate is actually, an opposite one, to strengthen the Bosnia-Herzegovina institutions.'[8]

The artificial nature of Bosnian institutions has meant that they cannot play any role in creating new mechanisms of inter-ethnic co-operation. In fact, the lack of influence or say over policy decisions for elected representatives, or guarantees of security for their constituencies, has perpetuated the fragmentation of political power and reliance on personal and local networks of support which were prevalent during the Bosnian war (Woodward, 1995:236–7). The lack of cohering political structures has forced Bosnian people to rely on more narrow and parochial survival mechanisms, which has meant that ethnicity has maintained its wartime relevance as a political resource. The 'new feudalism' noted by some commentators, and the continued existence of weak para-state structures in Muslim and Croat areas of the Federation, is symptomatic of the vacuum of integrative institutional power at state and entity level rather than some internal disintegrative dynamic (Deacon and Stubbs, 1998). Where earlier 'neutral' Western intervention undermined and weakened federal government and republic structures of political cohesion, the heavy-handed protectorate powers being exercised in Bosnia appear to have had exactly the same results.

Conclusion: Disintegration and International Intervention

There has been little critical consideration of the international community's facilitation of the disintegration of Yugoslavia and the role that over-extended international regulation has had in institutionalising ethnic divisions and weakening political structures across the region. In Bosnia and Kosovo the international institutions running the political process argue that they can govern the region better than elected governments can. This elitist view of the incapacity of Balkan people to cope with democracy and state sovereignty has not been challenged by the critics of international engagement in the Balkans. In fact, the most vociferous critics of international policy go further in arguing that there is still too much power in the hands of elected state leaders in Bosnia and across the region (Chandler, 1999b).

This study would suggest that criticisms that international intervention in the region has not gone far enough, that there has been too much respect for state sovereignty or too much legitimacy given to elected representatives, turn reality on its head. Conflict in the region has been fuelled through international intervention which has undermined the democratic state institutions necessary to cohere and integrate society and maintain law and order. This point is forcefully made by Michael Ignatieff (1998:45), who argues that the cause of Balkan conflict has been the external pressures which have led to the collapse or weakening of states in the region, making inter-ethnic accommodation more difficult and, in turn, fuelling nationalist fears and ethnic tensions. To conclude, from problems of inter-ethnic co-operation, that there should be less power in the hands of elected state and regional authorities, as liberal interventionists do, leads to policies which can exacerbate, rather than resolve, the crisis. This was again demonstrated by the course of events in the Serbian province of Kosovo, where 'neutral' Western intervention encouraged the demands of Albanian separatists and undermined the authority of state institutions leading to the withdrawal of Serb security forces. This led to a further breakdown in order in the province, armed conflict and further, highly destructive, international involvement. As the ongoing crisis in Kosovo illustrates, Western intervention in former Yugoslavia has created a vicious circle where one destabilising intervention has been followed by another as international institutions have set the framework of fragmentation.

The lesson for the future may well be that the growing liberal perspective, which sees state sovereignty as 'the traditional enemy of the human rights movement', could be in need of reassessment to take into account the need for democratic and regionally accountable mechanisms of conflict prevention and inter-ethnic co-operation (Robertson, 1999:151). There is an alternative to the cycle of greater international mandates, further regional fragmentation and the establishment of a new set of protectorates in the Balkans – that of allowing elected representatives in the region greater freedom to negotiate their own solutions. The experience of Yugoslav disintegration over the last ten years suggests that respect for state sovereignty may be important, for, like democracy, in Churchill's words, it is 'the worst form of government apart from all the others'. When state sovereignty has been undermined by international intervention, whether ostensibly neutral or stridently interventionist, this has acted to intensify and institutionalise ethnic and regional divisions.

Notes

1. See Woodward (1995:104–5). Woodward's text is one of best treatments of the breakup of Yugoslavia up to the Dayton Agreement. Several points in this chapter owe much to her work.
2. See, for example, *Unfinished Peace: Report of the International Commission on the Balkans*, Washington, DC: Carnegie Endowment for International Peace, 1996.
3. For a more detailed survey of the Dayton provisions and their implementation see Chandler (1999a).
4. *Office of the High Representative Bulletin*, 62, 11 October 1997.
5. Lee Hockstader, 'A Bosnian Town in Limbo', *Washington Post*, 8 October 1998.
6. Bosnia and Herzegovina TV News Summary, 15 July 1998.
7. Report of the High Representative for Implementation of the Bosnian Peace Agreement to the Secretary-General of the United Nations, 11 July 1997, par. 24.
8. Bosnia and Herzegovina TV News Summary, 10 November 1997.

3

Mirjana Skoco and William Woodger

War Crimes

The 1990s has been the decade of international criminal tribunals. From a total of zero[1] at the end of the Cold War, tribunals have been established for former Yugoslavia and Rwanda, steps have been taken to set up an International Criminal Court, and there have been discussions about tribunals for Cambodia, East Timor and Iraq. What is expected of such tribunals? The 1994 *Yearbook* of the International Criminal Tribunal for Former Yugoslavia (ICTY)[2] states its purpose as: 'to do justice, to deter further crimes, and to contribute to the restoration and maintenance of peace'. It also states:

> the only civilised alternative to [the] desire for revenge is to render justice: to conduct a fair trial by a truly independent and impartial tribunal and to punish those found guilty. If no fair trial is held, feelings of hatred and resentment seething below the surface will, sooner or later, erupt and lead to renewed violence.

The then ICTY president, Judge Antonio Cassese, told the United Nations General Assembly on 14 November 1994:

> international justice can guarantee absolute independence and objectivity and a correct application of ... legal standards. Often the national courts of the state or states where the gross breaches have occurred may not be in a position to render impartial justice, free from emotional or political overtones ... International justice thus becomes indispensable, the more so because the crimes at issue are on such a scale as to concern the whole international community.

Even accepting the tribunal's flattering view of itself and its debased view of others – uncivilised beings who cannot avoid killing in revenge, let alone bias in court proceedings – how well does the ICTY, the role model tribunal, live up to its own expectations?

The ICTY was the first international tribunal to be established since Nuremberg and Tokyo after the Second World War. Yet the law it applies is 40 years and more old. For equality of treatment, this presumes no breaches of that law in the intervening period, yet the competence of the ICTY only extends to the territory of former Yugoslavia, and only from a specific starting point, 1 January 1991. Yugoslavs were therefore not treated equally – it was the application of law only for them. The ICTY, established in May 1993, was to try crimes allegedly committed before the court existed, but excluding events which led to the war. It also excluded events in the capitals of powerful nations, in their tussle to decide whether Yugoslavia should exist as a state, or else which constituents were valid as new states (Cohen, 1995:217–22, 237–40; Woodward, 1995:146–7). This arguably so severely limits the ICTY's capacity to understand the wars, that it seems unlikely the tribunal could play any constructive role in aiding reconciliation.

Thus, equality of treatment is an element of fairness that the ICTY does not meet. The main counter to this point is twofold: fairness is simply asserted in terms of how the ICTY will act, as with Cassese; and it is asserted that Yugoslavia is a unique case, supported by the scale of reported atrocity (Beigbeder, 1999:147; Boutros-Ghali, 1999:76). This effectively circular argument ignores the massive political, diplomatic and media concentration on the region, emphasised by the relative non-interest in some 30 other ongoing conflicts. Ignoring the latter, and accepting for the purpose of further enquiry that something inherently unfair can act fairly, how does the record of the tribunal stand?

The Experience So Far

Even one example of unfair treatment should cause embarrassment to the ICTY, but lack of critical media scrutiny has meant its many failures have not been widely publicised. After one defendant, Goran Lajic, had been detained for three months, the Prosecutor admitted at the pre-trial hearing that nine out of the ten witnesses could not identify him. In the trial of Dusan Tadic an anonymous prosecution witness turned out to have been trained to give evidence while in prison in Bosnia, whereupon the Prosecutor withdrew his 147 pages of evidence without explaining why he had ever thought the witness credible in the first place. The case against 'Gruban' – an alleged Bosnian Serb rapist – had to be dropped when it was revealed that he was a fictional character, from Miodrag Bulatovic's novel Hero on a Donkey.[3]

According to Geoffrey Robertson (1999:280) the tribunal's Rules of Procedure and Evidence 'provide a model of "due process" in criminal courts'. Yet they have been amended on 20 separate dates. Indeed, they had already been amended on eight occasions before the first trial, that of Tadic, began on 7 May 1996. The case of Bosnian Serb General Djordje Djukic demonstrates clearly that breaking its own rules is not a problem for the tribunal: the Rules are simply changed to legitimise any similar case in the future. At different times Djukic was regarded as a witness, a suspect and an accused, sometimes simultaneously, because under the Rules, the ICTY had no correct way to handle him. The Prosecutor wanted to 'turn' a senior Bosnian Serb officer to give evidence against former Bosnian Serb president and army chief, Radovan Karadzic and Ratko Mladic. With such a prize in view, due process, rights and legality were abused.

Djukic was detained by Bosnian government police at a checkpoint on the road to Sarajevo airport on 30 January 1996, despite the road being under international control, and the Dayton Peace Agreement guaranteeing freedom of movement. There was no warrant for his arrest, and he had not been previously named in any of the many war crimes allegations. Djukic's 'crime' was that he was a general in the Bosnian Serb Army, something the surprised policemen only realised when they looked at his identity card. Following this questionable arrest and a period of detention in Sarajevo, Djukic was interviewed, with no offer of legal counsel, by a tribunal investigator, and asked to go to The Hague. To be asked to make such a decision, involving travelling to another country and detention in a foreign jail, without legal advice, is at best sharp practice.

The then Chief Prosecutor Richard Goldstone asked the tribunal for an arrest warrant on 7 February, voicing his 'appreciation for the continuing co-operation' of the Bosnian government.[4] Goldstone thus legitimised Djukic's capture and subsequent treatment. Under the Rules, however, it was not possible to arrest a suspect without an indictment. Rule 40 allowed arrest of suspects, and Rule 54 gives very broad powers to the ICTY, but Rule 55, which regulates arrest warrants, refers specifically to the 'accused', that is, indicted, and makes no mention of suspects. Nevertheless, arrest and transfer orders were issued. An unregulated arrest warrant is no better than arbitrary arrest, and extradition without all manner of supporting legal documents simply would not occur in a domestic jurisdiction. The ICTY is the only court in the world which can simply order extradition and expect it to happen without question. While in The Hague, Djukic was unable to appear in court in Sarajevo on charges in connection with the war. Although empowered to halt proceedings in a domestic court, the ICTY refused. The hearings on extending his detention in Sarajevo therefore continued while the tribunal prevented him appearing. Simultaneous court proceedings and loss of the right to appear at proceedings against him are both unacceptable.

ICTY spokesman Christian Chartier said the detention was 'not bound by any time limit', though he hoped Djukic would be indicted or released 'within weeks'.[5] Goldstone added that the 'rules of the tribunal do not provide any specific limits to the length of time persons may be held in custody in these circumstances'.[6] Unlimited detention without trial would also not occur in a domestic jurisdiction. According to Goldstone and Chartier, Djukic had been arrested as a suspect, and this was duly reported in the world's media. Yet a copy of the arrest and transfer orders would have revealed that Djukic was supposedly a 'witness' under Rule 90 *bis*. Under this Rule, witnesses can only be detained in relation to a case in progress before the court, and the detention period is limited to that of the original national court, in this case 30 days. There were no scheduled trials for the whole of 1996 in which

Djukic could have appeared as a witness. Even the pretext for the unregulated orders was false.

At a hearing three weeks later Djukic categorically stated he would not agree to be a witness, so Goldstone prepared an indictment against him. This looks like a threat: say what we want, or we'll find something to charge you with. The indictment itself was vague. Responding to a defence motion for Djukic's release, a judge invited Goldstone to make 'such modifications as he deems necessary if he intends to maintain the counts appearing in paragraph 7 of the indictment'.[7] However, this paragraph contained the *only* counts against Djukic: Goldstone had raised, and an ICTY judge had only recently confirmed, an indictment which did not even satisfy a second judge.

The ICTY has thus serially abused its own Rules, and hence its professed concern for due process and the rights of the accused. In tacit acknowledgement of these abuses of the Rules, they were later changed in what could be called 'The Djukic Amendments'.[8] Importantly, there was (and still is) no legal procedure by which Djukic could seek redress for this treatment at the hands of the Tribunal. In a revealing comment on their experiences with the ICTY, his lawyers said they would have preferred him to be returned for trial by a Bosnian Federation court in Sarajevo. They felt they could win their case of illegal arrest and detention in Sarajevo under domestic law, in contrast to their prospects in The Hague, where it was clear to them that the ICTY's own Rules were insufficiently defined and respected to afford their client either certainty or fairness.[9]

Kosovo: The Political Tribunal

The ICTY's claim to jurisdiction over Kosovo is based on two 'accidents'. First, the tribunal was established during the wars in Croatia and Bosnia for the 'territory of the former Yugoslavia', and five years later another conflict flared up there. Second, the time period covered by ICTY jurisdiction was supposed to end when the UN Security Council declared the wars in Croatia and Bosnia over,[10] yet despite the fact they actually ended in 1995 the Security Council had still to make this decision when the Kosovo conflict broke out in early 1998. In exercising its supposed authority in Kosovo, the ICTY sought help from Nato. This benefited both parties: the ICTY obtained easier access to 'evidence' by its association with Nato military intelligence, and Nato obtained legitimacy from its association with the ICTY as an important legal organ of the international community. Co-operation with the ICTY endorsed Nato's war propaganda, casting Nato as a policeman breaking up a fight, rather than a vigilante intervening without legal sanction and making a bad situation catastrophically worse.[11]

The then Chief Prosecutor Louise Arbour, however, claimed the tribunal was acting independently:

It is inconceivable in reality, quite apart from it being very unethical ... that we would in fact agree to be guided by the political will of those who may want to advance an agenda ... The real danger is whether we would fall into that inadvertently by being in the hands of information-providers who might have an agenda that we would not be able to discern.

This declaration of independence was undercut by the fact that Arbour made it from the platform of the British Ministry of Defence briefing on 20 April 1999. Whilst unable to support Nato's war directly, she did manage to mention the 'morality of the enterprise'. Arbour said she was 'not terribly worried' about the danger of being manipulated by information-providers because 'extremely stringent rules of evidence' would mean that 'we certainly will not be advancing any case against anybody on the basis of unsubstantiated, unverifiable, uncorroborated allegation'. Arguably this assurance must be regarded with scepticism.

British and American politicians who favoured the Nato military intervention in Kosovo certainly acted as if the ICTY was 'their' tribunal. Apparently feeling it had the authority to decide whether, and for what, people would be indicted, the US government stated: 'We will make a decision on whether Yugoslav actions against ethnic Albanians constitute genocide once we have sufficient information on which to base a judgement. The ICTY will indict those responsible for crimes against humanity and genocide.'[12] Similarly, British Foreign Secretary Robin Cook warned 'those with responsibility in Kosovo' could face prosecution 'unless they halt now the reprisals and start to obey the laws of human decency and of humanitarian law', implying he had the power to make the issuing of charges conditional.[13] Cook promised to call Arbour with the 'reports' he had, and two days later she announced the indictment of Zeljko Raznjatovic (Arkan).

On ICTY precedent, there are certainly grounds for indicting Nato leaders. To give but one example, on 8 March 1996 the ICTY issued a decision against Milan Martic, former president of the Republic of Serbian Krajina, for launching a rocket cluster bomb attack on military targets in Zagreb in May 1995. An international arrest warrant was issued for Martic on the grounds that in 'respect of its accuracy and striking force, the use of the Orkan rocket in this case was not designed to hit military targets but to terrorize the civilians of Zagreb'.[14] A similar case could be made over Nato's cluster-bombing of Nis on 7 May 1999, in which a market and a hospital were hit in separate strikes. The Nato bombs were a long way from their alleged target, the airport, and more than a mile apart from each other. Yet it is certain that Nato leaders will not face indictment. Instead, the Nato-led force occupying Kosovo has been granted the status of 'assistant' to the ICTY's investigators.

Announcing the indictment of President Slobodan Milosevic and other Yugoslav leaders on 27 May 1999, Arbour said she was 'mindful of the impact that this indictment may have on the peace process'. The 'impact' was not thought to result from the tribunal working in close co-operation with

Nato and its individual members. Rather, it resulted from Milosevic's guilt, which Arbour implicitly presumed whilst formally upholding the presumption of innocence:

> Although the accused are entitled to the benefit of the presumption of innocence until they are convicted, the evidence upon which this indictment was confirmed raises serious questions about their suitability to be the guarantors of any deal, let alone a peace agreement. They have not been rendered less suitable by the indictment. The indictment has simply exposed their unsuitability.[15]

The misapplication by the ICTY of the 'innocent until convicted' formula has the effect of transforming that concept into a sterile technicality which in practice – perversely – actually presumes guilt. The presumption of innocence is important because it involves the recognition that, under any legal system, charges will sometimes be brought against innocent people. Everyone must be treated as innocent because they may well be. For Arbour, the concept does not exist: indictment is enough. Hence she declared on 31 March that people linked with Arkan 'will be tainted by their association with an indicted war criminal'.[16]

Alongside Milosevic, Nikola Sainovic, a deputy prime minister of Yugoslavia, was also indicted, though it is difficult to see why. Despite being described at the 29 March MoD briefing as 'in effect the person who runs the effort in Kosovo' and 'possibly the most important member of the team', Sainovic is not named in the indictment as having 'superior authority' or command responsibility. His indictment seems to be based on the fact he 'held prominent positions' in Milosevic's political party and the Yugoslav and Serbian governments; he signed the October 1998 agreement allowing OSCE observers into Kosovo; he was a member of the delegation to the February 1999 Rambouillet talks; Western diplomats were told to talk to him about Kosovo; and ... that's it. Sainovic's indictment was ordered because of the need to show that the expulsion of ethnic Albanians from Kosovo was part of a long-standing plan, not a response to the Nato bombing campaign. Its real justification is political, not judicial.

The Media and the ICTY

Media criticism of the tribunal since it was established has been limited to complaints about the lack of UN funding and the failure of Nato forces to arrest or kill enough indictees. Such 'criticisms' are actually entirely supportive of the ICTY itself, and the sorts of problems discussed above are almost never mentioned in news coverage. Instead, journalistic principles have been abandoned in the media's zeal for 'war crimes' stories.

Like Arbour, journalists have eroded the concept of 'innocent until proved guilty'. In reporting domestic trials, they are careful not to lay themselves open to accusations of prejudging the case. Before being found guilty, defendants are not described in the media as 'criminals', since their innocence must be assumed until guilt is proven. When it comes to war crimes, however, normal protocols are forgotten, and defendants are routinely described as 'indicted war criminals', the approximate equivalent of 'charged murderers'. Djukic, for example, was the second of '53 indicted criminals' in custody according to *The Times* (2 March 1996). An 'indictment' is merely a charge, yet a 'criminal' is someone who has been found guilty.

The implicit presumption of guilt reflects reporters' enthusiasm for the work of the ICTY. As Goldstone acknowledges, most journalists 'wished the tribunal to succeed and ... responded to my calls for positive and supportive coverage' (Gutman and Rieff, 1999:14). It is therefore hardly surprising that the international media should be seen by many Yugoslavs as an arm of powerful Western institutions such as Nato and the ICTY. Goldstone comments on the way a close association with the tribunal may undermine media independence:

> Like aid workers and Red Cross or Red Crescent delegates, if reporters become identified as would-be witnesses, their safety and future ability to be present at a field of battle will be compromised ... I would therefore support a rule of law to protect journalists from becoming unwilling witnesses. (Gutman and Rieff, 1999:16)

In practice journalists have been entirely willing witnesses before the ICTY – which Goldstone is supportive of, without explaining why the same problems should not arise. On 8 October 1999 the ICTY ruled that evidence from a former Red Cross employee who had presented himself as a willing prosecution witness was inadmissible, precisely on the grounds that testifying would compromise the aid organisation's 'impartiality, neutrality and independence'.[17] Journalists and media organisations would normally claim the same 'impartiality, neutrality and independence', yet the *Guardian*'s Ed Vulliamy and former BBC journalist Martin Bell both testified before the tribunal about their experiences in Bosnia, and news organisations such as ABC and ITN have willingly contributed documentaries, news reports and unbroadcast 'rushes' to the ICTY and its forerunner, the UN Commission of Experts.

Similarly, many journalists covering Kosovo routinely concluded their reports with assurances that their 'evidence' would be handed over to ICTY investigators, and in some instances reporters represented themselves as volunteer 'detectives' for the tribunal.[18] This stands in contrast to journalists' attitudes to the September 1999 case of Ed Moloney – a reporter for the *Sunday Tribune* in Northern Ireland – who refused to give the police notes he had made during an interview with a man subsequently charged with murder. Britain's National Union of Journalists voiced outrage over the request, and Moloney stated bluntly that he was a journalist, not a detective. Yet in reporting Yugoslavia, reporters such as Vulliamy and Bell happily abandoned their role as public observers, becoming participants who aimed to influence events. As Goldstone concedes, 'without media support the tribunal would have floundered' (Gutman and Rieff, 1999:14).

Conclusion

The ICTY, claiming the highest legal standards, judging the most serious of allegations, does not seem fair or independent. It stands outside society, unlike most national courts which are accepted by the majority as having a proper role. With the international tribunals, large majorities in the countries to which they apply law do not accept them as impartial – indeed, they see them as biased, and a tool against them. War crimes law *is* used by politicians as a tool, and has always been used by them to legitimise war. They aim to ensure that the 'horror of war' is not an argument against war itself: if war is fought well, then war is an acceptable solution. Particularly in a civil war, and by no means just in the Balkans, those who fought and victims on all sides somehow have to resolve the extreme problems created by an extreme situation and draw a line under the conflict. The performance of the ICTY to date indicates that it contributes little to – and indeed impedes – this process.

Notes

1. The International Court of Justice adjudicates disputes between states, issuing non-binding judgments against them, so is necessarily excluded from this discussion.
2. Its formal name is the 'International Tribunal for the Prosecution of Persons Responsible for Serious Violations of International Humanitarian Law Committed in the Territories of the Former Yugoslavia since 1991'. The first short-name used was the 'International Tribunal for the Former Yugoslavia', but later the word 'Criminal', which does not appear in the formal name, was added.
3. See Kristen Sellars, 'The Tyranny of Human Rights', *Spectator*, 28 August 1999.
4. CC/PIO/031-E, The Hague, 7 February 1996.
5. Weekly press briefing of the spokesman for the ICTY, 13 February 1996.
6. CC/PIO/033-E, The Hague, 14 February 1996.
7. Decision by Trial Chamber I on preliminary motions of the accused, 26 April 1996.
8. Rules of Procedure and Evidence, as amended 25 June and 5 July 1996.
9. Interview by William Woodger with Djukic's son, Belgrade, Easter 1997.
10. S/Res 827, 1993, paragraph 2.
11. It is clear that Nato was breaching international law, because it was only after the bombing started that politicians started to argue that earlier UN Security Council Resolutions could be interpreted as authorising military action.
12. US Information Agency Fact Sheet: Ethnic Cleansing In Kosovo, 1 April 1999.
13. MoD Briefing, 29 March 1999.
14. ICTY Bulletin No. 4, 15 March 1996.
15. JL/PIU/404-E, The Hague, 27 May 1999.
16. CC/PIU/392-E, The Hague, 31 March 1999.
17. JL/PIS/439-E, The Hague, 8 October 1999.
18. See, for example, John Sweeney's film for Channel Four's *Dispatches*, 4 November 1999.

4

Peter Gowan

The War and its Aftermath

The Nato air war against Yugoslavia lasted for 78 days, from 24 March until 10 June 1999. The Nato powers were allied to the Kosovo Liberation Army (KLA) and the air campaign was linked to a KLA ground campaign within Kosovo against Serbian security forces and the Yugoslav army.

Nato's Balkan war was not only a military action. It was simultaneously a major intervention in European and world politics, throwing down three political challenges: questioning the core legal rules of the inter-state system by attacking a sovereign state without a United Nations Security Council (UNSC) mandate; challenging Russia not only as a UNSC member, but also by violating clauses in the Nato-Russia Founding Act and attacking a country with which Russia had friendly links;[1] and also challenging the political cohesion under US leadership of West and Central European states, testing US capacity to lead in European politics by maintaining the cohesion of its subordinate allies. At stake in the war was therefore not only the future of the Western Balkans but the evolution of the European and international political order.

Despite the avalanche of media coverage of this military conflict, a great deal of data relevant to a full analysis and evaluation of the military and diplomatic aspects of the war remains, at present, unavailable to researchers (Cordesman, 1999). In broad outline, the military side of the war was fought in two theatres: within Kosovo itself, where Nato air strikes were combined with KLA activity and where the Yugoslav army and Serbian security forces concentrated upon striking at the KLA and its actual or potential sources of civilian support while seeking to protect its military assets from Nato air power; and secondly, within non-Kosovo Yugoslavia, and especially within Serbia, where Nato air strikes were directed first at military targets, then at civilian and economic infrastructures – transport systems, public utilities, factories and other civilian targets such as TV and radio stations.

The Nato air war was overwhelmingly a US effort. The US flew over 80 per cent of the strike sorties, over 90 per cent of the electronic warfare missions, fired over 80 per cent of the guided air weapons and launched over 95 per cent of the Cruise missiles (ibid.). The European Nato member states thus had only an auxiliary role in the direct military effort and both command structures and decision-making on the targeting of air strikes and on the termination of the air war were effectively in American hands.

As far as the Yugoslav side was concerned, it was both militarily and politically almost entirely isolated. This is another way of saying that the Russian government decided not to take military action to assist Yugoslavia, nor to supply it with weapons systems that could have created difficulties for Nato warplanes. As the Russian general staff indicated at the start of the war, Russia did have the military capability to transform the military equation, but decided not to do so, and as the war progressed, reduced its support for core Yugoslav political demands.

On the political-diplomatic side US predominance within Nato was less overwhelming but was greatly strengthened by Nato's rule that the ending of the war had to be a unanimous decision, thus giving the US a veto. The other key players were the German and French governments. And as the war continued, the international political role of the Russian government became increasingly important as it became clear that Nato military action could not lead to an unconditional Yugoslav surrender in the short term.

Evaluation Against Aims

The difficulty of evaluating the Nato war against the Yugoslav/Serbian state lies in establishing what the political goals of the Nato states and of Yugoslavia/Serbia were in conducting the war. The public statements of government leaders about their war aims do not necessarily express the real operational goals of policy in this war any more than in any other. At the same time, information about the US government's decision-making on war aims and means remains classified. Nevertheless, an interim interpretation of aims can be reached through making the reasonable assumption that the US government made a rational calculation on how to harmonise operational means and goals. From this assumption we can engage in backward mapping from actual policy outputs back to policy goals and thus gain some basis for establishing aims against which the war can be evaluated. Such an assumption of rationality in the case of US policy on this war is all the more reasonable since we know that the US administration spent some 14 months preparing the military campaign and its political repercussions in painstaking detail (*Washington Post*, 23 March 1999).

The Nato powers publicly declared the aim of the air war to be purely humanitarian. In the first days of the war this declared humanitarian goal was presented in direct and immediate terms: Nato said it was bombing Yugoslav/Serbian forces to prevent them from attacking the Kosovo Albanian population. Yet the means Nato employed for this supposed purpose – an alliance with the KLA combined with high altitude bombing of Kosovo when weather permitted – had an effect opposite to the declaratory aim: Serbian security forces launched a full-scale offensive against the KLA and forcibly expelled hundreds of thousands of Albanians from Kosovo. This was an outcome which Pentagon chiefs had foreseen as likely, before the war was launched. As the *Washington Post* reported on 5 April 1999:

> Privately even the staunchest advocates of air power amongst the four star commanders doubted that air power alone could do much to budge Milosevic in the near term. They noted the challenges of sending planes against widely dispersed ground forces that were carrying out door to door terror.

The Defense Secretary, William Cohen, also advised, before the war started, that there would have to be a long bombing campaign. The *Washington Post* (11 April) explained: 'Aides say Cohen never counted on the operation being over quickly.'

Thus the declaratory aim of the air war could not have been its operational aim. If humanitarian aims are held to have played any governing operational role, then it must have been that of a humanitarian end result through an eventual Nato occupation of Kosovo. This may be described as a humanitarian paradox: Nato was prepared to precipitate a humanitarian catastrophe and even, according to some Nato leaders, a 'genocidal' catastrophe, for humanitarian goals to be achieved when the Yugoslav leadership was eventually coerced into accepting a Nato occupation of Kosovo. The fact that such a paradox is not permissible within a humanitarian, ethical justification for war may account for the fact that Nato leaders insisted at the start of the war that they believed President Slobodan Milosevic accepted that Nato should occupy Kosovo and actually would welcome the bombing as a means of persuading Serbian public opinion that there was no choice but to accept the occupation. This, in turn, however, undermines the argument that the purpose of the bombing was to stop Milosevic from perpetrating a humanitarian catastrophe.

These declaratory contradictions on the part of US and Nato leaders leave us with a conundrum as to the real operational motives for the war on Nato's part.[2] The only certain, coherent link between evident Nato means and goals is that between the bombing campaign against the Yugoslav state and the goal of gaining eventual Nato occupation of Kosovo. The various declaratory rationales mentioned above seem to belong more properly to means of legitimation of the war *vis-à-vis* various politically relevant audiences, as follows:

1. The rationale in terms of direct humanitarian intervention to prevent a humanitarian catastrophe in Kosovo had great significance for Nato attempts to gain some semblance of international legal legitimation of a war that violated core legal rules of the inter-state system. What, in international law, was an act of unprovoked aggression against a sovereign state in violation of the UN Charter might be justified by the claim that international law could be overridden by the need militarily to try to prevent an imminent genocide in Kosovo.

2. The suggestion from General Wesley Clark that he had intelligence information indicating that Milosevic welcomed the bombing as a means of
   gaining Serbian acceptance of Nato occupation of Kosovo seems to have
   been designed to win support for the air war from Nato governments in
   Europe which were opposed to the campaign.
3. The claims, after the bombing started, that the Yugoslav/Serbian authorities were engaged in genocide within Kosovo seems to have been designed
   to gain enduring popular legitimation within Nato countries for a long
   bombing war. These claims, made by British and American leaders, were
   reinforced by the decision of the UN Security Council's International
   Criminal Tribunal for Former Yugoslavia (ICTY) to indict Milosevic for
   war crimes at the end of the war.

The actions of the Serbian/Yugoslav state in Kosovo in response to the Nato
attack served to provide the Nato states with *ex post facto* popular legitimation of the attack on Yugoslavia amongst the Nato populations themselves.
The air campaign led to the expulsion of some 850,000 Albanians from
Kosovo as well as some killings and atrocities against sections of the Albanian
population and some destruction of Albanian property by Yugoslav forces and
paramilitaries.

Yugoslav spokespersons acknowledged during and after the war that some
atrocities had been committed against Kosovo Albanians in the first days of
the war, but claimed these were the work of rogue elements and were not
authorised by state authorities. They insisted that Serbian security and
military forces' actions in Kosovo were dictated exclusively by military neces-
sities, notably efforts to crush the KLA and secure defensive positions along
their borders. They further claimed that most of the Albanians flooding into
Macedonia and Albania were refugees from the internal fighting and from
the Nato bombing.

Authoritative, independent assessment of the scale and nature of the
Yugoslav/Serbian state operations against Kosovo Albanians during the war
is not yet possible. During the war Nato media reports claimed that as many
as 100,000 Kosovo Albanians had been slaughtered by Serbian security
forces (Agence France Presse, 3 August). After the war Nato spokespeople
gave figures of 10,000 or more people killed by Serbian security forces and
buried in approximately 100 sites.[3] At the start of August, UN administrator Bernard Kouchner claimed a figure of 11,000 deaths and argued that he
derived this figure from ICTY sources. But ICTY deputy prosecutor Graham
Blewitt contradicted Kouchner's claim, saying the ICTY had not provided any
such estimates and stating that: 'The only thing that we have said is that the
figure for the victims of war crimes is more likely to be in the thousands than
in the hundreds' (Agence France Presse, 3 August). The ICTY indictment of
Milosevic as a war criminal, on the basis of Nato-supplied data cited about
350 people dead, far less than the number of civilians killed by Nato bombing.

The logic of the war, as Nato experts acknowledge, gave an increasingly important role to KLA ground forces, whose task was to target Yugoslav troop concentrations for Nato air strikes, and to draw Yugoslav military forces into open combat thus making them vulnerable to air strikes. Some military experts even claim this KLA role played an important part in bringing Belgrade to the negotiating table. Thus the Yugoslav army had powerful military incentives for seeking to destroy KLA networks and units in Kosovo. So disentangling data on which of the Kosovo Albanian dead were KLA fighters and which were non-combatant civilians is a central evaluative issue. Like the Nato authorities, the Yugoslav authorities could also claim that the killing of civilians in many cases could have the status of 'collateral damage' – independent estimates of the numbers of civilians killed by Nato bombing ran not in the hundreds but at over a thousand. Although the figure of 10,000 Kosovo Albanian deaths thus lacks any established factual basis it does correspond exactly to Western estimates of the number of Serbian casualties from Nato's 37,000 bombing sorties.[4]

What is, however, beyond doubt, is that the 78-day Nato war marked a qualitative escalation in the killings on both sides in the Kosovo conflict. While in the whole of 1998 between 1,000 and 2,000 people were killed on both sides in that conflict, the deaths during the two and a half month war ran to many times these figures.[5] Yugoslav government figures of the numbers of Yugoslav civilians killed by the Nato bombing are 2,600.

As the US Joint Chiefs had predicted before the war, the bombing campaign against Yugoslav military assets within Kosovo proved ineffective. Nato's wartime statistics on the damage suffered by Yugoslav hardware proved greatly exaggerated.[6] Three months after the war Nato still claimed to have destroyed 93 tanks, 153 Armoured Personnel Carriers and almost 400 artillery pieces. But these claims are both unproven and are regarded as wildly exaggerated by Western independent experts, such as John Beaver from *Jane's Defence Weekly*, and other journalists who toured Kosovo extensively just after the arrival of Nato troops in Kosovo and reported that only 13 Yugoslav tanks had been knocked out and the retreating Yugoslav Army displayed an impressive array of tanks, artillery and other assets.

It was, indeed, the ineffectiveness of the bombing campaign within the Kosovo theatre which seems to have been a key motive for the US command to turn its main effort towards strategic bombing of Serbian economic and civil targets. Nato planes inflicted massive economic damage in Serbia, hitting 144 major industrial plants as well as Yugoslav TV and radio. According to Yugoslav sources 33 medical clinics or hospitals and 344 schools were bombed and evidence of widespread damage to these facilities has been confirmed by independent journalists. According to Belgrade, three out of every five targets of Nato bombing were civilian. Twelve days of systematic bombing by Nato destroyed the large Pancevo petrochemical plant, causing pollution levels 10,000 times the permitted safety levels in the surrounding region. The resulting destruction of the Yugoslav economy involved a loss of 40 per cent of total output and of 44 per cent of industrial output. It also inevitably entailed civilian deaths and casualties. Many of these were classed by Nato as accidental. Nato claims 20 cases of collateral civilian casualties. Anthony Cordesman of the Centre for Strategic and International Studies in Washington says this is false: there were over 100 incidents of collateral civilian casualties.[7]

War Diplomacy

Apart from ensuring Yugoslavia's continued political isolation within Southeast Europe and a semblance of political stability in such states as Macedonia and Albania, the major diplomatic issues during the war were concerned with Nato-Russian relations and internal Nato unity. As far as the latter was concerned, the key issues were from the start about the terms for ending the air war.

From very early on in the air war, the German government, as well as the Italian and Greek governments, indicated terms for suspending the bombing which differed from those of the US and British governments. While initially the French government kept its distance from German ideas for ending the war, President Jacques Chirac later shifted and this enabled a more vigorous German diplomatic effort to seek a negotiated settlement.[8] German efforts in this direction were, at the same time, constantly focused upon achieving a common position with the Russian government, and it was the achievement of this German-Russian common position that led eventually to the diplomatic breakthrough that ended the war.

Russian policy was, from the first, the object of intense activity by the various Nato powers. The American Deputy Secretary of State, Strobe Talbott, spent most of the war in Moscow. The first American objective was to gain Russian military passivity in the face of the Nato attack. To achieve this, the Clinton administration offered Moscow the prospect of large IMF financial support (*Financial Times*, 30 March 1999). US diplomacy can no doubt also be credited with helping in the replacement of Yevgeny Primakov as Prime Minister and in Yeltsin's decision to make Viktor Chernomyrdin Russia's envoy in charge of seeking a diplomatic solution. These steps were a signal triumph for American diplomacy, and they had a major impact on the course and final settlement of the war, pulling Moscow towards an ending of the war acceptable to Nato.

But the Clinton administration seems to have been divided, as the war progressed, as to acceptable terms for ending the war. Efforts to end the war through concessions to Belgrade were led, within the Nato alliance, by the German government. Bonn worked intensively for weeks to construct a joint G7–Russian document outlining areas of general agreement between these eight powers in the hope that this would lay the basis for a new peace initiative. As the document indicated, this initiative would involve a return to the UN Security Council and an acceptance on Nato's part of overall UNSC authority.

Although State Department officials in Europe seemed to support the G8 text, it was strongly criticised by unnamed administration sources in Washington the following day. And the US military strike against the Chinese Embassy in Belgrade destroyed the possibility of carrying forward the German–Russian initiative for a new UNSC resolution.[9] It also gave the Clinton administration at least a month's diplomatic breathing space in which to escalate the bombing in the hope of achieving a military breakthrough that could evade the need for substantial political concessions.

The German government then turned to establishing a secret back-channel to Belgrade, using a Swedish businessman as its intermediary and involving the Finnish President. These efforts brought a secret agreement on peace terms between Bonn and President Milosevic. In what appears to have been a carefully stage-managed German plan, the Bonn government arranged for the official, public mission to clinch the peace deal with Yugoslavia to coincide with a meeting of the European Council. At the same time, the German Chancellor made a public demand for a public inquiry into the US bombing of the Chinese Embassy, a demand which was all the more remarkable given that the Chinese government itself had dropped the demand for such an inquiry as a precondition for Chinese acceptance of any Western UNSC resolution on Kosovo. It thus seems likely that Chancellor Gerhard Schröder's call for an inquiry was designed to put pressure on Washington to accept the peace terms agreed between Bonn and Belgrade: if the German government had made public the information supplied to it by the Chinese government about the bombing, this could have polarised the Nato alliance from top to bottom.

The North Atlantic Council was bypassed and the divided Clinton administration was left with the choice of accepting the peace deal or finding itself in open political confrontation with the EU 15, including the British government. It continued bombing for a further week, but eventually accepted the German-brokered deal.

The End of the War

Under the terms of the agreement, two central objectives of the Nato powers were gained: the withdrawal of Serbian and Yugoslav military and state personnel from Kosovo and the entry into Kosovo of a predominantly Nato force, establishing a *de facto* Nato protectorate. Since the Yugoslav authorities had opposed both these steps before and during the war, their achievement was a defeat for the Yugoslav-Serbian state and was presented as a triumph for the Nato military campaign.

Yet a more detailed assessment of the diplomatic settlement of the conflict raises a number of complexities and interpretative problems. The Yugoslav government itself claimed that it agreed to the settlement because Nato made sweeping political concessions. From a Yugoslav point of view, as we shall see, these concessions were substantial. But they were less substantial for the Nato powers: the interests most damaged were those of the KLA.

Thus the agreement ending the war seems to have been partly the result of the damage inflicted by Nato on Serbia proper and partly the result of the Nato concessions on the future status of Kosovo and of the KLA. But there is also some evidence that the Yugoslav leadership believed it had the possibility of using the terms of the UNSC resolution ending the war and an alliance with elements in the Russian military and security apparatus to gain a strong or dominant Russian bridgehead in Northern Kosovo.

The peace terms did indeed include some substantial concessions to Yugoslavia/Serbia on the part of the Nato powers. Nato abandoned some central political positions which it had insisted upon at Rambouillet and at the start of the war. These concessions require careful examination. The most important were the following:

1. Rambouillet envisaged a three-year transition in Kosovo towards a referendum on independence. The peace terms envisaged no referendum and a continuation of Serbian sovereignty over Kosovo, including the return of Serbian state personnel.
2. Rambouillet recognised the KLA and its leadership as the political representatives of the Kosovo Albanian majority and as a provisional government of Kosovo. The peace terms did not recognise the KLA as a political authority.
3. Rambouillet did not recognise any role for the UN Security Council in the affairs of Kosovo. The peace terms placed Kosovo and the Nato occupation force under UNSC authority, and indeed did not explicitly acknowledge Nato as having any overall authority within Kosovo.
4. Rambouillet did not recognise any independent role for Russian forces within Kosovo. The peace terms gave Russia the right to an independent presence of Russian forces within Kosovo.
5. Rambouillet gave Nato forces the right to operate throughout Serbia proper. The peace terms deny Nato military forces any right to enter Serbia proper.

These five points do mark a major political shift on Nato's part, and have enabled the Yugoslav government to claim that their decision to repudiate Rambouillet and to opt for military resistance achieved very substantial political gains. Of this there can be little doubt. But these Yugoslav gains in the peace agreement did not represent a major failure on Nato's part to achieve its core operational objective in the Kosovo war.

As Henry Kissinger and many others have pointed out, some of Nato's Rambouillet terms seem to have been designed to be 'deal-breakers', designed to ensure that the Yugoslav government would reject the terms while the KLA would emerge from the breakdown on Nato's side. In this category of demands would fall point 5: the right of Nato military forces to move across the whole of Yugoslavia. This replica of the Austro-Hungarian ultimatum to Serbia which triggered the First World War was hardly a serious political goal of the Nato air campaign: it would have implied Nato occupation of Belgrade. It thus ensured a Yugoslav rejection of Rambouillet, but could easily be subsequently dropped.

More important for understanding the nature of the whole war in political terms is an appreciation of the Nato powers' real attitude towards the independence and KLA control of Kosovo. Nato's concessions on these two issues in the final peace terms were of great political importance to the Yugoslav government. But this does not necessarily at all mean that these concessions marked a climb-down by the Nato powers from their real political objectives in launching the war. While public opinion within the Nato zone more or less took it for granted that Nato supported the Kosovo Albanians and the KLA, the Nato powers did not, in fact, support either the central political aspiration of the Kosovo Albanians or the programmatic goals of the KLA. As far as the Clinton administration was concerned, it wished to gain the military support of the KLA in a war with Yugoslavia, but it was at best ambivalent if not downright hostile to the Kosovo Albanian goal of independence and unity of all Albanians. And the West European members of the alliance had shown themselves to be hostile to independence for Kosovo.

An absolutely central political paradox of the Nato war against Yugoslavia was thus that the United States administration was determined to launch a war against the Yugoslav state on the political terrain of the national question in Kosovo while simultaneously tending to agree with the Yugoslav state on the cardinal political issues involved in the Kosovo national question. Thus the shift in Nato's stance away from a Kosovo referendum, away from a KLA government, and towards continued Serbian sovereignty over Kosovo, did not mark a political retreat by Nato at all: simply a shift away from political support for the KLA's goals.

Nato and the National Question

The political problem at the root of the Kosovo conflict was a national question: the desire of the majority of the ethnic Albanian population to leave the Federal Republic of Yugoslavia. This was a deep-seated historical problem that long antedated the rise of Milosevic. The Kosovo Albanian separatist tendency was not, as many assume, simply a response to political repression. It revived precisely in a period throughout the 1970s when Kosovo Albanians enjoyed sweeping national cultural and political rights. And it produced an upheaval in Kosovo in the early 1980s, before Milosevic rose to power. Kosovo Albanian nationalist separatism and harassment of the Serbian minority in Kosovo was indeed in large part responsible for Milosevic's rise to power (Vickers, 1998).

The link between the Clinton administration and the KLA in the late 1990s derived from a common hostility to the Milosevic regime in Belgrade, not from American support for the KLA's separatist, Greater Albania programme.

The Clinton administration sought to obscure the centrality of the national question by presenting the source of the conflict as lying with the Milosevic government, thus implying that once the Yugoslav/Serbian leadership had been overthrown, all Kosovo's problems could disappear. Nato's emphasis on the air war being purely 'humanitarian' also served the purpose of obscuring the real political sources of the Kosovo conflict. So too did Nato attempts to present the Milosevic leadership as having 'genocidal' goals in Kosovo – a charge which in fact had no basis in the record of the Serbian Socialist Party on the issue (though it did have some basis in the record of some other actors in Serbian politics, including some who had been supported in the past by Western powers).[10]

Nato resistance to Kosovo Albanian demands for independence derived from a number of considerations: Nato feared the possibility of a Greater Albania which would destabilise Macedonia and the wider balance in the Western Balkans. The US feared that self-determination for Kosovo could lead to the unravelling of the Dayton agreement, which rejected self-determination for the Bosnian Serbs and also rejected the incorporation of Bosnian Croats into Croatia. And the redrawing of Yugoslav boundaries would also violate the entire OSCE position on the inviolability of existing European frontiers, except when frontier alterations were made by mutual consent.

Russia's Role and the UN

The areas where the peace terms that brought the conflict to an end could have involved real retreats on the part of Nato lay in two other areas: the placing of Kosovo under UN authority and the recognition of a direct and independent Russian role in post-war Kosovo. Both issues divided the Nato alliance and both were linked: if Russian forces had used the UNSC resolution to gain a large measure of independent control in Northern Kosovo, the UN Mandate over Kosovo could have been made strong through Nato's need to bargain with Russia over mandate implementation. Without a significant, independent Russian power in Kosovo, the UN Mandate could be undermined by KFOR and the Western powers.

These issues led to a flash-point which could have plunged Nato into a full-scale confrontation with Russia, or have thrown Nato into a deep internal crisis, when Russian forces occupied Pristina airport. General Clark pressed for a direct military confrontation at Pristina airport. But the British government, siding with the other West European states, opposed Clark and the Clinton administration backed down, later deciding on Clark's early retirement as Nato Commander-in-Chief.[11] But the result of the confrontation and America's ability to ensure that the Romanian and Bulgarian governments denied Russia overflight rights to reinforce its Pristina bridgehead ultimately led to a Russian political defeat. It lost an independent role in Kosovo, conceded control to Nato and ensured that Nato, not the UNSC Mandate would govern protectorate policy within Kosovo.

The return of the UNSC to a central place on the Kosovo issue at the end of the war did, nevertheless, have wider political significance. For the Clinton administration the war was also a political act to establish a new set of political rules and rights in the European and the wider international theatres. Within Europe, from the angle of the Clinton administration, the war was part of a pattern of actions designed to make an American-led Nato the politically sovereign authority over the main political conflicts facing Europe. This project entailed the exclusion of Russia from Nato and thus from Europe's central political institution. Nato enlargement into Poland and its acceptance of its own right to engage in military action outside the frontiers of its member states both assured Nato its European political dominance and ensured that Russia would be an excluded and dissatisfied power.

Yet there remained a loophole in these new arrangements won by the US in the 1990s: a number of European Nato states, notably Italy, Germany and France, continued to insist that Nato decisions on military action should be subordinated to decisions of the UN Security Council – a stance which simply reflected the established rules of the post-war international order. Yet the effect of this West European insistence that Nato be bound by Security Council mandates was to bring Russia back into play in European politics through its seat on the UNSC. The Clinton administration wished to break free from that constraint in and through the Kosovo war.

This desire to break with the established rules of the UN Charter on the part of the Clinton administration was not, of course, confined to issues within the European theatre. No less important was its aim of breaking free of UNSC constraints for military intervention in other parts of the world. For the United States, such intervention is not envisaged as being carried out unilaterally. The Clinton administration desires to avoid international political isolation by having West European states' military involvement in such actions, more for their symbolic political role than for the sake of making use of their military assets. The ongoing Anglo-American bombing campaign against Iraq outside UNSC mandate demonstrates this goal. And during the Nato war in the Western Balkans Tony Blair gave vivid expression to this general aim of overthrowing the cardinal rules of the UN-centred world order, especially in an April 1999 speech in Chicago where he explained: 'Globalisation is not just economic. It is also a political and security phenomenon.' The new order, he insisted, requires an 'important qualification' to the principle of 'non-interference in the internal affairs of other countries'.

It was in this area of its wider political war aims that the United States government was forced to retreat by having to acknowledge, at least on paper, the continued ascendancy of the UNSC and of the UN Charter over Nato. President Milosevic's claim at the end of the war that Yugoslav resistance to the Nato attack had restored the authority of the UN carries some force.

But the significance of the US government's retreat on the issue of UN authority should not be exaggerated. In some Nato states, notably Britain and France, the war created a positive enthusiasm for the use of military force outside

UN authority against governments alleged to be guilty of genocidal human rights abuses. This is a valuable political bridgehead for future attacks like the Kosovo war. Secondly, the partial restoration of the authority of the UNSC must not obscure the fact that actual UN administrative authority within post-war Kosovo is something that the US and Britain have the ability to subvert. Despite protests from Kofi Annan, for example, Bernard Kouchner has flagrantly violated the terms of the peace agreement and subsequent UN resolution by replacing the Yugoslav dinar with the German Deutschmark.

The New Post-War Political Conflicts in the Western Balkans

With the signing of the peace agreement bringing the Yugoslav/Serbian withdrawal, the US administration, supported by the British government, ensured that the end of hostilities would be followed by a continued political confrontation with the Yugoslav/Serbian state, geared to overthrowing the Milosevic leadership and the Serbian Socialist Party. Furthermore, Nato's shift of position from the Rambouillet terms and from the KLA's goals on the national question was a signal to the KLA leadership to radicalise their tactics in order to achieve their goal of independence under KLA leadership. Both these features of the war's conclusion have had serious humanitarian consequences for the peoples of the region.

The decision to brand the Yugoslav leader an 'indicted war criminal' became the pretext for the Nato states to impose a blockade on a Serbia whose civilian economy was already devastated by the Nato bombing campaign. In contrast with the Anglo-American policy towards Iraq, the Nato powers seem unlikely to be prepared to see hundreds of thousands of Serbia's population starving to death or dying of disease. But the aim is clearly to inflict sufficient suffering upon the population to generate disorders and movements to overthrow the country's elected government. The second Nato – and specifically American – tactic is greatly to step up its funding of opposition movements and leaders seeking to overthrow the government as well as its jamming of Yugoslav media and its funding of pro-Nato media.[12] The third tactic is to encourage the leadership of Yugoslavia's other republic, Montenegro, to threaten to break away from Yugoslavia altogether.

The European Union has decided to support these campaigns. But so far the results appear mixed: the blockade will no doubt be effective in causing extreme hardship for large parts of the population of Serbia, but at the time of writing the attempt by US-funded opposition leaders to mobilise a popular movement capable of overthrowing the Serbian Socialist Party governments seems ineffective. US hopes and efforts may therefore turn towards seeking to recruit elements within the Yugoslav state machine (especially within the army and security forces) to stage a *coup d'état*, no doubt backed by assurances that it will prevent its ICTY from pressing war crimes charges against those who co-operate.

Nato's removal of a sure path towards KLA-led independence for Kosovo has prompted the KLA leadership to take radical measures to consolidate their grip on the whole of Kosovo's population, pursuing a covert but very effective campaign of ethnic terror against Serbs, Roma and other non-Albanian groups within Kosovo. This KLA campaign has not been acknowledged by Nato's KFOR leaders within Kosovo. They have suggested instead that the terror has been spontaneous mass revenge by ordinary Kosovo Albanians. Yet there is clear evidence that the campaign against Serbs, Roma and other ethnic minorities has been organised and systematic and that many ordinary Albanians have been appalled by it.

The Yugoslav newspaper *Borba* reported on 19 August 1999:

more than 200,000 Serbs, Montenegrins and other non-Albanians have been expelled from the Province. In these two months, the terrorists have killed over 200 and wounded more than 400 civilians, women, children and elderly people, mostly Serbs and other non-Albanian residents. About 40,000 private homes and dwellings have been looted, demolished or burned, while 40 Serbian churches and medieval monasteries, many of which have been declared as part of European cultural heritage have been burned down or demolished. As many as 80,000 Serbs and other non-Albanian citizens have been intimidated and forced to leave their jobs.

These figures are broadly confirmed by Western journalists and human rights monitors, and some put the total numbers of refugees fleeing the province even higher.[13] It is also now recognised that this has been an organised, covert campaign. Both Human Rights Watch and the European Roma Rights Centre have identified KLA members as the perpetrators of the attacks, killings and rapes of Serbs and Roma (Associated Press, 3 August 1999). And *USA Today* reporter Jack Kelley, who witnessed a KLA campaign of terror against one family, reported unequivocally that KLA units were carrying out a 'systematic ethnic cleansing campaign' (3 August).

From the point of view of the KLA leadership, the campaign is not only rational but central to their efforts to gain full independence in the face of Nato resistance to their goal. By ethnically homogenising the province, the KLA has the possibility of declaring and asserting independence whatever Nato's future wishes. If substantial groups of Serbs, Roma, Montenegrins and other minorities remained within the province, these efforts could far more easily be blocked in the future by Nato powers in the name of defending minority rights. At the same time, the KLA leadership, by acting swiftly to cleanse the province, has been able to take advantage of the fact that it would be politically impossible for Nato's leadership, and especially for the Clinton administration, to blame the KLA directly for the terror. To do so would result in pressures to indict the KLA leadership for crimes against humanity at the ICTY, while KFOR is simultaneously relying upon the KLA to establish order in the province and could face a bloody guerrilla campaign against its own forces if it rounded up the KLA leadership for war crimes.

This configuration of circumstances places difficult dilemmas before Nato. It has given itself the clear challenge of overthrowing the Yugoslav government: a government in Belgrade pliant to US regional goals is now an inescapable necessity for stabilising US influence in Southeast Europe. At the same time, KFOR does not politically control Kosovo: that control is in the hands of a KLA with a murderous agenda of ethnic cleansing and a readiness, if necessary, to turn against Nato. The secure achievement of Nato's regional goals can hardly be compatible with the long-term strengthening of the KLA political leadership's authority over Kosovo.

KFOR will be fully aware of the KLA's crimes against humanity in Kosovo. The fact that it is turning a blind eye in public to this evidence may be viewed by some as programmatic support for such ethnic cleansing. But this seems unlikely. More probable is that the KFOR stance is tactical: publishing the evidence would result in calls for KLA leaders to be indicted by the ICTY, creating utter confusion in Western public opinion. At the same time, it could lead to a confrontation between KFOR and the KLA in which KFOR would suffer casualties and which could ultimately destroy its entire operation. Thus, the priority for the Nato governments must at this stage be to maintain a detente with the KLA while continuing to direct their main political effort to overthrowing the Yugoslav government. Once that is achieved, the political focus could turn back to tackling the KLA.

This interpretation of US tactics enables us to make sense of a number of current features of Nato policy. It was reported in September 1999 that senior US government officials were leaning towards supporting the goal of Kosovo independence.[14] The French government promptly repudiated any such idea, insisting on defending UNSC resolution 1244, which categorically states that Kosovo will remain within Yugoslav sovereignty.[15] These moves could be viewed as attempts to increase pressure on political forces within Serbia to overthrow Milosevic or risk losing Kosovo forever. The other side of this signal could be that Milosevic's removal could lead to a break with the KLA and even a crack-down upon it. Similarly, the US is hinting that if Milosevic stays it will ensure the breakaway of Montenegro from Yugoslavia, while if Milosevic is overthrown Montenegro would remain within the federation. And the blockade is no doubt believed to be the most powerful weapon of all for destroying the current political position of the majority of the Serbian population.

The Wider European Aftermath

If the US government can replace the current Yugoslav regime with one friendly to US definitions of the region's past and future and if at the same time the US can maintain Nato unity, the 78-day Nato air war will have been a substantial, though not unqualified success for US political strategy in

Europe. This success will consolidate support for Nato under US leadership within public opinion in most of the Nato countries. It will demonstrate throughout Southeast and Eastern Europe that the US is the hegemonic power in Europe, and the West European states should not be taken seriously as political partners. And because the polarisation between Nato and Russia during the war did not lead to outright conflict – which could very likely have split Nato irretrievably – the war has, if anything, served to consolidate the new division of Europe which the Clinton administration pushed for with its drive to enlarge Nato into Poland. The more that there is a risk of military conflicts in the East in the future, the more Western Europe's continuing dependence on the link with the US seems necessary.

At the same time, the war had entailed political costs. The way in which the Clinton administration used a national conflict within a state for its own power-political purposes has sent an alarming message to other states around the world, the great bulk of which are very far from being nationally homogeneous. The brazen way in which the US and Nato were ready to overthrow the legal cornerstones of the existing international order has also increased suspicion and hostility amongst many other states. It could also be argued that US enthusiasm to use the Kosovo war to showcase its new techniques of electronic warfare was, on balance, unwise, since the 'Revolution in Warfare' was shown to have a number of flaws against a sophisticated opponent like the Yugoslav army. It must also be doubted that the undermining of international law is an unequivocal US interest.

Within the European region, the West European states, feeling humiliated in front of their own populations by the US assertion of its European dominance, could have been expected to follow the war with a round of rhetoric about turning the EU into a great cohesive and independent political force in international affairs. Yet, as Strobe Talbott's speech at the Royal Institute for International Affairs in early October 1999 demonstrated, the effort by President Chirac and other West European leaders to move beyond rhetoric and take steps that could enable the EU to act in the defence field independently of the US has been a cause of disquiet in the Clinton administration.[16] Retiring Nato Secretary-General Javier Solana has also declared himself dismayed by suspicions in Washington over West European moves in this area.[17] The fact that the Blair administration appears to support the development of a defence policy-making authority within the Council of Ministers of the EU, involving regular meetings of military staffs as well as defence ministers is a cause of concern to Washington. So too must be the news of a merger of French and German defence industries in the aerospace field, assuming the merger comes off.

Less dramatically challenging but no less serious a problem could arise from a steady erosion of West European support for the US drive against Serbia. There are many small signs of such potential erosion, from the lack of deployment of troops and police in Kosovo in the numbers initially endorsed, through the evident coolness of some West European states towards the US policy of seeking to maximise the suffering of Serbia's population to drive it onto the streets against Milosevic.[18] But it is also seen in the evident lack of commitment of EU governments to offering a new economic deal for Southeast Europe or to relaxing their trade regime significantly towards the East Central and East European region.

But the likelihood is that, as so often in the past, US diplomacy will successfully ensure that its West European allies lack sufficient cohesion to mount a significant challenge to restored US European hegemony through Nato. Instead, they will act as they did over Kosovo: bandwagon with the US while building up fall-back positions so that if and when US initiatives turn out to be blunders, the major West European states can exploit these blunders as opportunities to further their own regional power.

In conclusion, the new, post-Cold War American imperial expansion under the banner of bringing civilised and humane values to the less civilised parts of the world has made a significant advance through the war against Yugoslavia. But it is too early to say what all the implications of the air war will be, except that the social and political development of the Balkan region has been set back for at least a decade if not far longer and a deep division has opened in Europe, at least for the moment, between the big Slav nations in the East and the Nato powers.

Notes

1. On the Nato-Russia Founding Act, see Fergus Carr, 'Nato and the Russian Federation in the new Europe', in Czech Atlantic Commission (Prague): *Nato Summit, 1997 and Further Enhancement of European Security* (Cesky Krumlov, 22–26 October 1997). See also Gowan (1999).

2. Many supporters of the war hoped these contradictions could be overcome through a Nato ground invasion. But the public rhetoric of leaders like Blair on this issue was propagandistic: a ground invasion could not have been mounted and was never seriously contemplated. As the British General Sir Michael Rose pointed out, Nato lacked sufficient military forces trained and motivated for high-intensity warfare.

3. On 18 June Associated Press reported claims that at least 10,000 Albanians were killed in more than 100 massacres; Reuters reported on 2 July that 'peacekeepers' had catalogued more than 100 sites where Albanians 'are thought to have been massacred and buried'; the *New York Times* on the same day carried a similar report of 'at least 10,000 people' slaughtered by Serbian forces 'during their three month campaign to drive the Albanians from Kosovo'.

4. See David Binder: 'Balkan balance sheet doesn't add up', MSNBC (US), 29 July 1999 [http://www.msnbc.com/news/295110.asp]. Noam Chomsky (1999:20) quotes Robert Hayden, director of the Center for Russian and European Studies at Pittsburgh University: 'The casualties among Serb civilians in the first three weeks are higher than all the casualties on both sides in Kosovo in the three months which led up to this war, and yet these three months were supposed to be a humanitarian catastrophe.'

5. The Stockholm International Peace Research Institute reports the number of deaths in the fighting in Kosovo in 1998 was 1,000 to 2,000. The US State Department calculates 2,000. The Yugoslav government has documented details of over 600 Serb officials and civilians killed by the KLA before the Nato attack.

6. Nato claimed towards the end of the war to have destroyed more than 50 per cent of Yugoslav artillery and more than a third of Yugoslav armoured vehicles.

7. Cordesman (1999). See also *78 Days: An Audit of War*, BBC2, 17 October 1999.

8. The first German plan for suspending the bombing, put forward within the EU, was leaked by British or American officials to the press before it had been fully discussed. Following the leak the French government stated that it did not support the German plan.

9. The suggestion that the missile strikes on the Chinese Embassy were an accident produced by outdated maps was never credible: US military attaches in Belgrade had dined at the Embassy a number of times before the war and the strikes on the Embassy were unusual in being authorised from Washington outside the Nato targeting machinery. The *Observer* newspaper (17 October 1999) has claimed the strikes were a US response to Chinese signals help for the Yugoslav army. But this factor, if true, does not explain such a major US step. The diplomatic factor seems more likely to have been decisive: namely that the US attack on the Chinese Embassy was an operation of the same type as the British decision to sink the *General Belgrano* battleship at the start of the Falklands War – both had the effect of scuppering what looked like promising diplomatic initiatives for peace settlements. The British action was precisely designed to achieve that purpose.

10. On Serbian politics in the 1990s, see Thomas (1999).

11. On the confrontation within Nato over Pristina Airport, see Ian Brodie, 'Generals at war over Kosovo raid', *The Times*, 2 August 1999. Of British general Mike Jackson's response to Clark, Brodie reports: '"I'm not going to start the Third World War for you", the British general was reported to have told General Clark after refusing his orders to send assault troops and helicopters into Pristina airport to block the Russian forces.'

12. On US Congressional plans to offer the Serbian opposition $100 million, see *Financial Times*, 19 August 1999. On US special envoy Robert Gelbard's meetings with the Serbian opposition, see Dusan Stojanovic. 'US envoy trying "to unite" Serb Opposition in closed meetings in Montenegro', Associated Press, 4 August 1999. The opposition leaders he met were Democratic Party leader Zoran Djindjic, Social Democratic Party president Vuk Obradovic and Civic Alliance head Vesna Pesic.

13. See, for example, Scott Glover, 'Anti-Serb Crime Patterns Point to "Ethnic Cleansing"', *Los Angeles Times*, 15 August 1999.

14. See the *Washington Post*'s 23 September 1999 report that the Clinton administration was leaning towards Kosovo independence; and Barry Schweid, 'Kosovo Breakaway Gaining Support', Associated Press, 24 September 1999.

15. See: 'France says it still opposes Kosovo independence', Reuters, 24 September 1999. The statement is more ambivalent than it seems: though asserting that Kosovo is part of Yugoslavia, the French government could interpret a Montenegrin secession as ending the existence of Yugoslavia and thus clearing the way for Kosovo's independence.

16. See Strobe Talbott, Deputy Secretary of State, 'Remarks at a conference on the Future of Nato', The Royal Institute of International Affairs, 7 October 1999. See also William Drozdiak, 'Nato Chief Leaves Changed Alliance for EU Post', *Washington Post*, 6 October 1999.

17. The *Washington Post* reported of Solana on 6 October 1999: 'He believes a large part of his new job will be to resolve potential misunderstandings with the United States as Europe strives to develop a common foreign and security policy. Solana said he is dismayed by the suspicions and skepticism he encountered during recent consultations with US policymakers.'

18. Signs of this have been seen in attempts by some governments to go against the US blockade policy over fuel supplies, commercial aircraft flights and even clearing the Danube of the destroyed bridges. The *Washington Post* reported on 12 October 1999: 'Last week, US Secretary of State Madeleine K. Albright spoke with some of her European counterparts – including British Foreign Secretary Robin Cook, French Foreign Minister Hubert Védrine and German Foreign Minister Joschka Fischer – to warn against any weakening of economic sanctions against Yugoslavia.'

Part II

Seeing the Enemy

5

Richard Keeble

New Militarism and the Manufacture of Warfare

The Nato/Yugoslav conflict which erupted in the Balkans in March 1999 can hardly be called a war, as commonly understood. While Nato suffered no casualties, thousands of Yugoslavs were killed: many more were traumatised; and military sites, broadcast stations, hospitals, homes were bombed. Nato had no credible enemy, its planes merely picked off undefended 'targets'. The nature and significance of the 'war' were, essentially, manufactured in the realms of myth, rhetoric and media spectacle.

The Making of New Militarism

The Balkans slaughter, in fact, represented a critical moment for a distinctly new kind of militarism which emerged in the US and UK in the 1980s.

The Decline of Soviet Military Power

The most important factor behind the formation of this 'new militarism' was the decline of the Soviet Union as a superpower. The Soviets' failure to intervene in Poland to crush the Solidarity movement in 1981 gave a clear indication to the West of the military impotence of its 'Great Enemy'. Thereafter, with the US the sole superpower and desperate to win a 'big war', in part to 'kick the Vietnam syndrome', enemies have had to be invented. This is, however, not pointing to a massive elite conspiracy. Rather, the manufacture of warfare is the result of complex ideological, political and economic factors.

Nor is it an entirely new phenomenon. To a large extent, the Cold War was manufactured to legitimise the dominant positions and privileges of the elites (largely linked to the military/industrial complexes) in both West and East. As Curtis (1995:29) demonstrates, the secret planning documents are often explicit about the absence of any real threat from the Soviet Union to Western interests in the Third World. In reality, the primary threats to Anglo-American interests in the Third World arose from independent nationalist movements. Curtis continues:

It would be certainly incorrect to describe the promulgation of the 'Soviet threat' as a conspiracy fabricated for public consumption. Though there are clear specific cases where supposed Soviet machinations were purposely concocted by Western leaders, it was more generally the case that the basic ideological framework in which the concept was promoted was internally digested by those actually making policy. This internalisation of state ideology was also largely effected by 'independent' commentators in the media and academia, an internalisation that further served to reinforce the required doctrine. (ibid.:34)

New militarism continues yet significantly develops this process of manufacturing warfare.

Satisfying the Military/Industrial Complex

As Shaw (1987:150) argues, the enormous political and economic power exerted by the military/industrial complexes in the US and UK means that militarism has become a core, defining reality for these societies. Yet the dominant ideology represents the state as being inherently peaceful – though vulnerable to aggression from abnormal states outside and irrational, uncivilised enemies within.

In the UK defence spending rose by 28 per cent between 1978 and 1986 (Derbyshire and Derbyshire, 1988:176). By the 1990s, the military/industrial complex had grown so enormous that the defence industry accounted for 11 per cent of industrial production, defence exports were worth up to £33 billion a year and defence-related jobs amounted to 600,000. The Ministry of Defence was the third largest landowner in the country, the largest customer for British industry and the largest employer of bureaucrats (Paxman, 1990:237).

Similarly, US global power since the early 1950s has been built on the militarisation of the economy. The boom in military spending, begun during the Korean War, continued relentlessly during the Cold War years. By 1990, more than 30,000 US companies were engaged in military production while roughly 3,725,000 jobs were in the defence industries. And 70 per cent of all money spent on research and development was spent on defence work (Drucker, 1993:126). Moreover, given the integration of the media industries' interests with those of the military/industrial complex and the importance of the media's role in celebrating militarism, it is worth identifying the media/military/industrial complex as a critical factor behind the formation of new militarism (Keeble 1997: 24–6).

Economic Warfare: Setting the Stage for US/UK Military Interventions

With the advent of the Reagan administration in the US and the Thatcher government in Britain, the elites in these two countries were determined to roll back the successes of Third World revolutionaries during the previous decade. The offensive was multi-pronged. In the first instance there was secret economic warfare. The global economic recession precipitated by the oil price increases of 1973 and 1979 overturned the global balance of power and initially the Third World made extraordinary gains – with 14 revolutions shaking the imperial powers (Halliday, 1986:92). In response, they completely altered their economic orientation to the Third World. From being suppliers of $50 billion a year of capital to the Third World in the two decades leading up to the mid-1970s, the imperial powers moved to drawing $100 billion a year from the Third World by the 1990s. The $150 billion shift was equivalent to the entire balance of payments of the United States, 15 times the annual investment of Iraq or Egypt. The result was the massive rise in global poverty and Third World instability (Baker, 1991:3–8). Michel Chossudovsky (1998) has further demonstrated how the US-dominated International Monetary Fund, World Bank and World Trade Organisation throughout the 1980s and 1990s set out to revamp national economies along free market lines, destroying entire countries (such as Somalia, Rwanda and Yugoslavia) in the process. And so the stage was set for US/UK military adventurism.

Secret Wars

The anti-Third World offensive was also conducted through a massive campaign of covert military action (known in the jargon as Low Intensity Conflict) – far away from the media glare. Indeed, over a series of new militarist adventures in the 1980s media/military relationships evolved in the US and UK, so that by the time of the Gulf conflict of 1991 spectacular, symbolically potent, overt conflict could be conducted in as much secrecy as covert warfare. Under Reagan, the morale of covert action warriors, badly dented by Vietnam, was quickly restored. By 1985 the CIA was the fastest growing major agency in the federal government (Knightley, 1986:366). Bob Woodward's history of the CIA's covert wars of the 1980s (1987:310–11) details a complex web of clandestine activity. And both Prades (1986:383) and Treverton (1987:14) suggest that by the mid-1980s the CIA was engaged in at least 40 major covert operations – virtually all of them ignored by the media.

In the UK also, the advent of the Thatcher government was accompanied by massive new investment in covert warfare and intelligence (Dorril, 1993). Symbolically, the 'no compromise' strong state tone of the decade was set with a spectacular assault by the Special Air Service Regiment (SAS) on the Iranian embassy in London to rescue hostages. And they became instant media heroes, remaining so ever since. Steve Peak (1982) points out that the Falklands 'war' of 1982 was the 88th deployment of British troops since 1945. In fact, since 1945, the UK – and US – have deployed troops somewhere in the globe at least once every year, usually away from the media glare.

The Shift from Mass Conscription

This new emphasis on covert warfare accompanied the shift away from mass conscription. Traditional militarism of the Second World War, in which the mass of the population participated in the war effort, either as soldiers or civilians, threw up some serious democratic crises for the Western elites. The old elites were discredited by appeasement and collaboration with the Nazis. Progressive movements and trade union militancy flourished in both Britain and the US (Harris, 1984:66; Hellinger and Judd, 1991:156–60). On the Continent, a 'transnational revolutionary mood' emerged between 1943 and 1947 (Gunn, 1989:7–8; Kaldor, 1990:86). Significantly mass conscription during the Vietnam War (though not a total war for the US) was also accompanied by social dislocation – with the emergence of student radicalism, black radicalism and urban riots. Since then, the military emphasis has been on avoiding Vietnam-type confrontations. Technological development has been the army's top priority. Men have increasingly given way on the 'battle front' to the computerised machine. Short, manufactured, spectacular new militarist wars have evolved from the early 1980s to reinforce the power of the political and economic elites and the marginalisation of the mass of the public.

The Press and the Illusion of Participation

The shift to covert systems and volunteer forces using high-tech weapons, backed up by the nuclear 'deterrent', signalled in both the US and UK a growing separation of the state and military establishment from the public. The populist press, serving as the propaganda arm of the state, helped create the illusion of participatory citizenship. Moreover, the media play other important roles in the new militarist societies by engaging the public in a form of glamorised, substitute warfare. Instead of mass active participation in militarist wars, the public is mobilised through the consumption of heavily censored media (much of the censorship being self-imposed by journalists) whose role is to manufacture the spectacle of warfare (Combs, 1993). People react to this propaganda offensive with a mixture of enthusiasm, confusion, contempt, apathy and scepticism. Yet crucially, public opinion polling and consumption of media spectacles provide the illusion of participation just as satellite technology provides the illusion of 'real live' coverage of the conflict.

MacKenzie (1984) has described the 'spectacular theatre' of nineteenth-century British militarism when press representations of heroic imperialist adventures in distant colonies had a considerable entertainment element. But Victorian newspapers and magazines did not have the social penetration of today's mass media. Victorian militarism, however, was reinforced through a wide range of institutions and social activities: the Salvation Army, Church Army and uniformed youth organisations, rifle clubs, ceremonial and drill units in factories. By the 1980s this institutional and social militarism had given way to a new consumerist, entertainment militarism in which the mass media, ideologically aligned to a strong and increasingly secretive state, had assumed a dominant ideological and strategic role.

The New Militarist Adventures of the 1980s

The Manufacture of the Falklands War

Just before the Task Force set sail for the South Atlantic in April 1982 to rout the suddenly demonised 'Argies', Margaret Thatcher was being polled as the least popular post-war prime minister. Very few people had even heard of the Falklands Islands. Moreover, Argentina at the time was closely allied to the West, deeply embroiled in supporting the Contra terrorists for the Reagan administration in Nicaragua (Woodward, 1987:172–7, 187–9; Andrew, 1995:465). Britain's national security was hardly at stake in this 'bizarre little war', as Reginald and Elliot describe it (1985:5) against a puny Third World state – whose powers were grossly exaggerated – for control of a group of islands populated largely by penguins.

Yet the media helped transform the petty squabble into a spectacular, heroic war. As Shaw (1987:154) comments (in effect, identifying the shift from the old to new militarism):

> While Britain in the Second World War can be seen as the archetype 'citizen war' of total war through democratic mobilisation, the Falklands are the vindication of small professional armed forces, acting on behalf of the nation but needing no real mass participation to carry out their tasks. For the vast majority involvement was limited to the utterly passive, vicarious consumption of exceptionally closely filtered news and the expression of support in opinion polls.

Contrived delays in the transmission of television images meant this was largely seen as a bloodless war (Greenberg and Smith, 1982; McNair, 1995:176). But not all the censorship was imposed by the state. Morrison and Tumber (1988) show how, in the end, the 29 British reporters assigned to the Task Force pool came to identify closely with the military. Moreover, the patriotic imperative, so deeply rooted in the dominant political and media culture, together with journalistic self-censorship and the hyper-jingoism of the pops, all served to transform the squabble into a form of spectator sport (Luckham, 1983:18).

Grenada, Libya and Panama

The Falklands conflict was to set an important precedent for a series of military adventures by the US, culminating in the Gulf massacres of 1991. On 22 October 1983 US forces invaded Grenada in Operation Urgent Fury; on 14 April

1986, 30 US Air Force and Navy bombers struck Tripoli and Benghazi in a raid codenamed El Dorado Canyon; on 20 December 1989, 24,000 US troops invaded Panama making it the largest US military operation since Vietnam. Each of these strikes bore the crucial hallmarks of the new militarism.

- They were all 'quickie attacks'. The Libya bombings lasted just eleven minutes. All the others were over within days.
- They were all largely risk-free and fought from the air. All resulted in appalling civilian casualties. Yet the propaganda – in Orwellian style – claimed the raids were for essentially peaceful purposes. Casualty figures were covered up and the military hardware was constantly represented as 'precise', 'surgical' and 'modern' and 'clean'.
- Media and military strategies were closely integrated. With journalists denied access to planes, the massacres were hidden behind the military's media manipulation and misinformation.
- The massive displays of US force bore little relation to the threats posed. For instance, for the Grenada invasion 7,300 US military personnel and 300 police from Jamaica, Barbados and St Lucia were involved. As Smith (1994:64) comments: 'Virtually every element in the US military played a role: airforce, navy, army (82nd Airborne), Marines, Army Rangers, Navy Seals and Delta force. If the Los Angeles Police Department had requested a role they would probably have gotten a piece of the action.'
- The threats posed to US/Western interests were either grossly exaggerated or non-existent. For instance, on the second day of the Grenada invasion, the mainstream press reported official sources as saying that soldiers were meeting substantial resistance from 1,100 Cuban troops with '4,340 more on the way', while a 'reign of terror' was endangering US medical students on the island. All of this 'information' was later found to be lies.
- Central to the new militarist strategy was the demonisation of the leaders of the 'enemy' states. In the case of Grenada, they were 'communists'. Colonel Gadaffi was demonised in the US and UK mainstream media throughout the early 1980s as a 'terrorist warlord' and his supposed links with the Soviet Union were constantly stressed. Immediately before the raids Reagan dubbed him a 'mad dog'. Over the Panama invasion, the propaganda constantly focused on the demonised personality of 'drug-trafficker' Noriega (Dickson, 1994:813). Significantly, the coverage downplayed the history of US links with Noriega. He had been recruited by the CIA's chief of station in Lima, Peru, in 1959 to provide information on fellow students at the Peruvian Military Academy and his contacts with US drug barons and officials were close, particularly while George Bush briefly headed the CIA during the Ford administration (1975–76). But by 1989, Noriega had angered the Bush administration by refusing to back Colonel Oliver

North's moves against the Sandinistas of Nicaragua. In all these cases, the 'human interest' bias of the coverage served to simplify the event into a battle between good and evil and marginalise any critical consideration of previous Western support for these states.
- All the operations were celebrated in ecstatic language throughout the mainstream media. Administration lies were rarely challenged just as the global protests against the actions were rarely reported.

The Manufacture of the Gulf War, 1991

According to the French theorist Jean Baudrillard, the contemporary postmodern culture is one of hyper-reality, of re-production and simulation rather than production. Over the Gulf conflict he controversially argued that there was no war (1995). Yet drawing on different perspectives here, a similar conclusion can be drawn. For the US-led forces there was no credible enemy. The Iraqi army was constantly represented in the propaganda as a million strong, the fourth largest in the world, battle-hardened after the eight-year war with Iran. In fact, they were war-weary. When in January and February 1991 Iraqi soldiers were deserting in droves and succumbing to one slaughter after another the US/UK press still predicted the largest ground battle since the Second World War. Images of enormous Iraqi defences with massive berms and a highly sophisticated system of underground trenches filled the media. In the end there was nothing more than a rout, a walkover, a barbaric slaughter buried beneath the fiction of heroic warfare.

Moreover, a major war was needed by the US (backed by the UK and other allies) to assert its primacy in the New World Order as invented by President Bush after the Iraqi invasion of Kuwait. The US's position, basically underpinned by military power and massively burdened by debt and recession, was coming under increasing threat from the more civilian-oriented economies of Germany and Japan. War could then be seen as a symbolic assertion (though essentially defensive) of US military and media power in the world. And even a mythical 'war' could serve to destroy the social/economic infrastructure of Iraq which, while posing no threat to the West, was seen as a threat by the Israeli elite. A 'war' could serve as a lesson to future Middle Eastern governments who considered challenging the US right of access to oil reserves. Vietnam was the war that got out of control. Desert Storm, in contrast, was the US attempt to wage the perfect new militarist war: to control it and give it a contrived, happy ending.

Central to the manufacture of the war was the propaganda focus on the demonised personality of Saddam Hussein, President of Iraq. He was personally represented as a global threat, a monster, an evil madman daring to challenge the New World Order, the new Hitler. Suddenly after the invasion of Kuwait, *he* became the Big Enemy. This focus on a demonised Saddam served to direct all blame for the conflict on to one man (Schostak, 1993:85; Keeble, 1997:61–80; 1998).

The military control over the press, together with journalists' self-censorship, were other crucial factors facilitating the manufacture of the war (Kellner, 1992; Thomson, 1992). Very few journalists were allowed to travel with the troops in tightly organised pools; those who did were kept far from any of the massacres. Most reporters were confined to hotels in Saudi Arabia. Those who tried to evade these constraints were harassed by the authorities – and sometimes even by other colleagues. Given the absence of any credible enemy, the military were left conducting the war as if it were theatre or a film. This is exactly how Fuad Nahdi, one of the *Los Angeles Times*' reporters in Riyadh, described it:

> The first press conference of the day would be at 7.30 am. From then on you knew exactly what the line for the day was going to be. The script had been written beforehand and I felt like the reviewer of a good play or film.

So the censorship regime served essentially ideological, symbolic purposes – it was the expression of the arbitrary, monopoly power of the military over the conduct of the war.

How many Iraqis were slaughtered in the conflict will never be known: some reports suggested over 200,000. Yet the attacks were represented in the propaganda as smart violence in defence of global order – which actually saved lives. In contrast, Iraqi violence was indiscriminate and anarchic (Aksoy and Robins, 1991).

Another important factor allowing the manufacture of the war was the firm media consensus in support. All the mainstream media in the US and UK backed the military action, though in the UK the *Guardian* maintained a certain scepticism throughout. Immediately following the Kuwait invasion on 2 August 1990, the press in both countries went on a virtual war footing. Diplomacy was repudiated, but with the media's help it was falsely established that the 'villain' was refusing to negotiate.

The Contradictions of the New Militarism Post-1991

With the decline of Russian military power continuing throughout the 1990s, and with the imperial powers determined to extend the reach of transnational capitalism throughout the world, particularly to countries of the former Eastern Bloc, the manufacture of warfare remained a constant strategy. The Clinton years saw little shift in the militarist consensus. The annual military budget was as high as $270 billion, roughly equivalent to what was being spent during the Cold War (except during the Korean and Vietnam conflicts) (Gray, 1997:31–2). And Cox (1995:123) concludes that on military matters 'Clinton has proved to be remarkably hard-nosed; in fact, in this area there is not a great deal to distinguish his policies from those of his Republican pre-decessor.' In Britain, the Labour government of Tony Blair, despite all the rhetoric about 'ethical' policies, continued the new militarist strategies of its Tory predecessors.

Many analysts have focused on the development by the Pentagon of the 'Rogue Nation' doctrine to replace the Cold War strategies as a way of legitimising military expenditure. Michael Klare (1998:12) comments: 'Since 1990, US military policy has been governed by one over-arching premise: that US and international security is primarily threatened by the "rogue states" of the Third World.' He adds pointedly (ibid.:14) that none had engaged in unambiguously aggressive behaviour since 1990 and most seemed determined to establish good relations with the West. A survey by the US State Department, published in April 1993, even found no evidence that Sudan had sponsored or conducted terrorist acts. Four months later, Sudan joined the list of rogue states (Füredi, 1994:34). Significantly, in August 1998, sites in Sudan – and Afghanistan – became the target of unprovoked attacks by US cruise missiles following the African embassy bombings. As Edward Herman (1998) comments: 'When the evidence assembled after the 1998 bombing of the pharmaceutical factory in the Sudan showed that the US claims justifying the attack were false and based on incompetently gathered and evaluated data, there was very little if any criticism in the mainstream media.'

But, while many elements of new militarism continued into the 1990s, there were also important changes. The propaganda legitimising the military adventures still dwelt constantly on a demonised 'Saddam' during attacks on Iraq but for actions elsewhere there was a shift to 'peacekeeping', 'peace-enforcing', 'monitoring an exclusion zone', 'defending democracy' and 'humanitarianism'. Significant cracks appeared in the elite consensus over the new militarism. And the US/UK military alliance, whether operating through the UN, Nato or 'unilaterally', also faced some significant setbacks.

The Somali Disaster

America's intervention in Somalia proved one of its most humiliating disasters and revealed serious cracks in the elite over new militarism. Operation Restore Hope was launched in November 1992, supposedly to tackle the humanitarian disaster unfolding in Somalia after a coup removed the dictator General Siyad Barre in January 1991. It was in reality an attempt to legitimise the new militarism under the cloak of 'peacekeeping' and 'humanitarianism'. In May 1993, a full UN peacekeeping operation took over from the increasingly embattled US forces (Hill and Malik, 1996). But US appointees dominated the military command structure and, significantly, the assault on the forces of the demonised Somali leader General Aideed on 3 October, which left 18 US soldiers dead and more than 70 injured (as well as thousands of Somalis dead and injured) was entirely planned from the headquarters of the US Special Operations in Florida (Wesley, 1997). The deployment of massive military force was, according to the new militarist strategy, aimed at securing a quick victory against a puny enemy. It all went wrong. And after US forces became embroiled in the civil war and suffered casualties they made a quick exit leaving Somalia to its fate.

Defending Democracy in Haiti?

Significant cracks also appeared in the elite consensus over the Haiti operation of September 1994. After the elected leader, Father Jean Bertrand Aristide, was removed in a coup in September 1991, the US had refused to intervene against the military and political elite, many of whom were CIA 'assets'. Then, in an excessive display of force, US troops invaded the island, supposedly to 'defend democracy' and restore Aristide. But the soldiers, with no army to fight, concentrated on defending wealthy properties and shops from looters and simply watched as Aristide supporters were attacked by local militiamen. Moreover, Aristide's radicalism had faded in the three years since the coup and he became a willing tool of US imperialism signing an IMF loan package, agreeing to co-operate with the US and members of the Haiti military to maintain order and granting an amnesty to the coup leaders (Clement, 1997).

'Saddam' the Necessary Bogeyman

Much of the new militarist strategy in the 1990s was directed at Iraq, which became the focus of regular manufactured crises (Carapico, 1998). In January and June 1993, September 1996 and December 1998 US jets attacked sites in Iraq with rapid, risk-free actions and only an 11th hour intervention by UN Secretary-General Kofi Annan prevented strikes after a media-hyped crisis exploded in January–February 1998. With US-led forces creating the Kurdish enclave in the north of the country immediately after the end of the massacres in 1991 and later an 'exclusion zone' in the south, US policy towards Iraq concentrated, paradoxically, on building up a demonised 'Saddam' as the necessary bogeyman for the military/industrial complex and the Iraqi state as a counter to Iran to the East. Bombing attacks continued on a daily basis throughout 1999, becoming an institutionalised phenomenon barely worth a mention in the media.

Yet it became increasingly difficult for the elite to sustain the lies on which new militarist adventures were based and significant cracks began to appear in the consensus over Iraq. The media maintained almost unanimous support for the June 1993 attacks on Baghdad after reports appeared in mainstream newspapers (fed by US intelligence and so impossible to verify independently) that Iraq had plotted to assassinate former US President Bush during a trip to Kuwait in April (Kellner, 1993; 1995). The consensus also held firm during September 1996 when another 'Saddam scare' erupted after Iraqi troops were reported to have invaded Kurdistan in support of the KDP Kurdish faction headed by Massoud Barzani against the Iranian-backed PUK faction led by Jalal al-Talabani. Again US missiles hit Iraqi 'targets'. Then, in the following month, the PUK faction regained its lost strongholds and the crisis suddenly disappeared from the media.

During the January–February 1998 crisis, when the media were full of manufactured reports of Saddam's deadly stockpile of chemical weapons 'that could wipe out all life on earth', a range of critical voices were heard. And during the Desert Fox attacks of December 1998, in Britain, newspapers such as the *Independent on Sunday*, the *Guardian* and the *Observer* opposed the action while, in the US also, many commentators found the launching of the attacks on the eve of President Clinton's impeachment debate too much of a co-incidence and a cynical ploy to win public support.

The US/UK-led attacks on Yugoslavia in 1999 can now be seen to carry the distinct marks of the new militarist strategy. They were risk-free and conducted entirely from the air (as were Nato's earlier strikes against Bosnian Serbs in 1995). Celebrated as 'humanitarian' and 'precise', the attacks were, in fact, part of an attempt by a newly enlarged Nato to celebrate its 50 years' anniversary with a symbolic victory in a manufactured 'war'. Moreover, the 'war' was an attempt by the US to re-establish its dominant global role after a series of serious setbacks while it could also help Premier Tony Blair, in the UK, and Chancellor Gerhard Schröder, in Germany, achieve their own parochial ends. Just as the deployment of ground troops during the Gulf massacres of 1991 was needed for the manufacture of the 'Big War', so the demonisation of the Serbs and, in particular, Yugoslav President Milosevic as the 'evil, new Hitler' helped legitimise the excessive use of force against defenceless 'targets'. Significantly the media consensus this time held firm with virtually all the mainstream media in the US and UK supporting the action. In Britain only the *Independent on Sunday* dared to stand outside this consensus. And within a few weeks of the ending of the air strikes, its editor was sacked.

6

Mick Hume

Nazifying the Serbs, from Bosnia to Kosovo

What one media commentator dubbed 'the war of Simpson's voice' (*Observer*, 18 April 1999) became an important sub-plot of coverage of the Kosovo conflict, after anonymous government sources rubbished the BBC's John Simpson for allegedly broadcasting 'pro-Serb' reports from Belgrade. In the House of Commons, in the heat of this war of words, Tory MP Edward Garnier asked Prime Minister Tony Blair publicly to repeat the allegations against Simpson which had been widely ascribed to the Prime Minister's official spokesman, Alastair Campbell. 'He's entitled to present what report he likes', Blair said of John Simpson in reply to Garnier, 'and we are perfectly entitled to say that these reports are provided under the guidance and instruction of the Serbs. That is the proper way to conduct a democracy.'

The Prime Minister's remarks were reported as an 'emphatic' defence of a journalist's right to free speech (*Guardian*, 22 April). But look again at what he said: that Simpson's reports were not simply being compiled by him under certain restrictions imposed by the Serbian authorities, but were actually being 'provided under the guidance and instruction of the Serbs'. The clear implication was that the Serbs were not just negatively telling Simpson what he could not report – they were positively dictating what he did broadcast. That sounds like a serious slander against the BBC's most senior foreign correspondent, made under cover of parliamentary privilege.

The government's outbursts against Simpson provided a revealing insight into its mindset. It confirmed the almost paranoid levels of insecurity inside a New Labour government which apparently felt the need continually to lash out over the reporting of Kosovo, despite the fact that the media were overwhelmingly on-message. It also demonstrated the black and white terms in which Blair and his supporters viewed the conflict.

How was it possible for a presumably sensible Prime Minister to imply that somebody like Simpson, who won an OBE from John Major's government for his reporting of the 1991 Gulf War, was a Serbian stooge? For the government, as Blair made clear from the start, the war over Kosovo was a moral crusade: it was 'no longer just a military conflict. It is a battle between good and evil; between civilisation and barbarity' (*Sunday Telegraph*, 4 April). The Serbs were not just the enemy, they were Evil incarnate. In such an apocalyptic confrontation, there could be no observers or innocent bystanders. If you were not wholeheartedly committed to the side of the Nato angels, you were deemed to be in the camp of Slobodan Beelzebub. In this sense, the casual slandering of John Simpson was a telling sign of how thoroughly the authorities in the Nato countries, aided and abetted by too many in the media, had demonised the Serbs.

How did this come about? Modern societies do not, on the whole, believe in the devil himself. Even the established Western churches have had to revise their view of hell and damnation in our more secular times. What we do believe in, however, are Nazis, as the modern agents of hell on earth.

The most effective way to demonise anybody today is to link them somehow to the Nazi experience. The accusation that President Milosevic's Serbia was carrying out 'another Holocaust' in Kosovo was the culmination of a long campaign to Nazify the Serbs, which had escalated throughout the conflicts in the former Yugoslavia. A significant part of the responsibility for this Nazification campaign has to lie with those sections of the media that have been guilty of displaying an anti-Serb bias, described by Nik Gowing (1997:25) as the 'secret shame' of the journalism community during the Bosnian civil war.

The clearest way in which the Serbs have been linked with the Nazis has been through accusations that they have committed genocide, first in Bosnia and then in Kosovo. From the start of the war against the Serbs, British government ministers appearing at the daily press briefings seemed hardly able to open their mouths without mentioning the 'G' word. During one brief morning session in March, Defence Secretary George Robertson told reporters that Nato was facing 'a regime which is intent on genocide'; that the sole purpose of the air strikes was 'to stop the genocidal violence' and the 'ethnic extermination'; that the air war would continue until 'the genocidal attacking stops'; that Nato was united in its determination 'to stop this ethnic cleansing extermination policy'; and that Serbian commanders should look to their consciences and refuse to obey 'these genocidal orders'.[1]

Foreign Secretary Robin Cook seemed equally determined to link present-day Serbs with the Nazis of the past. As recently as February 1999, in response to an allegation from the German Culture Minister that modern Britain remained obsessed with the Second World War as its 'spiritual core', Cook had promised not to mention the war. 'I have never at any point in any of my speeches referred back to the last war and I can give an undertaking that we won't', said the Foreign Secretary (*Telegraph*, 16 February). By April, however, in the midst of the war over Kosovo, it sometimes appeared that he could allude to nothing else. Nato unity, Cook told the Ministry of Defence press briefing, was based on:

> our common belief that the revival of fascism which we have witnessed in Kosovo must have no place in the modern Europe. Nato was born in the

aftermath of the defeat of fascism and genocide in Europe. Nato will not allow this century to end with a triumph for fascism and genocide.[2]

New Labour's German allies, the Social Democrats, also weighed in with some ominous historical references. German Defence Minister Rudolf Scharping claimed there was 'serious evidence' in Kosovo of 'concentration camps like there were in Bosnia', and of 'systematic extermination that recalls in a horrible way what was done in the name of Germany at the beginning of World War II'. Predictably others replied in kind, Serbian TV renaming the Nato alliance the 'Nazi American Terrorist Organisation'.

Where Nato politicians tended to imply that there were parallels between the Serbs and the Nazis, the newspapers insisted upon it and added the dreaded 'H' word. On 29 March the *Daily Mail*'s front page reported, beneath a picture of Kosovo Albanian children in a lorry, headlined 'Flight from Genocide': 'Their terrified and bewildered faces evoke memories of the Holocaust.' On 1 April, the *Daily Mirror* ran a front-page picture of refugees with a mother and child picked out in black and white, *Schindler's List* style. Under the headline '1939 or 1999?' it reported that 'Nazi style terror came to Kosovo yesterday in a horrific echo of the wartime Holocaust.' That same day, the *Sun* bluntly headlined its Kosovo spread 'Nazis 1999 – Serb cruelty has chilling echoes of the Holocaust.' By now, the pattern was well-established.

The continual, deliberate talk of genocide in the coverage of Kosovo was much more significant than the usual wartime rhetoric. In terms of international law, the allegation of genocide has important implications. As the *New York Times* (4 April) reported:

> Policy-makers in the United States and Europe are invoking the word to help provide a legal justification for their military campaign against Serbia. It is one based in part on concepts of humanitarian law, where no word is more evocative.

In particular, the United Nations Genocide Convention of 1948 could allow for international intervention to prevent it.

In political terms, the way that the authorities and the media bombarded us with the language of genocide and concentration camps was even more significant. These words invoke modern moral absolutes – perhaps the only ones that are still recognised as such in our relativist times. If there is genocide, it will be widely accepted without question that there must be intervention and retribution. The deployment of this language was designed to give an air of moral certainty to Nato's war against Serbia. Yet its real effect could only be to cloud and confuse the key issues further.

'Genocide' is not just another word for brutality, making people homeless, putting people on trains, or even murder. It means, according to the *Oxford English Dictionary* and in popular parlance, 'annihilation of a race'. The word was first used in the 1940s, specifically to describe the Nazi campaign to wipe out European Jewry (a campaign which also took a dreadful toll on other groups). Similarly, for more than half a century, 'concentration camp' has not meant a place where large numbers of people are concentrated, even if it is against their will. Everybody who uses such language should know that it will be taken to mean a death camp, on the Nazi model, designed for the industrial implementation of a policy of genocide.

To deploy that language, with all of the historical baggage that comes with it, is automatically to suggest that the Milosevic regime should be put on a par with the Nazis. Those who have tried to compare Hitler's Germany with Milosevic's Serbia in this way risk losing all sense of perspective and proportion. Hitler's Germany was the dominant economic and military state in Europe, a superpower of its age which applied all of its might to pursue the imperialist goals of colonial conquest and racial superiority. Milosevic's Yugoslavia, by contrast, is an inefficient and economically powerless state, desperately trying to hang on to what remains of its greatly diminished territory after a decade of war and sanctions.

There can be no serious comparison between the crimes of the Nazis and what the Serbs have done. During the Kosovo conflict, the Nato governments and their allies in the media tended to use the rhetoric of genocide to substitute for the lack of much hard evidence to support stories of Serb atrocities against ethnic Albanians. Since the conflict ended, it has become clearer that – as some of us suggested at the time – many of these stories were a familiar mixture of half-truths, rumours and fabrications common to every modern war. During the war, the media splashed claims by Nato ministers and generals that up to 100,000 ethnic Albanians could have been killed by the Serbs in Kosovo. 'We've now seen about 100,000 military-aged men missing', American Defense Secretary William Cohen told CBS on 16 May, 'They may have been murdered.' Since then, the estimated numbers killed have been dramatically reduced – a process attracting far less news interest in Britain and America than the inflating of the death toll did.

In August 1999, Spanish forensic experts who had gone to Kosovo to help investigate massacres poured scorn on the official estimates of the death toll. One reportedly told El Pais that they had been instructed 'to prepare ourselves to perform more than 2,000 autopsies. We only found 187 cadavers and now we are going to return [to Spain].' Another said, 'I have been reading the data from the UN. They began with 44,000 deaths. Then they lowered it to 22,000. And now they are going with 11,000. I look forward to seeing what the final count will really be.' For this forensic scientist, the search for mass graves had turned into 'a semantic pirouette by the war propaganda machines, because we did not find one – not one – mass grave'.[3]

One of the worst rumoured mass graves was in the mines of Trepca, Northern Kosovo, where the Serbs were rumoured to have dumped or destroyed the bodies of up to 700 ethnic Albanians. When the horror stories about Trepca broke, in June 1999, the *Mirror* explicitly put this site on a par with the death camps of the Holocaust. 'Trepca – the name will live alongside those of Belsen, Auschwitz and Treblinka', the paper said: 'It will be etched in the memories of those whose loved ones met a bestial end in true Nazi Final Solution fashion' (18 June). Four months later, in October 1999, the International War Crimes Tribunal at The Hague had to announce that its investigations had found no bodies at all in the Trepca mines.

The exaggeration of the casualties caused by the Serbs in Kosovo follows a pattern established during the Bosnian civil war. Many of those journalists who accuse the Bosnian Serbs of genocide claim that a quarter of a million died in that conflict, most of them Bosnian Muslims. The respected Stockholm International Peace Research Institute put the total casualty figure for all sides in Bosnia at a much lower 30,000–50,000.[4] Serbs did commit atrocities in both Bosnia and Kosovo (as did others), and there were many tragic deaths. But to try to compare these conflicts with the Nazi annihilation of the Jews is a serious distortion. In terms of sheer casualty numbers alone, it is akin to equating a motorway accident with a major earthquake.

The tendency for reporters to compare the two, with talk of 'echoes of the Holocaust' and 'genocide' carried out in 'true Nazi Final Solution fashion' has seriously distorted the popular image of the Balkans today. It has helped to brand the Serbs as the evil new Nazis. Once that has been achieved, there is no need for (indeed, there is no tolerance of) any further discussion of the issues. Never mind about the real situation on the ground, or the role of the Western states in exacerbating the conflict; if there are Nazis involved, what more do we need to know? Anything becomes permissible to put a stop to them. Branding the Serbs as Nazis has thus become an excuse for ignorance – not least among journalists.

But the damage does not stop there. Comparisons between the Serbs and the Nazis distort not just the present, but also the past. They have risked belittling the horror of the real Holocaust, by putting the slaughter of six million Jews and many others in the Nazi death camps on a par with a local conflict, bloody though it may be, in Kosovo or Bosnia. This diminishing of the Final Solution is what ultimately concerns me most about the Nazification of the Serbs. As the cries of 'genocide' in Kosovo grew louder, the diminishing of the Holocaust that this comparison implied became an issue of concern for others in the media.

'The sufferings of the Jews in the Second World War were special: effectively without precedent, almost without parallel', wrote Felipe Fernandez-Armesto. By contrast, 'Serb war objectives are depressingly familiar' (*Independent on Sunday*, 4 April). Whilst supporting the Nato intervention, Nazi camp survivor and Nobel Laureate Elie Wiesel also complained about the comparisons with the Final Solution, insisting that 'The Holocaust was conceived to annihilate the last Jew on the planet. Does anyone believe that Milosevic and his accomplices seriously planned to exterminate all the Bosnians, all the Albanians, all the Muslims in the world?' (*Newsweek*, 12 April). 'It's not that I believe Jews have the monopoly on suffering', complained Manhattan writer Julia Gorin in the *Jewish World Review* (29 April), 'But some comparisons to the Holocaust are beyond offensive – especially when they're used to manipulate public support for a war that is as absurd as it is unjust.' By comparing the Kosovo conflict with the Nazi experience, suggested Fergal Keane of the BBC, 'we not only deny the awful singularity of the Holocaust but we reduce ourselves to the realm of absurd comparison ... It is bad history and it makes for bad politics' (*Independent*, 17 April).

Despite these and other dissenting voices, however, the media bear a heavy burden of responsibility for the way that constantly accusing the Serbs of genocide has been used, both to distort perceptions of the situation in the Balkans, and effectively to rewrite the history of the Holocaust. Some journalists spent the war acting as little more than copy typists for Nato, writing up briefings from ministers and generals and spinning the official line across the front page. The loss of perspective brought on by indulging these casual comparisons between the Serbs and the Nazis is nowhere clearer than in the press stories mentioned above, where various papers compared the experience of ethnic Albanians fleeing or being shipped out of Kosovo to that of the Jews being transported to Nazi death camps. As Julie Burchill commented at the time, in her '40 reasons why the Serbs are not the new Nazis and the Kosovars are not the new Jews': 'the Nazis did not put Jews on the train to Israel, as the Serbs are now putting ethnic Albanian Kosovars on the train to Albania' (*Guardian*, 10 April).

Yet in the wave of Second World War nostalgia that engulfed the debate about Kosovo, to question the emotionally correct line on any of this was to risk being accused of 'appeasement' or even 'Holocaust denial'. Much of the media proved deaf to the pleas for perspective issuing from somebody like 76-year-old Aca Singer, head of the Federation of Jewish Communities in Yugoslavia, who lost 65 members of his family in the Holocaust. Sheltering from Nato bombs in Belgrade, he told of his fury at the way in which the word 'genocide' was being degraded by all sides in the conflict. 'I don't at all agree that this is genocide', he said of the wars in Croatia, Bosnia and Kosovo:

> There was no effort to wipe out an entire race – men, women and children – merely because of their ethnic or religious identity. Both the Serbs and the Albanians pressure us for sympathy and comparison. Both sides it seems want to be Jews. I put myself on neither side.

And Blair and Clinton, he added with disgust, by comparing Serb actions in Kosovo to mass murder by the Nazis, 'are also manipulating with the Jews' (*New York Times*, 9 April).

That is undoubtedly true. Yet it was not Blair or Clinton who started 'manipulating with the Jews' in order to Nazify the Serbs in the Western imagination. It was a process that began before either of them was in power – back during the Bosnian civil war at the start of the 1990s. Journalists were not simply complicit with their governments in that process of Nazification – some of them were responsible for starting it.

In Bosnia, a generation of crusading journalists set the pattern for seeing the complex conflicts in the Balkans as a simple morality play, to be understood and reported in terms of Good against Evil. These war reporters urged Western governments to intervene forcefully against the Serbs at a time when none was keen to do so. While the media crusaders took it upon themselves to campaign for military intervention, drawing parallels between the modern Serbs and the fascists of the 1930s, they did not see fit to take up arms themselves, as the International Brigades had done during the Spanish Civil War. As a result, they deservedly earned the unflattering title of 'Laptop Bombardiers'.

The selective atrocity stories and images that much of the media sent back from Bosnia, coupled with the emotive arguments put forward by the commentators who signed up to what became known as the Something-Must-Be-Done Club, set the pattern for Nazifying the Serbs. At the time, more astute media observers noted the dangerous tendency to moralise the Bosnian civil war. Andrew Thompson of BBC's *Newsnight* summed it up as 'the regular presentation of one side as bad (the Serbs) and one side as good (everyone else)'.[5] Nik Gowing, diplomatic editor at Channel Four News during the conflict, has noted that 'In Bosnia, above all, there is more evidence than many media personnel care to admit that journalists embarked on crusades and became partial' (Gowing, 1997:26) Misha Glenny, author of *The Fall of Yugoslavia*, who worked for the BBC World Service during the Bosnian civil war, complained that, in the absence of any serious media discussion of why the Serbs were fighting, 'the general impression is because they are stark, raving, mad, vicious, mean bastards'.[6] Anybody who thinks that is an exaggeration should go back and re-read the way that award-winning broadsheet journalists described the Bosnian Serbs as aliens from 'the disturbed universe of evil' (Maass, 1996:37), running 'satanic' concentration camps (Ed Vulliamy, *New Statesman*, 25 April 1997).

Perhaps the key moment in the media's branding of the Serbs as the new Nazis, jackbooting their way across the Balkans, came in August 1992. When ITN broadcast pictures of some gaunt Bosnian Muslims and barbed wire at a transit camp in northern Bosnia, the world's media – which had been avidly awaiting such a sign – seized upon them as proof that the Serbs were organising another Holocaust. In Britain, the *Mirror* headlined the story as the discovery of 'Belsen '92' (7 August 1992). In the USA, ABC News broadcast the ITN pictures with a commentary that suggested they 'hint at the atrocities of the past. But this is not history, this is Bosnia. Pictures from the camps: a glimpse into genocide' (6 August 1992). After that episode, according to Simpson (1998:444–5), for many journalists 'the hunt was on in Bosnia for Nazi-style atrocities':

a climate was created in which it was very hard to understand what was really going on, because everything came to be seen through the filter of the Holocaust. And so we had stories about extermination camps and mass rape camps, as though the Bosnian Serbs were capable of a Germanic level of organisation.

From the summer of 1992, the media's thoroughgoing demonisation of the Serbs helped to set in motion a dynamic of increasing Western intervention in the civil wars in the former Yugoslavia. The Serbs = Nazis stories published and broadcast through the 1990s were to play a significant part in paving the way for Nato's 'just war' in the spring of 1999.

Whatever crimes President Milosevic is guilty of, his regime bears no sensible comparison with the Third Reich. Why, then, have sections of the media tried so hard for so long to demonise the Serbs as the new Nazis? It has nothing to do with any 'national psychosis' on their part, but quite a lot to do with the state of the mind of the Western journalists themselves.

In our uncertain, anxious times, when everybody observes that there is a moral vacuum at the heart of Western society, a new breed of journalists and politicians have taken it upon themselves to try to fill that gap through foreign crusades. By finding a sense of moral certainty in somebody else's conflict, and identifying with a faraway cause that could be posed in stark terms of Good versus Evil, they have sought to compensate for the lack of purpose and solid values in their own societies. And in a society like Britain, what greater moral cause could there be than a re-run of the Second World War, this time preferably against a relative pushover like Serbia?[7]

The fact that this anti-Nazi crusade was staged primarily for the benefit of the Westerners involved is clear enough when one hears journalists talk about Kosovo as the 'test for our generation' (*Guardian*, 26 March 1999); or when one reads Ed Vulliamy (*Guardian*, 10 April 1993) talk about the war in Bosnia as his chance to walk in his father's footsteps:

My father had the honour of fighting fascism; I have instead the strange privilege of meeting the people who are fighting a pale but unmistakable imitation of the Third Reich but have only the sons of the appeasers of 1938 to turn to.

The crusading journalists who started a new school of interventionist reporting over Bosnia have done more than they could ever have expected to shape the development of Anglo-American foreign policy through the 1990s. This is not because of the peculiar power of their writing and broadcasts, so much as the peculiar circumstances of the time. In our alienated age, when politics passes most people by, it has proved possible for a relatively small number of crusading media commentators to exert a disproportionate influence on foreign policy. The Something-Must-Be-Done club has thus been able to punch well above its weight – especially under a New Labour government which eagerly took up the challenge and set off in search of what

Tony Blair called a 'moral purpose' in Kosovo, several years after the frontline troops of the new press corps did the same thing in Bosnia.

No doubt there are those in the media who feel self-satisfied about the success of their moralistic campaign to Nazify the Serbs in the Western imagination. They might like to consider the consequences for an issue that ought to be close to their hearts – that of press freedom. When you are dealing with Evil, you do not feel any need to indulge such luxuries as free speech and open democratic discussion. When you are fighting the new Nazis, you do not want to tolerate dissent. Throughout the war over Kosovo, journalists and others who tried to ask awkward questions were likely to find themselves treated as some kind of fascist fifth columnists by the authorities. George Robertson implied to BBC Radio's John Humphrys that his abrasive interviews would not have been tolerated in the Second World War; Cabinet minister Clare Short said the 'outrageous' critics of the Kosovo war effort were 'the equivalent to the people who appeased Hitler'. Indeed, anybody who questioned the Nato orthodoxy tended to be treated as the Lord Haw-Haws of the Kosovo war. Perhaps they were fortunate that the government only slandered them, instead of trying to have them strung up for treason.

Notes

1. Ministry of Defence Briefing, 28 March 1999.
2. Ibid., 13 April 1999.
3. See John Laughland, 'The Massacres that Never Were', *Spectator*, 30 October 1999; Jon Swain, 'Lost in the Kosovo Numbers Game', *Sunday Times*, 31 October 1999.
4. Stockholm International Peace Research Institute, *Annual Report*, 1996.
5. Letter to the *Spectator*, 12 March 1994.
6. Interview for Channel Four documentary, *Journalists at War*, August 1993.
7. For a detailed analysis of these trends see Hume (1997).

Mirjana Skoco and William Woodger

The Military and the Media

Vietnam spawned the myth of an 'anti-war' media, although in general journalists have never really been critical of wars fought by their own country. The military's misperception that journalists 'lost' the Vietnam War for the US jolted them into a search for methods to control the media. Direct control, from the Falklands and Grenada through Panama and the Gulf, did not provide the solution, since media quiescence during the fighting did not preclude retrospective criticism, and the military have an exaggerated fear that a bad press – even after the fact – can negate a military victory. As one US Army Colonel puts it: 'It is conceivable that a commander could win the battle and lose the information war by excluding or attempting to exclude the media from his operations' (Willey, 1998–99). Instead of direct control – for instance, through censorship of journalists' copy – the US military now favour the idea of 'working with' the media. Today's generation of military thinkers are far more likely to acknowledge that 'reporters did not lose the Vietnam War for America' (ibid.), and even to admit that 'misinformation provided to the media led to a military credibility gap'.[1] This chapter examines contemporary US military strategy for managing relations with the media, and reflects on the experience of Kosovo.

Learning from the Gulf War

Though stoutly supporting the military during the Persian Gulf War, journalists also resented what they saw as undue interference and control, and found that a professional concern to get newsworthy stories could bring them into conflict with the military. Afterwards, media criticism was swift, high-powered, and damning. On 15 April 1991 Washington bureau chiefs complained to Secretary of State Dick Cheney that the 'the flow of information to the public was blocked, impeded or diminished' by the Department of Defense during the conflict.[2] They also established a working group, which reported that: 'In a free society, there is simply no place for such overwhelming control by the government.'[3] In contrast, the DoD's Pete Williams praised Gulf War coverage as 'the best ever' (MacArthur, 1993:152). There followed months of talks between the working group and the DoD, culminating in the mutual agreement of nine principles of combat coverage, the first of which was 'open and independent reporting'.[4] How could such apparently opposing views ever come together? What incentive could there be for the military to give up the 'the spoils of the information war' (Taylor, 1992:278)?

Mainstream US military thinking now accepts that the media are able to tell 'our story'. As Rear Admiral Brent Baker puts it:

> Play the media game. Understand there are times for a low profile, but more often, a media opportunity to tell your story should not be lost because of fear. We need to tell people, through the media, what we are about.[5]

It must also be emphasised that media criticism of the military is not what it seems. Given timely delivery of news stories, information from official military sources and access to the front, there is little evidence to suggest the media would complain about attempts to prevent more radical criticism. Good old patriotism limits critical reporting once 'our boys' are in harm's way, and almost no reporters question why the military is going to war. Apparent media satisfaction with the new principles of combat coverage hides real problems which still exist. The shift towards 'open reporting' is handled with instructions that 'commanders must ... issue guidance about what information [journalists] will receive'.[6] The corollary of open reporting is 'security at source' – in other words, no real information will be revealed. Journalists will have limited access to operations when it suits the military, and this will ensure that 'good news' stories achieve prominent coverage, whilst everything else is excluded. Despite the balance being in the military's favour, a McCormick Tribune Foundation conference in 1997 declared that 'conferees appeared to be in agreement that relations between the military and the media are perhaps the best ever'.[7]

Learning to Love the Enemy

The US military is actively schooling itself in how to use the media as a weapon. In 1983, Lieutenant Commander Arthur A. Humphries wrote in the *Naval War College Review* that the military must never be 'neglectful of the news correspondents ... the news media can be a useful tool, or even a weapon, in prosecuting a war psychologically so that the operators don't have to use their more severe weapons' (MacArthur, 1993:145). Since the Gulf, this idea has been taken up seriously, and expanded to include methods to obtain the 'positive' stories for the home audience. Rather than fighting the media, the military are playing on the fact that the media are generally supportive of American military might. The military intends to co-opt the media for their own purposes – the media supposedly benefit by receiving, or being led to report, a greater number of 'quality' stories.

The process includes 'understanding' the media. According to journalist Warren P. Strobel, the military have 'gotten very smart':

They saw that from here on ... reporters are something they're going to have to deal with and they decided they were going to study us to death and get inside our heads and figure us out. And low [sic] and behold, they've done a better job of that than civilian [sic] counterpart.[8]

At the US Army Command and General Staff College, course A751, 'Military and the Media', provides 27 hours 'designed to enlighten military officers about the relationship between news media and the military'. To pass the course, the 'student' must 'accept the idea that the media has been and will be a player on the battlefield and that leaders must plan for and react to the actions of reporters'. The College also runs sessions on 'the news media and public opinion as influences on the national security decision making process', and 'the role of the media in Information Warfare'. Colonel Jon H. Moilanen notes how 'information operations' have 'taken center stage in the annual training exercise as students learn to deal with hostile and aggressive media during interviews, briefings and in other role-playing scenarios' (1998–99). According to Moilanen, Public Affairs (PA) 'contributes to maintaining a well-informed and supportive American and regional audience, coalition and global community'.

A similar orientation is evident in military research projects and internal journals. Commenting on a military study, Lieutenant Colonel Frank J. Stech (1994) argues indirectly for the manipulation of the media, hoping that the military will be:

> well-schooled in the guidelines for creating compelling and persuasive visual images, in the requirements for framing credible news stories, and in the semiotic uses of signs and symbols – i.e., that they practice tactics and operational arts developed explicitly for CNN war-fighting needs.

No longer expected merely to fight wars, the military now have to be skilled semioticians as well. Stech also notes that for 'CNN wars' policy must have a 'human face':

> If our policies fail to reflect a human face, if the cold calculations of our leaders envision no compelling stories of human values, then in a world of CNN war the force of public support ... for those policies will be questionable at best.

The notion of cold, calculated policy sold to the public through 'compelling stories of human values' may sound familiar to media audiences after Kosovo. However, Major Raymond R. Hill advises that such tasks should be left to politicians:

> do not overstate information to garner support or act as a cheerleader to maintain public support. To do so risks loss of credibility, a mistake that

haunted the US military leadership during Vietnam. Political leaders must handle any cheerleading tasks.[9]

Lest this be taken as an indication of the military's intention genuinely to inform the public, Hill notes that an advantage of providing information to the media is that 'a glut of information hides those inadvertent security leaks that occur during media coverage'. He goes on to suggest that 'the military can quickly establish some element of control using information':

> For instance, use unclassified web pages on the Internet. This is already common within the Department of Defense. Extend this capability during conflicts to provide published information, press releases, briefing transcripts, and prepared responses to video or picture images.

Hill also highlights the value of having journalists on one's side, arguing that:

> independent media reporting can assist the military effort by providing: intelligence; proof of atrocities and violations of laws of armed conflict; assistance rallying local, national, and international support for nation building efforts; or monitoring of civil affairs issues. The media can assist military efforts if the military plans for and requests such assistance. Captain Haddock nailed the issue ... when she stated, '... we must understand their strength and exploit that strength as a weapon'.

Judging from Kosovo, current practice is clearly following these trends.

Department of Defense guidelines for the Public Affairs Office (PAO) note that 'one bad news item is remembered forever, while 100 good news items seem to be forgotten'.[10] 'Bad' stories, in military eyes, are ones the media just get 'wrong'. To help avoid them, officers are told:

> Your command or agency has an important story to tell to the American people who support your activities. Your soldiers and employees and their activities are 'news' to both local and national audiences. You are the most believable spokesman to represent them. Preparation and practice on your part will result in newsworthy, informative articles and programs that may be seen by millions of viewers and readers.

The PAO guidelines also suggest that 'Leaders must learn to take time to articulate their positions to the media. They must use short, simple language that the media will use and the public will understand.' The 'opportunity' of a media interview is to be prepared for by, among other things: finding out who the reporter is and why the interview was requested; establishing ground rules for the interview; anticipating questions and responses; and using PAO or other staff as devil's advocates, if possible practising before a camera and playing it back to staff to conduct a critique. Other helpful hints include what to wear for an interview (make sure your socks are long enough – if you cross your legs, you don't want your shins to outshine your shoes!), never go 'off the record' with a reporter you don't know, never lie to a reporter, don't discuss hypothetical situations or speculate.

For the battlefield, Public Affairs go beyond detailed advice on how to talk to the media. Whilst it is not possible to examine Public Affairs plans for actual military operations, it is possible to obtain unclassified plans from military exercises, such as the 1999 Pacific Strike exercise. Here, the Commander's Guidance is to 'allow free access ... by news media in order to accurately demonstrate the ability and resolve of this force to the American people and the rest of the world'.[11] Of course, the new openness is illusory. Although 'censorship and media security review are prohibited', this is only because 'security at the source is in effect'. Information will be given to the media via 'on the record' briefings, but 'security at source' means that nothing worthy of being 'off the record' will be revealed. Furthermore, despite forbidding censorship, Appendix 3 to the Public Affairs plan for Pacific Strike lists numerous things the media must promise not to report, on pain of being ejected from the battle zone. The list includes: specific numerical information; details of operations, including those cancelled or postponed (noting that this means cancelled operations can *never* be reported, at least until announced by politicians or senior military figures); specific rules of engagement; information on intelligence collection; general descriptions of point of origin and type of aircraft; missing aircraft or ships whilst rescue is being planned or carried out; specific operating methods and tactics; any photographs or visual media showing faces of dead, wounded, prisoners or civilian internees. The exercise plan also includes 'Command Messages' outlining the overall rationale for Public Affairs Officers to put forward, including the 'Moral high ground' – the US military even *practises* only 'moral' and 'legitimate' actions, and practises selling these to journalists.

Learning to Work with Friends

The vast majority of Public Affairs Officers are in 'reserve' contingents of the armed forces, including the National Guard – because many PA specialists also have full time jobs as journalists or other media workers. Those best able to represent the military to journalists are other journalists in military uniform. Unlike the military, journalists have no institutional structures within which to discuss, plan, and teach themselves how to report, or how to counter the systematic public affairs training of the military. There are foundations and conferences, but the thrust in these discussions is more about how to work with the military, not about how to deal with the way the military works with journalists. Commercial media also have few funds available, even if there was the will to challenge. In any case, where would the payback be, with the military becoming so anxious to 'facilitate' reporting?

Nevertheless, the extent to which journalists are accepting their role in the cosy relationship proposed by the military is a little surprising.

In 1994 the Pentagon opened the doors of its military colleges to private citizens. The first private citizen to attend the prestigious National War College, in 1995, was the Associated Press's Susanne Schafer, funded by a $25,000 AP study grant. Schafer was followed in 1996 by Lisa Burgess under a Freedom Forum grant. Announcing the grant, the Forum's Charles L. Overby, said that 'better training and education of journalists are keys to improving the adversarial media-military relationship' and Burgess added that it was essential, as the sole representative of the media in the college, to represent herself as 'professional, dedicated, ethical and involved'.[12] The Forum's move followed their publication of an influential report, *America's Team: The Odd Couple*, which recommended setting up a foundation-funded organisation to 'facilitate' the media–military relationship, funding more military study for selected journalists and the publication of a manual to go to all media editors, with a pocket edition for journalists (Aukofer and Lawrence, 1995). Clifford H. Bernath, principal Deputy Secretary of Defense for Public Affairs, called the report 'a significant milestone in defining today's relationship between the military and the media', indicating not only the lack of threat that journalists present to the military under such plans, but also the positive PR implications for the military.[13] Frank Aukofer suggests that not only should journalists monitor military courses and take part in military seminars, but that 'local media leaders should invite military personnel to visit their facilities, participate in editorial boards' and 'put some combat commanders in newsrooms to see how we operate'.[14]

The post-Grenada pool system was much criticised by journalists, who disliked the control the pool allowed the military to exercise, and resented sharing their best material with competitors. Yet in Bosnia, TV journalists themselves established the Sarajevo Agency Pool in 1992 (which ran until August 1995), despite fierce debates about it penalising the brave and rewarding the indolent, and pressure from editors outside the war zone (Bell, 1995: 63–6). According to Patrick Sloyan (1999), two weeks into the Kosovo air war, the 'normally somnolent news hierarchy' was 'pounding Clinton's desk' with requests for more information about the war. One of their requests was for a pool system. Sloyan suggests that the request could have been a mistake (an understatement, surely) in light of the experience of the pool system during the Gulf War. But over Kosovo, the media elite's response to limited military information was simply to get closer to the military, with no worries this time, unlike in Bosnia, about the competitive aspects of journalism.

Learning from Kosovo

Nato spokesman Jamie Shea has outlined his lessons from the war:

> Do not expect perfection in dealing with the press ... we are obliged to stay on-the-record whereas the media want ... the 'inside story' ... therefore Nato's

press strategy has to be geared towards the optimal selling of the Alliance's basic arguments and the optimal playing down of the manifold criticisms from the media.[15]

It is hard to credit, but Nato believes it received poor coverage from the media of Nato countries during the bombing of Yugoslavia. As US military planners had warned, coalition operations were not yet, but would need to, come under the same Public Affairs doctrines as the American military. It is clear they will in the future.

Nato has a sophisticated media strategy now, but did not at the start of the bombing campaign. Speaking in September 1999, Shea explained that half his office had been in Washington preparing for Nato's fiftieth anniversary, leaving only three people in Brussels. Nato anticipated a short bombing campaign and, amazingly, maintain they did not expect the world's media to be very interested, so were not ready for the 400 journalists who set up in the Nato car park. But by the end of the war, Nato had made considerable efforts to put a media strategy in place. After the mid-April Djakovica refugee convoy bombing, which vividly exposed Nato's media shortcomings, various specialists were despatched from Washington and London to overhaul the public relations set-up. Shea wants to prevent a negative story 'playing for days' due to 'lack of information', which he felt the military men were not giving him because they did not know how important the media was. He now argues for the institutionalisation of the 'SHAPE information network', that he and Alastair Campbell, Tony Blair's Press Secretary, established within Nato's operational HQ in Mons, Belgium. This was a 'spy' system, whereby Nato officers reported to Brussels outside normal communication channels and chain of command, allowing Shea's press office more information on what the military command within Nato was doing.

Shea is proud of the way Nato was able to 'occupy the media space', creating a situation whereby 'nobody in the world who was a regular TV viewer could escape the Nato message'. But in future, he suggests, Nato needs to be 'more dynamic and creative' in obtaining access to enemy media in order to 'level the playing field'. This arises from the surprising thought that it is unfair if the Western media carry information (such as interviews, or pictures of bomb damage and casualties) from an enemy without the enemy being obliged to show the Nato side as well: 'We need to have media planning for such a pro-active approach better prepared next time around.' Similarly, he suggests that 'the all-intrusive nature of press-relations to an Alliance conflict is still underplayed and under-exploited in Nato's crisis management exercises. We have to redefine these to give media activities and media training a much more central role in line with reality and our own experiences.' Nato's future media strategy is a combination of how they operated during the latter part of the bombing campaign and how they would have wished to have operated had they anticipated the scale of media interest from the outset.

Nato is certainly on the path to using the media as the US military do. The role of boosting public support was largely left to politicians, with Nato actively co-ordinating information released so that it would support the policy and statements of those politicians. At important points, such as the start of the campaign, or the final briefing on the Djakovica convoy bombing, it was the military commanders who took centre-stage, not the press spokesmen. Nato did impose reporting rules, preventing the unauthorised use of names and hometowns of Nato personnel, and US journalists complained – but they did not complain about the 'security' aspects that limit reporting of military build-ups and attacks to abstract phrases which reduce their impact.

However, despite its professed 'openness' and 'honesty', Nato's response to the bombing of a passenger train on 12 April shows that manipulation and suppression are never far away when necessary. Nato maintained the train had been travelling too fast for the missiles to be diverted, and played a videotape to prove the point: 'all of a sudden at the very last instant with less than a second to go he caught a flash of movement', said General Wesley Clark at the following day's press conference. However, in January 2000 it was revealed that the videotape had been played at three times the normal speed. In response Nato first said the 'error' had been caused by a 'technical problem' and although this had been noticed in October it had not been considered 'useful' to admit it (Agence France Presse, 6 January). Later, Nato changed its story, citing 'security reasons', as missile speeds could be calculated from the film (Channel Four News, 7 January). The different excuses given and the fact that Nato released other missile film with timing information (including, at the 18 April briefing, an example where a 'quick-thinking pilot' was able to abort an attack), suggests a cover-up and confirms that the defence initially given for 'accidentally' bombing the passenger train was entirely spurious. Military-friendly journalists failed to ask questions at the time, even when the bridge described to them by Clark as 'relatively long' appeared on the film as a very small one.

Conclusion

The military have been learning the lessons of how to deal with the media, and the media have been coming to terms with selling the 'positive' side of military exploits. In tacit acknowledgement of past mistakes, military personnel are now under orders to provide information, and to not lie or grandstand. The new 'openness' has been widely welcomed by the media, though ultimately, for all the rhetoric, it is the same as usual, with restrictions, misinformation and manipulation. This should come as no surprise, since the aim of the military is to present the case for prosecuting war effectively, not to question whether war is the solution.

According to Lieutenant-General Jay Garner, both the media and the military are 'absolutely fundamental to American democracy'.[16] The media's view of themselves as the 'fourth estate' implies a similar claim: that journalists will serve citizens with an informed debate, necessary for achieving consensus on the positive progress of society itself. The independence of the media from the government, military and other institutions is a mandatory precondition, and prior acceptance of a natural right to military intervention more than highlights the media's low expectation of the potential of their role. Creation of a media consensus on intervention, before having an informed debate with majority of its citizens is a serious recurrent failure of the media in foreign affairs which degrades democratic principles.

Notes

1. *The Future Military–Media Relationship: The Media as an Actor in War Execution*, A Research Paper Presented To The Research Department Air Command and Staff College In Partial Fulfilment of the Graduation Requirements of ACSC by Maj. Raymond R. Hill Jr., March 1997. Hill notes the 'fairly common (mis)perception among military officers that the media was a prime cause of defeat in Vietnam', and acknowledges that even 'the Army's official histories credit media reports as often more accurate than public statements of the administration'.
2. Pascale Combelles-Siegel, 'The Troubled Path to the Pentagon's Rules on Media Access to the Battlefield: Grenada to Today', 15 May 1996 [http://carlisle-www.army.mil/usassi/ssipubs/pubs96/medaacss/medaacss.pdf].
3. Ibid.
4. DODD 5122.5, Statement of DOD Principles for News Media Coverage of DOD Operations, 21 May 1992, Enclosure 3.
5. US DoD Public Affairs Office (PAO) Guidance. [http://carlisle-www.army.mil/usacsl/divisions/pki/legal/oplaw/z-appdxf.htm]
6. US DoD Joint Publication 107 (draft).
7. 'The Military and the Media: Facing the Future', Cantigny Conference Series, 1997 [http://www.rrmtf.org/conferences/facing.rtf].
8. *Media Vs. Military*, Common Ground Radio, broadcast 14 July 1998.
9. *The Future Military–Media Relationship: The Media as an Actor in War Execution*, A Research Paper Presented To The Research Department Air Command and Staff College in Partial Fulfilment of the Graduation Requirements of ACSC by Maj. Raymond R. Hill Jr., March 1997.
10. US DoD Public Affairs Office (PAO) Guidance [http://carlisle-www.army.mil/usacsl/divisions/pki/legal/oplaw/z-appdxf.htm].
11. ANNEX V (Public Affairs) to II Corps OPLAN 99–01, PACIFIC STRIKE [http://www-cgsc.army.mil/pw/CORPS/annexes/annexv.doc].
12. The Freedom Forum, *Forum News*, 24 June 1996.
13. 'Military Relying On First Amendment Center Report', First Amendment Center press release, 18 October 1996.
14. The Freedom Forum, *Forum News*, 24 June 1996.
15. Jamie Shea, 'The Kosovo Crisis and the Media: Reflections of a Nato Spokesman', Atlantic Council of the United Kingdom, 15 July 1999.
16. The Military and the Media: Facing the Future, Cantigny Conference Series, 1997 [http://www.rrmtf.org/conferences/facing.rtf].

8

Goran Gocic

Symbolic Warfare:
Nato versus the Serbian Media

The closest thing to democracy in Yugoslavia in the 1990s was the press. As elsewhere in Eastern Europe, the new media market was one of the most dynamic and radically transformed areas of public life. Indeed, the Yugoslav press went much further than their Western counterparts in criticising their own government. Particularly the new privately owned publications, such as *Dnevni telegraf, Danas, Nasa Borba, Blic* and *Glas*, remained both influential and apparently beyond the reach of the authorities for the second half of the decade. The same applies to radio stations, many of which were of an international standard. Television was somewhat different. Local channels in cities run by the opposition could break away from official agendas, but were too small to produce high-quality news programming. Belgrade's Studio B went furthest in this respect, but the only broadcaster with the technical and financial means to reach all the country's 4.5 million voters was the licence-funded state broadcaster Radio Televizija Srbije (RTS). RTS's three channels not only have a monopoly on broadcasting, but without serious competition within the country they have a virtual monopoly on information, especially for the rural populace without access to commercial terrestrial channels, satellite TV and the Internet.

The privately owned Yugoslav media have tended to be pro-Western, and in the run up to the Kosovo crisis broke the official silence about the situation inside the province, warning that Serbia could become branded a rogue state. Federal media legislation in October 1998 was in many ways a response to such coverage, and also targeted the Albanian-language press in Kosovo. Disproportionately high fines were introduced for ill-defined offences such as 'damaging the respectability of the country', aimed particularly against radical critics of the regime such as B92 radio and the *Dnevni telegraf*, which was fined and closed down several times. Other papers took no chances and either suspended publication or toned down their reporting.

However, it was Nato that made a pro-Western stance untenable for Yugoslav journalists, not only during the bombing, but in the longer term as well. As the bombs and missiles started to fall, the roles of privately owned pro-Western media and nationalistic state-run media were instantly reversed.

After a decade of crude propaganda RTS became an accidental hero, as Nato gave it an unexpected chance to redeem itself. 'Milosevic's lie machine' did not need to fabricate the nation's victimisation: the reality was horrific enough. Both RTS and President Milosevic undeservedly became 'heroes in opposing the New World Order' during the Kosovo war. Others could only follow suit with more moderate criticism of the West. *Dnevni telegraf* closed on the first day of bombing, and B92 underwent a coup in the middle of the war. Since the bombing has ended, RTS has resumed its usual odious party line, while the independent media have not recovered from the blow. The Milosevic–Nato joint action destroyed the free media in Serbia for the foreseeable future.

When the US F-117A stealth aircraft was shot down on 27 March 1999, the world's press carried the news on their front pages, and TV channels broadcast RTS pictures of the wreckage around the globe. Nato took a while to recover from the shock. Official statements sounded as if they had been scripted by Eugene Ionesco. At Nato's 28 March briefing, spokesman Jamie Shea described it as 'the incident concerning the crashing of an F-117A Nighthawk Stealth aircraft'. On 20 April Major General Bruce Carlson announced at a Pentagon briefing: 'We have eliminated an act of God and loss of consciousness by the pilot.' Shea later claimed these surreal denials were due to security reasons (that is, recovering the pilot).[1] In fact, however, the pilot had already been recovered before the 28 March briefing, where, in a desperate attempt to spin good news from bad, Shea expressed 'relief' and 'congratulations' over the 'excellent news' that the pilot had been rescued. Nato therefore had no 'security' reason to deny the plane had been shot down.

The shooting down of the F-117A allowed RTS to score its first and most dramatic media coup. The incident was of little military significance – it was only one aircraft – but was symbolically important. It showed that although a small and impoverished country like Yugoslavia could not challenge US power, it could *de facto* question America's *absolute power*. Furthermore, the capacity to provide pictures of the wreck meant that Nato denials could be exposed as lies. The Iraqis had also claimed to have downed US stealth aircraft, but without pictures it was difficult to make a case: US denials were enough to assure everyone that no planes had been shot down.[2] As the RTS pictures beamed around the world, street demonstrators in Yugoslavia added their own caustic comments on placards: 'Sorry, we did not know it was invisible.' Internet sites carried pictures of the wreck, sometimes captioned with a parody of the Windows '95 warning: 'This aircraft has performed an illegal operation and will be shot down.'

Both Yugoslav and Western media borrowed images and language from the Second World War. For both, fascism was not only a shorthand for evil, but also something which 'we' have already fought successfully. Western journalists parroted the standard line that Milosevic was the 'new Hitler', just as they had with Saddam Hussein in the Persian Gulf War. Meanwhile RTS addressed the aggressor as 'the fascist hordes', in the manner of populist wartime reporting about the German occupation, and Second World War films, such as *The Battle of Neretva* or *Sutjeska*, were carried on all channels. Nato leaders suggested that the West enjoyed the benefits of a free and independent media, and that propaganda was confined to the 'totalitarian' Yugoslav regime. In some respects, however, the opposite contrast may be drawn: while much Yugoslav propaganda was witty and ironic, some Nato efforts were comparatively crude. RTS designed numerous video clips, usually associating Nato with the Nazis. One showed Nato planes flying in a swastika formation; in another, President Clinton was shown delivering a speech, but with Adolf Hitler's face superimposed; and another used film of Hitler dancing with Eva Braun but with US Secretary of State Madeleine Albright's face inserted. Similar clips circulated on the Internet. In contrast, Nato leaflets thrown from aeroplanes were outdated and illiterate. Supposedly scary, and devoid of any irony or distance, they quickly became a source of comic relief for their 'target audience'. While the 19 richest democratic countries representing, as Tony Blair put it, 'civilisation', mounted a 1940s-style propaganda campaign, one impoverished dictatorship, representing 'barbarity', opted for MTV-style messages, delivered via digital technology and replete with Generation-X irony.

Of course, Nato was aware of and bothered by all this. According to Lilja Besos, who worked for the Spanish channel TV 5 during the bombing, Nato Secretary-General Javier Solana telephoned in person to complain when the station broadcast a series of RTS clips without adding any critical commentary.[3] General Wesley Clark later said he felt Nato had lost the propaganda war,[4] and BBC journalist Julie Read said that 'The only TV pictures I clearly remember from the war were dead people killed by Nato.'[5] Rattled by Yugoslav propaganda, Nato destroyed most of RTS's transmitters, bombed its buildings in Belgrade and Novi Sad, and severed the station's satellite link on Eutelsat (even though it had been paid for in advance, and Yugoslavia was one of its founding members). Nato also reportedly announced it would shut down Yugoslavia's Internet links, the first threat of the kind, although to have actually done so would have been practically impossible.[6]

Compared with other media, the Internet is much more difficult to control or to destroy. Indeed, this was the strategic thinking behind its development by the US Department of Defense's Advanced Research Project Agency. To some degree, the Internet reverted to its original military purposes during the Kosovo crisis. Serbian hackers temporarily jammed Nato's Website, and sent e-mails to corporate and military sites to jam their systems and infect them with viruses. One of the hundreds of anti-Nato Websites, www.vojvodina.com, offered links to the e-mail addresses of journalists and officials in Nato countries: 'the site even directs hackers to a site that sells software for sending blast messages, a key weapon of "spammers," who clog e-mail systems'.[7] Arguably, the medium gives an advantage to the militarily inferior side, which can offset its conventional weakness by transferring the war into cyberspace. A more wired country (such as the US) is more vulnerable than a less wired one (Yugoslavia). Aware of the dangers of Internet warfare, the US took counter-measures, mounting their own cyber attacks against Yugoslav government computers.[8] The CIA also reportedly planned to wage cyber war against Milosevic's foreign bank accounts.[9]

However, although Kosovo was dubbed 'the first Internet war', the significance of actions by Yugoslav hackers was again largely symbolic, signalling the vulnerability of Goliath, not really hurting him. The real Internet challenge came not from hackers but from the wired elite. Unique Internet communities gathered as a large number of Serbian expatriates started to exchange opinions and information and send it around the globe – information which bypassed any censorship, which was from the horse's mouth and which was presenting the case of the 'other' (non-Western) side. The Serbian gathering on the Net during the bombing was fundamentally different from the previous populist gatherings of party or nationalist rallies, or student protests. It was global, without age or geographical limits, and the Internet had its own war heroes, such as Monk Sava from Decani monastery in Kosovo, nicknamed a 'CyberMonk' by Western journalists. Mailing lists in Serbian and English produced heated debates, and along with a seemingly limitless number of Websites provided alternative sources of information, commentary and analysis.[10] Minority or endangered groups are better motivated to present their case on what is considered to be an 'alternative' and largely unregulated medium.

The disturbing consequence of the 'no casualty' doctrine is that the Western soldiers cease to be soldiers in the conventional sense, as advanced technology takes their place. Instead, they are joining politicians in becoming mannequins of power, that is, something more like 'demonstrators' or *actors*. This became apparent in Kosovo – from the pure Hollywood mock-invasion of US/Nato troops filmed in Greece, to the photo opportunities of posing as babysitters and cooks in refugee camps. It seems that their job is not combat, but *posing* in one way or another, for the cameras. By contrast, at a time when the average Western citizen would not go to war for any reason, most of the warriors around the world (that is, those who do not go to war for a salary, but out of necessity or conviction), especially those in non-client armies, are regarded as bloodthirsty criminals. Similarly, Western war reporters are not reporters any more (in the sense of being investigators and seekers after truth). Together with soldiers, they are agents serving the West's expansionist aims. Their duty is providing useful facts and sometimes misinformation rather than information, with the prime function of justifying the actions of their governments. It is precisely the (Western) media manipulator, the journalist, who wins the battle that is evaded by the (Western) soldier and lost by the (non-Western) warrior. The reporter is the one who can celebrate the war victory: the contemporary power, prestige and bay-wreath of the reporter's vocation are inherited from those of the archaic warrior. With the current development of the mass media, the warrior becomes some kind of demonised antagonist

who fills up the medium exclusively when war crimes are addressed. The pro-
tagonists are (usually civilian) victims, and the almighty reporter is a fiction
director who casts perpetrators and victims. Consequently, the media operative
on the ground now takes the risks that were traditionally attached to soldiers.
The increased number of journalists killed in local wars confirm this propo-
sition (the death toll of foreign journalists in Yugoslav civil wars is 76).[11]

The cyber war in Kosovo completed this chain reaction of vocational
inversions. The first-hand reports available on the Web from the Yugoslav
battlefield demonstrated the redundancy of paid journalism, showing how
'professional journalist' has become a dirty word, denoting a politically
corrupt, callous and irresponsible mercenary who slavishly follows official
agendas, or a crusader who recommends that countries should be destroyed
in order to save them. In contrast, many Internet posts, contributed free of
charge, were informative, fresh, touching, powerful, well-substantiated,
insightful, surprisingly well-written – all that professional journalism is
supposed to be.

Due to its huge technological advantage, the US has proved that it can lead
and win a war from the air alone and without losing a single soldier.
Increasingly, it is technological superiority (not courage or strength of
numbers, for example,) that dictates the outcome of war. Since the techno-
logically superior winner is known in advance, resistance significantly shifts
towards the realm of the symbolic. However, those who are able to manufacture or purchase superior technology also have the power of definition.
Since the US owns the global media – five of the world's six largest media corporations are American – they can decide who wears the white and who the
black hat, regardless of the facts. As killing becomes something conducted
by remote control, its representation turns war into a video game, an obscene
TV commodity. It is not only sanitised but, like violence in cinema, aestheti-
cised. As one Nato serviceman said of his first combat assignment in Kosovo:
'It's a lot of fun. I love my job. It was kind of playing a video game and riding
a roller-coaster at the same time.'[12] The Internet also confirms the trend toward
US dominance: traffic on the Web is 50 per cent commercial (dominance of
the industrialised West), 70 per cent American (ideological dominance) and
80 per cent in English (Anglo-American cultural dominance). The future consequences for cyber wars are consequently grim. Following Kosovo, more limited
(Intranet), rather than universal, access could become a frequent security
measure. Disseminating false information (even in the first person, in the form
of highly personal accounts) and destructive intrusions into computer systems
would not be limited to individual cyber terrorists, but could be mounted by
national cyber forces, supported by governments.[13]

It is much easier to organise a propaganda campaign when you are
defending than when you are attacking. Reviewing the Kosovo propaganda
war, it is evident that Yugoslavia scored some symbolic victories. For the first
time since the beginning of the Yugoslav crisis, the authorities introduced
some media management, limiting the access of foreign journalists,

controlling their whereabouts, occasionally censoring their reports and taking them to see the destruction caused by Nato bombing. No matter how devoted Western journalists were in supporting Nato's war effort, the media, after all, still need *a spectacle* – even pictures of Nato's victims are irresistible. Yet the US lost far less in its few media defeats than the Serbs won from their Pyrrhic symbolic victories. Even in the unlikely event that Nato lets Yugoslavia keep its little southern province, the Serbs – suffering the disastrous consequences of the bombing and with Kosovo still a powder keg – would still clearly be the losers.

Notes

1. Jamie Shea, speech to the Royal Institute of International Affairs, Chatam House, London, 28 September 1999.
2. The previous six 'losses' of F-117 aircraft were all 'accidents', according to Major General Bruce Carlson, DoD Briefing, 20 April 1999.
3. Interview with the author, 29 July 1999.
4. BBC *Newsnight*, 20 August 1999.
5. Interview with the author, 5 September 1999.
6. The threat was reported on a Serbian Net site, and has not been confirmed. For a sober assessment of the practicalities involved in carrying out the threat, see 'The "Internet War" Becomes More Literal', Stratfor commentary Archive, 12 May 1999, available at: http://www.stratfor.com/crisis/kosovo/commentary/c9905122050.htm.
7. Patrick Howe, 'War on the Web: Serb hackers blitz sites', *Arkansas Democrat Gazette*, 12 April 1999 (quoted from: http://www.ardemgaz.com/prev/balkan/abnet12.html).
8. After the war, General Hugh Shelton, chairman of the Joint Chiefs of Staff, admitted that 'US forces tried to confuse and break Belgrade government's computers.' *Voice of America*, 7 October 1999.
9. 'Clinton Reportedly OKs plan To Destabilize Milosevic', Reuters, 23 May 1999.
10. Examples included: www.yurope.com/kosovo/lista.html, www.srpska-mreza.com, and www.demokratska.org.yu.
11. Milos Vasic, Independent Journalists Association of Serbia, 23 April 1999.
12. *How the War Was Spun*, BBC 2, 16 October 1999.
13. Ben Venzke, 'Information Warrior', an interview with Winn Schwartau in *Wired*, August 1996, available at: http://www.wired.com/wired/archive/4.08/schwartau.html?pg=1&topic=).

Part III

Reporting the War Around the World

9

Seth Ackerman and Jim Naureckas

Following Washington's Script:
The United States Media and Kosovo

In times of war, there is always intense pressure for reporters to serve as propagandists rather than journalists. While the role of the journalist is to present the world in all its complexity, giving the public as much information as possible in order to facilitate a democratic debate, the propagandist simplifies the world in order to mobilise the public behind a common goal.

As the Rambouillet negotiations were getting underway in France in February 1999, Secretary of State Madeleine Albright laid out her view of the Kosovo conflict in a major address at the Institute for Peace in Washington. Albright, of course, is a diplomat, not a journalist. Her history of the Balkan conflict is not an effort to get at historical truth, but an attempt to further US foreign policy goals. She said:

> Yugoslavia's collapse and descent into violence and brutality began in Kosovo. It was by proclaiming Serbia's right to supreme authority there that Slobodan Milosevic burnished his ultranationalist credentials and began his rise to power. And one of his first acts as President of Serbia, in 1989, was to strip Kosovo of the autonomy it had enjoyed under the Yugoslav Constitution. His policies of ethnic polarisation and hate-mongering in Kosovo ushered in a decade of police repression and human rights abuses throughout Yugoslavia ...
>
> For 10 years, Kosovo's Albanian population fought a courageous, non-violent campaign to regain the rights they had lost ... But about one year ago, President Milosevic upped the ante by launching a brutal crackdown. Police and military forces were sent in to terrorise civilians, killing hundreds and driving hundreds of thousands from their homes. Under these conditions, many Kosovars abandoned non-violence and threw their support to the Kosovo Liberation Army, although its tactics too were sometimes brutal and indiscriminate.[1]

Though it contains elements of truth about the US's official enemy, Albright's account is filled with inversions, omissions and simplifications. For instance, she leaves out the events of the turbulent years preceding Milosevic's 1989 revocation of Kosovo's autonomy, a period marked by complaints from ethnic Serbs that they were being driven out of the province by Albanian nationalists. Albright also reverses the sequence of events leading up to Milosevic's 'brutal crackdown' on Kosovo in 1998. That crackdown, though brutal indeed, was a *response* to the Kosovo Liberation Army's first major military offensive in early 1998 – not a provocation which led to the KLA's uprising.

But what is most noteworthy about this expedient State Department history of Kosovo is how faithfully it was followed, in subsequent months, by the American press corps. When attempting to provide background to the Kosovo story, the US media followed Albright's lead in dating the modern history of the conflict to the late 1980s, when Slobodan Milosevic began using Serb-Albanian tensions for his own political ends; the strife of the 1970s and 1980s was effectively erased from the historical record. *New York Times* reporter Roger Cohen summarised the conflict this way: 'First, the Albanian majority wielded power, then Mr Milosevic stripped away that autonomy, and his police ruled Kosovo harshly for the last decade' (2 July 1999). A *Times* article on Kosovo's history by reporter Michael Kaufman skipped directly from the Second World War to '1987, when Slobodan Milosevic, now the Yugoslav president, first began exploiting and inflaming the historical rivalries of Albanians and Serbs'. In Kaufman's account, 'the conflict was relatively dormant until Mr Milosevic stirred up hostilities in 1989 by revoking the autonomous status that Kosovo had enjoyed in Serbia' (4 April 1999).

This spurious chronology is not only historical revisionism; it contradicts the *Times'* own earlier coverage of Kosovo. Reporter David Binder filed this report on 28 November 1982:

> In violence growing out of the Pristina University riots of March 1981, a score of people have been killed and hundreds injured. There have been almost weekly incidents of rape, arson, pillage and industrial sabotage, most seemingly designed to drive Kosovo's remaining indigenous Slavs – Serbs and Montenegrins – out of the province.

Describing an attempt to set fire to a twelve-year-old Serbian boy, Binder reported on 9 November 1982:

> Such incidents have prompted many of Kosovo's Slavic inhabitants to flee the province, thereby helping to fulfil a nationalist demand for an ethnically 'pure' Albanian Kosovo. The latest Belgrade estimate is that 20,000 Serbs and Montenegrins have left Kosovo for good since the 1981 riots.

'Ethnically pure', of course, is another way to translate the phrase 'ethnically clean' – as in 'ethnic cleansing'. The first use of this concept to appear in the Nexis news database was in relation to the Albanian nationalists' programme for Kosovo: 'The nationalists have a two-point platform', the *Times'* Marvine Howe quotes a Communist (and ethnically Albanian) official in Kosovo as saying, 'first to establish what they call an ethnically clean Albanian republic and then the merger with Albania to form a greater Albania' (12 July 1982). All of the half-dozen references in Nexis to 'ethnically clean' or 'ethnic cleansing' over the next seven years attribute the phrase to Albanian nationalists.

The *Times* returned to the Kosovo issue in 1986, when the paper's Henry Kamm reported that Slavic Yugoslavs 'blame ethnic Albanians ... for continuing assaults, rape and vandalism. They believe their aim is to drive non-Albanians out of the province.' He reported suspicions by Slavs that the autonomous Communist authorities in Kosovo were covering up anti-Slavic crimes, including arson at a nunnery and the brutal mutilation of a Serbian farmer. Kamm quoted a prescient 'Western diplomat' who described Kosovo as 'Yugoslavia's single greatest problem' (28 April 1986). By 1987, the *Times* was portraying a dire situation in Kosovo. David Binder reported on 1 November:

> Ethnic Albanians in the Government have manipulated public funds and regulations to take over land belonging to Serbs ... Slavic Orthodox churches have been attacked, and flags have been torn down. Wells have been poisoned and crops burned. Slavic boys have been knifed, and some young ethnic Albanians have been told by their elders to rape Serbian girls ...
>
> As Slavs flee the protracted violence, Kosovo is becoming what ethnic Albanian nationalists have been demanding for years, and especially strongly since the bloody rioting by ethnic Albanians in Pristina in 1981 – an 'ethnically pure' Albanian region, a 'Republic of Kosovo' in all but name.

This is the situation – at least as perceived by Serbs – that led to Milosevic's infamous 1987 speech promising protection of Serbs, and later resulted in the revocation of Kosovo's autonomy. Despite being easily available on Nexis, virtually none of this material found its way into contemporary US coverage of Kosovo, in the *New York Times* or anywhere else.[2]

Invisible Rebels

Journalists also followed Albright in her portrayal of the recent violence in Kosovo as an anti-Albanian pogrom, rather than a civil war between security forces and rebel guerrillas. Especially during the first weeks of Nato's bombing, when the overwhelming focus of US media coverage was on refugees and human rights abuses, the KLA's existence was often barely mentioned amid reports of expulsions and atrocities.

On 24 March 1999, the first day of the airstrikes, the *New York Times* ran a 500-word editorial endorsing the Nato campaign ('The Rationale for Airstrikes'). Although it made ample reference to the brutality of Serb forces, it did not once mention the KLA. 'Serbian forces are shelling and burning villages, forcing tens of thousands to flee. They have also been killing ethnic

Albanian civilians', the editorialists wrote. An uninformed reader would be left wondering what brought on the wave of violence. A 22 March *Times* article referred to Nato's plans for bombing 'elite Serbian units carrying out attacks on ethnic Albanians in Kosovo' and to 'tens of thousands of civilians now fleeing the offensive in Kosovo'. Only much later in the piece was there a single fleeting reference to 'rebel forces'. This tendency was particularly acute on US television, which focused primarily on images of huddled refugees and atrocity stories rather than reporting on the political and military situation inside Kosovo. During the early days of Nato's bombing, when Kosovo took up most of the evening network news broadcasts, it was not uncommon for entire broadcasts to go by without any reference to the Kosovo guerrillas or the civil war on the ground.[3]

The US media's transformation of Kosovo's civil war into a one-sided ethnic holocaust becomes clearer when one compares the *New York Times*' coverage of Kosovo with its treatment of a similar war – the Kurdish conflict in eastern Turkey. In one case, the *Times* assigns responsibility for the violence to the guerrillas; in the other case, the security forces putting down the rebellion are blamed. On 24 June 1999 the *New York Times* reported on the trial in Turkey of captured Kurdish guerrilla leader Abdullah Ocalan. The *Times* provided background on the war between Kurdish separatist guerrillas and Turkish security forces:

> The war that Ocalan has waged has cost more than 30,000 lives and made him the object of intense hatred. It has also made him a heroic figure to many Kurds who live in Turkey's southeast.

While here it is *Ocalan's* war that has cost 'more than 30,000 lives', in this 27 March *Times* depiction of the Kosovo conflict, the KLA simply disappears:

> The Serbian campaign against the ethnic Albanians has seen more than 2,000 killed in the last year, with hundreds of thousands of Kosovars driven from their homes, according to United Nations refugee officials.

Eliminating one party from the description of each of these conflicts does not help readers to understand the situations in all their complexity; but it does help to simplify the conflict so that those without additional information will see that the side supported by Washington are the 'good guys', and the other side are the 'bad guys'.

Diplomatic Rewriting

Nobody worked harder than Madeleine [Albright] at Rambouillet to try and achieve peace. And nobody should forget that President Milosevic had every opportunity to resolve this issue through dialogue. It was his refusal to negotiate in good faith that produced the conflict. (British Foreign Secretary Robin Cook, 22 April 1999)

In reporting diplomacy, too, American journalists read from the script written for them by Nato officials. On 23 March 1999, US envoy Richard Holbrooke was in Belgrade to deliver a final ultimatum to Yugoslav President Slobodan Milosevic: sign the Rambouillet plan – the document that emerged from the talks in France between the Yugoslav government, ethnic Albanians and the five-nation Contact Group – or be bombed. Milosevic's government refused to ratify the plan, which envisioned a very high degree of autonomy for Kosovo, and would have allowed Nato troops access to all of Yugoslavia. On 24 March the bombing began. But in the media, 24 March also marked the beginning of a remarkable process of historical revision in which the picture of the previous months of diplomacy at Rambouillet was seriously distorted. In order better to serve the war effort, establishment news outlets brazenly rewrote the history of pre-war negotiations, presenting Belgrade as rejectionist and the US as reasonable and accommodating.

One month earlier, at the close of the first round of Rambouillet talks, *New York Times* correspondent Steven Erlanger had summarised the diplomatic scene by noting that 'Mr Milosevic has shown himself at least as reasonable as the ethnic Albanians about a political settlement for Kosovo' (24 February 1999). He went on to note that Yugoslavia – via Milosevic's chief negotiator at Rambouillet, Milan Milutinovic – had shown flexibility on the main sticking point: the nature of an international peacekeeping force to implement a settlement in Kosovo:

> Already, the Serbian president, Milan Milutinovic, has said that, when negotiations resume on March 15, the Serbs are ready to discuss 'an international presence in Kosovo' to carry out political arrangements of any agreement. And other Serbs have floated ideas that include leavening Western forces with lots of Russians.

On the eve of war, however, Erlanger's reporting underwent a remarkable sea change. The journalist's 24 March dispatch was headlined 'US Negotiators Depart, Frustrated by Milosevic's Hard Line', giving precisely the opposite impression than his earlier reports – even though the Yugoslav position had not changed at all. The piece was full of quotes from US officials asserting Belgrade's obstinacy, charging that Milosevic had refused 'every opportunity' to avoid Nato bombing; that Milosevic stubbornly 'can't agree to a foreign force on Yugoslav soil because of history or politics or whatever'; and that 'if there had been any sign of compromise' the officials 'probably wouldn't be on the way to the airport right now'.

Yet only hours before Erlanger filed his dispatch, the Serbian leadership reaffirmed its earlier position – which Erlanger had a month previously called 'reasonable' – in a series of parliamentary resolutions. These rejected the

Rambouillet document, mainly because it envisioned the occupation of Kosovo by 28,000 Nato soldiers who would have the right to move throughout all of Yugoslavia. The resolutions denounced 'the demand to deploy Nato troops' and repudiated the notion of deploying 'foreign military troops' in Kosovo, which it called an 'occupation of Serbia'. But in a highly significant move, an accompanying resolution (called a 'decision') was passed, declaring that Serbia was:

> ready, immediately after the signing of the political settlement about self management [that is, Kosovo autonomy], negotiated and accepted by the representatives of all the national communities which live in Kosovo and Metohija, to consider the dimensions and character of the international presence in Kosmet, intended for the implementation of such a settlement.[4]

Although Erlanger's 24 March article reported that the Serbian parliament met 'to reject the idea of allowing foreign troops into Kosovo' and even quoted a hawkish Serb parliament member debating the issue, he omitted any mention of the other outcome of that debate: the resolutions urging an agreement on an 'international presence'. Those resolutions, which represent one of the most significant events in Kosovo's recent history, went unreported by virtually every major American news outlet. Curiously, Erlanger inconspicuously slipped a mention of the 23 March resolution into one of the final paragraphs of an 8 April *Times* dispatch, describing the parliament's statement as a call for 'United Nations forces'.[5]

The process of historical revision at the *Times* was completed when, as the war began, correspondent Jane Perlez took over day-to-day coverage of the diplomacy, making frequent assertions that Milosevic 'has absolutely refused to entertain an outside force in Kosovo, arguing that the province is sovereign territory of Serbia and Yugoslavia' (14 April 1999).

'They Need Some Bombing'

Meanwhile, with virtually no notice from the US media, the prospect of a compromise on the international force had been raised at Rambouillet and rejected out of hand by the US. Agence France Presse and the Russian ITAR-TASS news agency reported on 20 February that an unnamed Contact Group member had outlined a compromise: an international force for Kosovo under the flag of the United Nations or the Organisation for Security and Co-operation in Europe (OSCE), rather than under Nato. The Serbs signalled that they might accept such a force, but the US immediately ruled it out. Secretary of State Madeleine Albright was asked on CNN (21 February): 'Does it have to be [a] Nato-led force, or as some have suggested, perhaps a UN-led force or an OSCE … force? Does it specifically have to be Nato-run?' She replied: 'The United States position is that it has to be a Nato-led force. That is the basis of our participation in it.'

In one of the most significant and least known events of the Kosovo conflict, the US presented the Serbs with a new document on 22 February, only hours before the deadline for the end of the first round of talks. This document, which became known as the military portion of the 'Rambouillet agreement', was introduced without the knowledge of the Russians, with whom the Western nations were supposed to be cooperating; Russian negotiators immediately protested that they could not support the terms it contained. At the time, the story went unreported in the major news outlets. Several months later, on 26 July 1999, a *Newsweek* interview with Russian Foreign Minister Igor Ivanov, in which he described these events, was published only in the European edition of the magazine.

There is evidence that this part of the Rambouillet plan, which called for Nato troops to have far-ranging powers throughout all of Yugoslavia, was intentionally crafted to provoke a rejection by the Serbs, in order to create a pretext for Nato's bombing. A high-level US official reportedly told journalists at Rambouillet: 'We intentionally set the bar too high for the Serbs to comply. They need some bombing, and that's what they are going to get.'[6] Despite this inflexibility, three weeks into the war *Time* looked back nostalgically at the talks in France, lamenting that now 'the cautious compromise of Rambouillet seems a naïve pipe dream in a land where compromise has been banished' (19 April).

A rare admission of how little separated Yugoslavia's offers from the United States' demands was made by Thomas Friedman in his 'Foreign Affairs' column in the *New York Times* (11 May 1999) – though he presented it as evidence that Belgrade was being stubborn:

> If this war can be brought to a diplomatic solution soon, the Serbs, as they rebuild all their broken bridges, roads and factories, may start to ask: Was it worth it? Was it worth setting our country back a generation so that the peacekeepers in Kosovo would wear UN blue helmets and not Nato green ones?

It did not seem to occur to Friedman that Nato should have asked itself the same question.

Negotiation = Capitulation

The onset of war sent the diplomatic process back to square one, hardening positions on all sides. Yugoslavia was no longer putting out feelers about an 'international presence'. The diplomacy was treading the same ground that had been covered at Rambouillet. But establishment media, having airbrushed out the rapprochement achieved before the war, were compelled to present new developments as 'breakthroughs', though they were often the same agreements reached before 24 March.

On 7 May the *New York Times*' lead story was splashed across its front page in a bold, two-column headline: 'Russia in Accord on Need for Force to Patrol Kosovo'. The lead sentence: 'The West and Russia agreed for the first time today on the need for an international military presence in Kosovo to keep any eventual peace.' Although the US administration succeeded in portraying this development as a Russian capitulation to the American position, it was, in fact, precisely the opposite. Russia – which had been acting as an ally of the Serbs and as a mediator between them and Nato – had not changed its position at all. In signing the so-called 'G8 statement', Russia was merely agreeing to the deployment of 'effective international civil and security presences' in Kosovo – and, as Russian officials made clear, only with the permission of Belgrade. But this had been their position as far back as February, when they even signalled the prospect of sending Russian soldiers to partic- ipate in such a 'presence'.[7] In fact, the G8 statement was a significant setback for US policy, since it established the United Nations, and not Nato, as the ultimate guarantor of a settlement for Kosovo. But the US media were in no position to point this out, since they had obscured the crucial role that this tension – between the US's insistence on Nato supremacy and the European- Russian view that the UN should have ultimate authority – had played in the Kosovo crisis from the start.

Not only did the history of US diplomatic intransigence disappear from the media's coverage once the war began, but the concept of diplomacy itself was transformed. The notion that Nato as well as Yugoslavia should be expected to compromise seemed virtually unthinkable. Yugoslavia, on the other hand, was portrayed as inflexible when its overtures represented anything less than total capitulation. A routine dispatch in the *Washington Post* on 5 May reported that Nato and Russian 'efforts to formulate a diplomatic solution to the conflict picked up pace'; but the article could not report much progress, since:

> administration officials and [Russian envoy Viktor] Chernomyrdin remained at odds over what a settlement should look like and how it should be imple- mented. Further, there were few signs that Milosevic was significantly closer to accepting Nato demands.

A casual reader of this passage could be forgiven for feeling confused: it begins by referring to US 'efforts to formulate a diplomatic solution'; but 'diplomacy' here turns out to mean getting the Russians to obtain from Yugoslavia a full capitulation to Nato's 'demands'. Likewise, the *New York Times* reported on 3 May: '[Nato] officials said Milosevic's moves in the last three days' – including 'an interview in which he outlined his ideas for a settlement' – 'were an effort to show that he can be reasoned with. But so far, the Yugoslav leader has shown no flexibility on Nato's key demand: an inter- national security force in Kosovo, with Nato at its core.' Again, 'diplomacy' means capitulation, and compromise is ruled out.

Although this may have been the position of the mainstream media, it was not what the American public preferred: a CBS News poll taken on 11 May found that respondents agreed by a two-to-one margin that the 'United States and Nato should negotiate a compromise with Slobodan Milosevic in order to end the fighting in Yugoslavia.' On any mainstream American political talk show, such a statement would have been greeted by hoots of derision.

'Give War a Chance'

When the bombing began, Nato stressed the idea that Milosevic alone was responsible for the war, and that the air strikes were aimed only at him. 'We're not at war with anybody, and certainly not with the people of Yugoslavia', Nato spokesperson Jamie Shea insisted at a 5 April Nato briefing. At first, most of the US media went along with this line, presenting a rather colourless, opportunistic bureaucrat as a Hitlerian lunatic who had single-handedly launched war after war to satisfy his own personal hatreds. 'The Face of Evil' was how *Newsweek* described Milosevic on its 19 April cover. *Time*'s Lance Morrow, with astute grasp of the use of physical detail to inspire hate, described Milosevic's 'reddish, piggy eyes set in a big round head' (12 April). *Time* took him even lower down the bestiality scale in a 3 May cartoon of 'Slobbo the Nutt', a 'worm-like leader'.

From the beginning, however, there were prominent pundits and news outlets that took issue with the idea that Serbian civilians should not suffer from the bombing. In the 5 April edition of *Time*, for example, reporter Bruce Nelan questioned Nato's use of lighter bombs in the Yugoslav war, noting that:

> smaller bombs means there's less certainty about destroying the target in one attack. And if the pilot has to come back, that increases the risk to him in order to lessen the risk of civilians on the ground – a kind of Disneyland idea of customer service that rankles many war fighters at the Pentagon.

Not long into the war, Nato did relax the rules of engagement for the bombing campaign, quite predictably increasing the number of innocents killed by US bombs – a development that was cheered by some pundits. *New York Times* foreign affairs columnist Thomas Friedman wrote on 6 April that:

> people tend to change their minds and adjust their goals as they see the price they are paying mount. Twelve days of surgical bombing was never going to turn Serbia around. Let's see what 12 weeks of less than surgical bombing does. Give war a chance.

Likewise, *Washington Post* columnist Charles Krauthammer criticised the 'excruciating selectivity' of Nato's bombing raids and applauded the fact that 'finally they are hitting targets – power plants, fuel depots, bridges, airports,

television transmitters – that may indeed kill the enemy and civilians nearby'
(8 April).

Protocol 1, Section IV of the Geneva Convention sets forth the basic rule
protecting civilians: 'Parties to the conflict shall at all times distinguish
between the civilian population and combatants and between civilian objects
and military objectives and accordingly shall direct their operations only
against military objectives.'[8] In that light, consider the following appeal by
Thomas Friedman of the *New York Times* (23 April):

> Let's at least have a real air war. The idea that people are still holding rock
> concerts in Belgrade, or going out for Sunday merry-go-round rides, while
> their fellow Serbs are 'cleansing' Kosovo, is outrageous. It should be lights
> out in Belgrade: every power grid, water pipe, bridge, road and war-related
> factory has to be targeted.
>
> Like it or not, we are at war with the Serbian nation (the Serbs certainly
> think so), and the stakes have to be very clear: Every week you ravage Kosovo
> is another decade we will set your country back by pulverizing you. You
> want 1950? We can do 1950. You want 1389? We can do 1389 too.

Or Bill O'Reilly, the top-rated commentator on the Fox News Channel (26 April):

> If Nato is not able to wear down this Milosevic in the next few weeks, I believe
> that we have to go in there and drop leaflets on Belgrade and other cities
> and say, 'Listen, you guys have got to move because we're now going to
> come in and we're going to just level your country. The whole infra-
> structure is going.'
>
> Rather than put ground forces at risk where we're going to see 5,000
> Americans dead, I would rather destroy their infrastructure, totally destroy
> it. Any target is OK. I'd warn the people, just as we did with Japan, that
> it's coming, you've got to get out of there, OK, but I would level that
> country so that there would be nothing moving – no cars, no trains,
> nothing.

If the war crimes tribunal in The Hague were to obtain an internal Nato
memorandum directing military commanders to carry out a campaign like
the one suggested by the *New York Times*' premier foreign affairs commentator, the prosecutors would likely have no legal choice but to issue an
immediate war crimes indictment against the author of the document. As for
the campaign proposed by O'Reilly, it differs from the counterinsurgency
operations carried out by Milosevic's forces in Kosovo only in that it would
probably lead to far more civilian deaths.

The Kosovo war saw a disturbing resurgence among American correspondents of the concept of collective guilt. As *New York Times* columnist
Anthony Lewis put it: 'Nato air attacks have killed Serbian civilians. That is
regrettable. But it is a price that must be paid when a nation falls in behind

a criminal leader' (29 May). US media saw no contradiction between calling Milosevic a 'dictator' and holding the people of Yugoslavia morally responsible for his actions. After starting out with a paragraph worrying that Milosevic might 'retreat ... from Kosovo with his dictatorship intact', the *New York Times*' Blaine Harden went on to assert: 'It is worth remembering, though, that Mr Milosevic is an elected leader, having won three elections that were more or less fair' (9 May). Arguing with a member of Congress, Fox's O'Reilly declared: 'I don't understand why you don't think the Serb people should be held accountable for this dictator. He serves at their behest' (26 April).

Actually, in his current role as President of Yugoslavia, Milosevic was not popularly elected; he was chosen by the Yugoslav federal assembly, in an irregular vote in which he was the only candidate allowed. Perhaps a more direct indication of the level of Milosevic's support is the fact that an opposition coalition won the November 1996 local elections in 14 of Serbia's 19 largest cities, including many of the communities where Nato's attacks were concentrated. Still, there was a widespread sense that the Serbs, by failing to respond with outrage to reports of atrocities in Kosovo, had lost the moral standing to protest the Nato bombs falling on Belgrade. In a much-noted article in *The New Republic*, headlined 'Milosevic's Willing Executioners' (10 May), reporter Stacy Sullivan argued that the Serbian mentality comprises an 'intense sense of the collective guilt of the other Balkan ethnicities ... Thus, if the Muslims of Srebrenica were massacred, that is an appropriate form of retribution for [Muslim crimes against Serbs]. Cosmic payback.' It is not difficult to see the irony of such an argument appearing, just as Nato was escalating its attacks against civilian targets in Serbia, in an essay whose thesis holds that 'the silence of the intellectuals on the matter of war crimes raise[s] disturbing questions about the *culpability of Serbs as a whole*'.[9] 'Maybe we do have a quarrel with the Serbian people', the pull-quote said. The *New York Times*' Harden makes a similar case in a 9 May article with the ominous headline 'How to Cleanse Serbia' – though it is hard to take very seriously an analysis of the Balkans which, like Harden's, refers to Montenegro as an 'obscure' place.

How could the people of Serbia sit by while such terrible things are being done? In a country like the United States, where the government has sponsored massive atrocities in countries from Indonesia to Guatemala with only muted protests – where the Secretary of State replies to a report that half a million children have been killed in Iraq by sanctions with the statement that 'we think the price is worth it'[10] – this question should really not be such a puzzle.

'Accidents' Will Happen

Certainly the US media did not waste much time worrying about possible US war crimes, or the carnage caused by Nato bombs. In one of the worst 'accidental' bombings of Yugoslav civilians by the US, some 80 ethnic Albanians were killed on 13 May in the Kosovo village of Korisa. But the Pentagon did not admit that it had in fact bombed the village until several days later. During the first news cycle, when the story was big news, US and Nato officials advanced a variety of cover stories in order to deny or reduce their guilt, and network news media were all too eager to carry these false stories.

NBC's Jim Miklaszewski on 14 May, the day after the bombing, reported that Nato officials are 'fairly certain' they did not bomb the village: 'Nato's still investigating, but privately, Pentagon officials believe the Serbs attacked the village with mortars or small artillery, and then laid the blame on Nato.' In modern warfare, of course, planes generally drop bombs on specified targets whose co-ordinates are precisely known. It is unlikely that it would take 15 minutes, let alone more than 24 hours, to determine whether a particular village had been the target of any air strikes. Meanwhile, officials were 'privately' giving ABC's John Cochran an entirely different story. He reported that same night:

> Privately, though, US officials say American planes apparently did bomb Korisa, where they say there were legitimate military targets, including troops and anti-aircraft artillery. Nato analysts are looking at the possibility that, after the bombing, the Serbs shelled the town with artillery to make the devastation appear even worse. The analysts say the pictures from the scene do not seem to match the damage they believe was caused by the bombs.

No substantiation was ever offered for the horrific charge that Yugoslavs had themselves shelled the site to worsen the carnage. After Nato officials dropped this claim and openly admitted that they had in fact bombed the Albanians, they settled on a new story to try to redirect the blame for the mass slaughter: the refugees were 'human shields' who were brought to a military facility in hopes that they would be killed and provide a propaganda victory for Yugoslavia.[11] But press accounts from the scene cast doubt on the idea that Korisa was a military target: the London *Independent*, reporting from the scene, noted on 16 May that 'Western journalists who visited the scene saw burnt scraps of flesh and the scattered possessions of villagers – but no sign of a military presence beyond a small number of soldiers apparently billeted in nearby homes.' Reports from journalists at the site suggest that Nato bombs were not aimed at any obvious military target, but at the tractors and wagons of the refugees – which from 15,000 feet are hard to distinguish from tanks and army trucks.[12]

Still, most of the press accepted the 'human shields' story with little questioning – including those news outlets that had reported Nato's original falsehoods without a hint of scepticism. The coverage of the Korisa bombing was consistent with reporting that gave empathetic, detailed coverage to atrocities or alleged atrocities committed by Nato's enemy, but cursory, often dismissive coverage to death and mayhem inflicted by Nato forces. Nevertheless, the *New York Times*' Michael Wines had no trouble drawing the moral from the US's 'victory over Communism and inhumanity' in Kosovo that there is 'a yawning gap between the West and much of the world on the value of a single human life'. For Wines, the war in Yugoslavia 'only underscored the deep ideological divide between an idealistic New World bent on ending inhumanity and an Old World equally fatalistic about unending conflict' (13 June 1999).

Reliable Sources

Given how closely the major US media identified with the Western military alliance, it is not surprising that Nato's political and military officials dominated most media debates. A FAIR (Fairness and Accuracy in Reporting) analysis of sources on ABC's *Nightline* and PBS's *NewsHour* during the first two weeks of the bombing found such sources were abundantly represented; on *NewsHour*, current or former US government and military officials, Nato representatives and Nato troops made up 39 per cent of sources, while on *Nightline* this group provided a majority – 55 per cent – of sources. [13] *NewsHour*'s Margaret Warner epitomised this general homogeneity when she introduced a panel on 31 March: 'We get four perspectives now on Nato's mission and options from four retired military leaders.'

By contrast, opponents of the air strikes received scant attention. Of 291 sources that appeared on the two shows during the study period, only 24 – or 8 per cent – were critics of the Nato air strikes. Critics were 10 per cent of sources on *NewsHour*, and only 5 per cent on *Nightline*. Only three critics appeared live as interview guests on *NewsHour*'s discussion segments during the study, and only one critic took part in *Nightline*'s debates. In the absence of opponents of the war, debate focused on whether or not Nato should supplement bombing with ground troops, while questions about the basic ethics, legality and rationale of the bombing went largely unasked. Former Senator Bob Dole represented the typical 'opposition' voice when he said on *Nightline* (31 March), 'I just want President Clinton ... not to get wobbly.'

American and European journalists were well-represented, particularly in live discussions: they provided 17 per cent of all discussion sources on *Nightline* and a full 40 per cent on *NewsHour*. These discussions tended to focus on whether the US government was succeeding in swaying the American public, with journalists frequently providing suggestions on how the US government could cultivate more public support for the bombing. Academic experts – mainly think tank scholars and professors – made up only 2 per cent of sources on *NewsHour* and 5 per cent on *Nightline*. Just two experts appeared in live interviews on *NewsHour*, and no expert source was interviewed live on *Nightline*. While these percentages reflect a dearth of scholarly opinion in both shows, even the experts who were consulted did not add much diversity to the discussion; none spoke critically of Nato's actions.

On a 1 April *Nightline* episode that criticised Serbian media, Ted Koppel declared: 'The truth is more easily suppressed in an authoritarian country and more likely to emerge in a free country like ours.' But by generally excluding sources who would call into question the official version of events – the version that US media overwhelmingly embraced – Koppel demonstrated that the danger of unapproved truths emerging is something that can be avoided, even in a 'free' press.

Notes

1. Madeleine Albright, remarks at the US Institute for Peace, 4 February 1999.
2. To criticise US media for not recalling reports about ethnic violence aimed at ethnic Serbs is not, of course, to suggest that such violence legitimises later atrocities committed against ethnic Albanians. It is to insist that all victims of violence should be taken seriously in the press.
3. For example, *NBC Nightly News*, and *ABC World News Tonight*, 26 March 1999.
4. Kosovo and Metohija is the official name of Kosovo, abbreviated to Kosmet.
5. It should be noted that Steven Erlanger did some of the best on-the-ground reporting from Yugoslavia during the war.
6. Cato Institute conference, 18 May 1999. Former State Department official George Kenney wrote in the *Nation*, 14 June 1999: 'An unimpeachable press source ... told this [writer] that ... a senior State Department official had bragged that the United States "deliberately set the bar higher than the Serbs could accept". The Serbs needed, according to the official, a little bombing to see reason.'
7. ITAR-TASS, 18 February 1999.
8. Protocol Additional to the Geneva Conventions of 12 August 1949, and relating to the Protection of Victims of International Armed Conflicts (Protocol 1), 8 June 1977, article 48.
9. Emphasis added.
10. *60 Minutes*, CBS, 12 May 1996.
11. *New York Times*, 16 May 1999.
12. Paul Watson and John-Thor Dahlburg, *Los Angeles Times*, 15 May 1999; Julian Manyon, London *Independent*, 16 May 1999.
13. *Extra! Update*, June 1999. The survey, conducted by Margaret Farrand, was based on a search of the Nexis database for stories on the war between 25 March and 8 April, identifying both guests who were interviewed live and sources who spoke on taped segments.

10

Edward S. Herman and David Peterson

CNN: Selling Nato's War Globally

The Cable News Network (CNN) made a spectacular leap into prominence as a global news organisation during the 1990–91 Persian Gulf War, with its veteran journalist Peter Arnett reporting live on-the-spot from Baghdad, its already extensive global network of affiliates and outlets in place, and its then-unique 24-hours-a-day news service all contributing to making CNN the news service of choice and maximum influence during the war. CNN has grown substantially since then. By 1999, Time Warner Inc., CNN's parent company since 1996 and the world's largest media enterprise, proclaimed with some justification that 'CNN is the foremost news brand in the world', with CNN International (CNNI) now reaching more than 150 million households in more than 212 countries and territories – 'more viewers than all other cable news services combined'.[1]

Even in 1990–91, policy-makers and 'influentials'[2] watched CNN to learn about and transmit messages to the enemy as well as the public. The wide reach of its all-news format and ability to go 'live' at any time with 'breaking news' have made it easy for CNN to get policy-makers to co-operate with ready access, interviews, and even a scheduling of their daily events with an eye to gaining airtime on CNN.

CNN's importance from the Gulf War onward has even given rise to the notion of a 'CNN effect' or 'CNN factor' – the belief that CNN 'has become part of the events it covers' and that with its seeming omnipresence CNN 'has changed the way the world reacts to crisis'.[3] In this view, CNN's ability to focus an audience's attention can increase public pressure on political leaders, virtually forcing them to act. Viewed positively it would supposedly democratise policy-making, whereas for critics and policy-makers themselves it would hamper policy, forcing them to respond to a more volatile and uncontrolled public opinion.

But this notion of CNN leading policy not only fails to take into account the institutional constraints on CNN's policies and practices, it is also not consistent with the way in which CNN's agenda is formed, how it frames issues and its presentation of specific details in reporting on something like the Kosovo crisis. The bulk of this chapter will be devoted to an analysis of the latter set of issues. However, we can say in advance that CNN's performance before, during, and after Operation Allied Force, Nato's war against Yugoslavia in the spring of 1999, was well-geared to the demands of the leaders of CNN's state. There is perhaps no better symbol of the US–CNN relationship than the fact that in the midst of the Kosovo crisis, James Rubin, the top public relations officer of the US State Department, should marry Christiane Amanpour, CNN's leading foreign correspondent. In the mainstream US media this was not seen as in any way problematic, either suggesting probable bias on Amanpour's part or creating a conflict of interest.

CNN's Institutional Constraints

Time Warner makes no bones about the fact that its 'foremost business objective is to create value for our shareholders', that its top managers see cultivating the affluent Baby Boomers as a business imperative, and that increasing their share of the advertising market is a major route to profitability.[4] Neither Time Warner, its major advertisers, nor the major cable systems it supplies with news would be pleased if CNN stepped far out of line by allowing dissenting voices much play.

Another major constraint for CNN is the imperative that it attract viewers and keep them watching. This impels the network to adopt 'news-making' practices that stress action and visuals while avoiding both in-depth contextual reporting that may bore its audience and the presentation of unconventional points of view that may anger or alienate them. Superficiality and the conduiting of official propaganda also result from CNN's focus on 'breaking news', where speed precludes accuracy checks, meaningful context and the encouragement of serious criticism and debate.

Maintaining good terms with US officials is of paramount importance to CNN as it depends on the US government for commercial and diplomatic support as it expands abroad, and because much of its news comes from government decisions, press releases and reports. This exceptional degree of source dependency and the symbiotic relationship it produces makes for an uncritical media institution consciously allied with, and readily managed by, the government. CNN's 'professionalism' is largely reduced to making sure that the right news conferences are covered, that the appropriate guests are put on the air, and that everyone's names are spelled correctly.

CNN prides itself on being a 'global', not a US, news network. It has pushed to 'regionalise' its news operations around the world, and some half of its assignment desk personnel are not of US nationality (King, 1999:121). Nevertheless, ownership and control and its main office are in the United States and its dominant officials are US citizens. Policy, especially when US interests are at stake, flows from headquarters; and in cases such as Operation Allied Force, 'CNNI piggybacks on the domestic network, pre-empting most of its regional programming for the same breaking coverage one sees in the US'.[5] But this 'breaking news' coverage was overwhelmingly a version of 'press release journalism', based on 'live' news conferences, leaks from government sources, and interviews with US and Nato officials in Washington and Brussels passed along with minimal processing or presentation of relevant context. Such bias is defended by CNN officials on the grounds that what Nato officials had to say was newsworthy and that 'Viewers are intelligent and capable of making their own judgments – be it propaganda or truth' (King, 1999:123). But the difference between a propaganda agency and an independent news organisation is supposed to be that the latter filters out untruths, provides meaningful oppositional facts and analyses, and is not itself an instrument of propaganda. CNN did not pass this test in the Kosovo war.

The Nato–CNN Partnership

When US Special Envoy for Yugoslavia Richard Holbrooke lauded the mainstream US media for providing 'extraordinary and exemplary' coverage of the Kosovo war on 22 April 1999, he named CNN among the exemplars.[6] And with good reason. CNN's anchors and reporters almost without exception took the justice of the Nato war as obvious and were completely unaware of or unconcerned with their violation of the first principle of objectivity – that you can't take sides and serve as a virtual promoter of 'your' side. The result was that in word usage, assumptions, and choice and treatment of issues and sources, CNN and its reporters on the Kosovo war followed Nato's lead and served as a *de facto* public-information partner. These journalists never questioned Nato's motives, explored any hidden agendas, challenged Nato's claims of fact, or followed investigatory leads that did not conform to Nato propaganda requirements.

If Nato said that the bombings were motivated by 'humanitarianism', that was enough for CNN reporters, and CNN's Christiane Amanpour asserted that Nato's war was for 'the first time ... a war fought for human rights' (6 October 1999). That 'only a fraction of 1 percent of the [Nato] bombs went astray' was gospel for Amanpour simply because that is what Nato says (6 October). If Nato claimed that the Serb brutalities and expulsions that followed the bombing would have happened anyway, Amanpour took this as unquestioned truth ('this has been an offensive that has, you know, been planned for a long time', 3 April). That the Serbs were committing 'genocide' (Tom Mintier, 18 March; Miles O'Brien, 26 June), whereas Nato's military operations were regretfully doing only what was necessary and proper, was a premise of CNN anchors and reporters. And that Nato patiently sought a negotiated peace while Milosevic was the 'wild card' who 'may be testing Western resolve' and with whom the West was 'fed up' (Brent Sadler, 27 January; Andrea Koppel and Joie Chen, 29 January), was standard CNN usage.

Although CNN official Will King asserted that CNN explored 'issues from why wasn't Nato getting involved in other similar conflicts elsewhere in the world ... and was the Alliance legally justified' (1999:123), this was not true.

Kofi Annan raised the question of legality of Nato's action in a brief news conference that CNN carried live on 24 March, but the thrust of his remarks was thereafter ignored, as was the question of the legality of Nato's choice of targets to bomb. Contrary to King, there was no discussion of why humanitarian intervention, so-called, takes place in Kosovo but not for example in nearby Turkey, itself a Nato member and with a terrible human rights record throughout the 1990s.

CNN's journalists not only followed Nato's agenda and failed to ask critical questions, they also served as salespersons and promoters of the Nato war. Time and again they pressed Nato officials toward violent responses to Serb brutalities and unwillingness to negotiate, with Nato allegations on these latter points taken at face value. CNN's Judy Woodruff repeatedly asked Nato officials about the threat to Nato's credibility in the absence of forceful action (18 January 1999); Wolf Blitzer pressed unrelentingly for an introduction of Nato ground troops, raising the matter a dozen times in a single programme (4 April). Amanpour complained bitterly that General Wesley Clark 'had to lobby hard to get his political masters to escalate the bombing' and that there were '19 different leaders who insisted on vetting the bombing' (6 October), her last point a patent falsehood. When Nato bombing was constrained by bad weather, a CNN anchor expressed clear disappointment; and when delays were announced in the delivery of US Apache helicopters, CNN's correspondents were dismayed.[7] In short, CNN's personnel were rooting for the home team.

In its use of sources, too, CNN's pro-Nato tilt was immense. Based on a 38-day sample of CNN coverage of the Kosovo crisis and war, the table opposite shows that representation of Nato bloc officials, past and present, was an overwhelming 61 per cent, led by 257 US/UK official appearances (35.3 per cent) out of a 728 total. The US/UK official representation exceeded that of the Serbs by a 3.4 to 1 ratio. But this greatly understates the difference in representation, for two reasons. One is that on average US/UK spokespersons were given almost triple the time given the Serb officials to state their case, so that adjusting for this difference the ratio of representation jumps to 9 to 1.

An equally important factor is the difference in CNN's treatment of Nato and Serb officials. The former were treated deferentially as spokespersons of a just cause, and the questions encouraged them to elaborate on their plans and claims, without challenge (except for the previously mentioned suggestions that more forceful action may be necessary to establish credibility). In contrast, when Serb spokespersons made claims and charges, although CNN treated them politely, they were often challenged with counter-arguments, and the issues they raised were not explored.

This failure to explore issues and present evidence and analyses contrary to those of Nato was reinforced by CNN's unwillingness to tap oppositional sources in the Nato countries themselves. As the table shows, of 15 important dissident commentators, only three had brief appearances on CNN in the sample period. These dissident sources quite possibly would have had more credibility to CNN's audience than Serb (or Russian) spokespersons, making their virtual exclusion from CNN an important form of closure of oppositional voices.

Sources tapped by CNN during the Kosovo war[*]

Source	Number of appearances	Percentage of appearances
Nato bloc officials	269	37.0
US/UK	(257)	(35.3)
Other Nato	(12)	(1.7)
Nato bloc ex-military	78	10.7
Other current or past US/UK officials	97	13.3
Total Nato bloc representation	(444)	(61.0)
Non-Nato bloc excluding Serbs and Albanians	29	4.0
Kosovo Albanians	37	5.1
Serbs	75	10.3
Other	143	19.6
15 major Western opponents of the war[**]	(5)	(0.7)
Total	728	100

Notes:
* Based on a sample of all CNN programmes on the Kosovo war for 38 days, from 14–31 March and 26 May–14 June.
** The 15 opponents of the war that we checked were: Phyllis Bennis, Francis Boyle, David Chandler, Noam Chomsky, Ramsey Clark, Marjorie Cohn, Régis Debray, Robert Fisk, Robert Hayden, Diana Johnstone, George Kenney, Jan Øberg, John Pilger, Benjamin Schwarz and Norman Solomon. Of these 15 people, only three, George Kenney (twice on 25 March, once on 27 March), Phyllis Bennis (3 June) and Ramsey Clark (7 June), turned up on CNN during the sample period.

CNN in the Kosovo War: Case Studies

How well or how poorly CNN, or any other 'news' organisation, carries out its purported mission is above all else an empirical question. So, how did CNN employ its considerable news-gathering tools in the Kosovo war? In what follows, we will present three short case studies, each of which suggests some unflattering conclusions.

The 'Peace Process': Rambouillet

The period from early February through 18 March 1999 was one in which a Nato-engineered 'peace process' – named the Rambouillet talks for the chateau outside of Paris where most of the meetings were held – was allegedly tried but failed.

But the truth was another matter. The actual 'peace process' comprised an ultimatum by Nato that Belgrade either agree to Nato's military occupation of Kosovo and loss of effective sovereign rights there or accept the consequences. As State Department spokesman James Rubin explained to CNN on 23 February:

> [T]o put the proper pressure on President Milosevic, we understand quite well [what] was necessary. And what's necessary is the very real prospects about Nato strikes. And that can happen if, and only if, the Kosovar Albanians agree to the agreement.

In the end, the leading Nato powers wanted to bomb Yugoslavia, and imposed negotiating conditions on the Serb delegation that assured their rejection by inserting a proviso in 'Appendix B' of the Rambouillet agreement/ultimatum that required Yugoslavia to permit Nato forces occupying rights throughout all of Yugoslavia, not just in Kosovo.[8] In the Serbs' eyes, this term amounted to a virtual declaration of war on Nato's part. A State Department official eventually acknowledged that there had been a deliberate 'raising of the bar' to assure rejection and to clear the ground for bombing.[9]

As late as 22 February, Serb negotiators had announced that they were ready to sign the 'Political' section of the agreement as it then stood. What they adamantly refused to accept was the 'Implementation' section's proviso that would have allowed Nato to occupy Kosovo.[10] For their part, the Kosovo Albanian delegation had rejected the 'Political' section precisely because it said nothing about a process that would lead to a referendum on the future status of Kosovo. But Nato had been counting on the Kosovo Albanians to sign on, openly conditioning any future attack on Serbia on whether or not the Albanian side came aboard. Otherwise, Nato's leadership feared that it would not have been able to muster the support it needed among Nato's other members to carry out its attack on Serbia. As Madeleine Albright explained, 'The Kosovar Albanians must do their part by giving a clear and unequivocal yes. It is up to them to create a black and white situation' (Agence France Presse, 24 February 1999).

Then over the night of 22–23 February, Nato inserted new terms into the agreement that called for 'a mechanism for a final settlement for Kosovo, on the basis of the will of the people', a last-second change that the Serbs interpreted to mean the eventual loss of Kosovo.[11] The Serbs had agreed to the 'Political' settlement in its prior form, but now rejected it because of the new terms. Then one month later, on 23 March, a vote by the Serbian National Assembly reaffirmed the basic political conditions to which the Serb delegation had agreed all along.[12] This vote suggested the strong possibility that a negotiated settlement to the crisis was still within reach. Nato flatly rejected the principles affirmed by the National Assembly. One day later, the bombing began.

How well did CNN handle this period of nominal diplomacy? As its journalists postulated Nato justice and confrontation with evil, CNN portrayed the entire process as one of Nato trying to get an evasive Milosevic to agree to a reasonable settlement. Is he 'getting the message?' (Gene Randall, 30 January). CNN wasn't interested in the subtleties of negotiating positions; they were even quite aware that Nato was trying to get the Albanians signed up to allow it to bomb Serbia. But CNN took this as quite reasonable. They reported without question Nato's claim that both sides had been threatened with Nato military action if they committed violence (Bernard Shaw, 26 January; Judy Woodruff and Nick Robertson, 27 January; Patricia Kelly, 28 January). And they consistently failed to note that military actions by the KLA served its interest in provoking Serb military responses, thus justifying Nato's attack on Serbia.

Altogether, in the months leading up to the bombing, CNN's reporting was closely geared to Nato's propaganda needs. First, the legality of Nato's threats to bomb and occupy Yugoslavia (or part of it) without Security Council sanction was off the Nato agenda and ignored by CNN, whose journalists took this Nato right for granted. Second, Nato's 'humanitarian' objective was accepted without question by CNN's reporters. Third, CNN followed Nato's lead throughout January–February, and up to the commencement of bombing on 24 March, by repeated and uncritical reporting of Serb atrocities in Kosovo, helping Nato to build a moral case for bombing. CNN's reporters never addressed the one-sidedness of Nato's threats and the built-in inducement to the Kosovo Liberation Army to provoke incidents. Fourth, CNN framed the 'peace process' as one of whether the Kosovo Albanians would sign the agreement, thus allowing Nato to pressure and bomb the Serbs. Thus CNN took as given Nato's spin that its ultimatum was meritorious and that Serb reluctance to join the Kosovo Albanians in agreeing to the terms was evidence of their misbehaviour and defiance. Finally, Nato's use of 'Appendix B' to 'raise the bar' was ignored by CNN, making the bombing appear solely the result of Serb recalcitrance.

The Racak Massacre

The story of the 'Racak massacre', which first surfaced on 16 January 1999, was a key episode in the build-up toward the Nato bombing.[13] It 'provoked an international outcry', according to a subsequent report by the OSCE, 'and altered the perspective of the international community towards the [Federal Republic of Yugoslavia] and Serbian authorities in Belgrade'.[14] The day before, a mixture of forces from the Yugoslav Army (VJ), the Ministry of the Interior (MUP), Special Police Units (PJP) and paramilitaries carried out what they termed a 'police' action in and around four villages south of the capital, Pristina (Racak, Petrovo, Malopoljce and Belince). The purpose of their mission was to 'arrest members of the terrorist group that last Sunday [10 January] attacked a police patrol, killing one policeman', the Serbian Media Centre reported at the time (Agence France Presse, 15 January). The VJ-MUP forces announced their action in advance to the OSCE monitors, and were accompanied on it by several OSCE observer cars and by an invited Associated Press team that filmed the events. There were exchanges of small-arms fire and 'savage fighting' (Deutsche Presse-Agentur, 16 January), including the use of tanks and heavy artillery by the Serb forces against the villages; however, most of the fighting took place in the surrounding woods. The earliest estimates of the death toll from this VJ-MUP operation ran anywhere from seven dead (the ethnic Albanian-run Kosovo Information Centre) to 'at least 15 KLA fighters' (the Serbian Media Centre).[15] Shortly thereafter, an official Serb communiqué claimed that 'several dozen' KLA fighters had been killed (Johnstone, 1999:56). At the end of the day, the VJ-MUP forces withdrew from the area, and KLA fighters quickly re-occupied the villages.

The next morning, local Kosovo Albanians took journalists and OSCE observers to a gully near Racak that contained a number of dead bodies, all wearing civilian clothes.[16] William Walker, the head of the OSCE's Kosovo Verification Mission, arrived at the scene and indignantly denounced the alleged massacre and mutilation of civilians. 'It looks like executions', he said. 'From what I personally saw, I do not hesitate to describe the event as a massacre – obviously a crime very much against humanity.'[17] (This is the same William Walker who, while serving as the US ambassador to El Salvador in 1989, said of the army's murder of six Jesuit priests, their housekeeper, and her daughter: 'Management control problems exist in a situation like this.' Walker more generally dismissed the massacres of unarmed civilians by the Salvadoran government with the flippant remark that 'in times like these of great emotion and great anger, things like this happen.')[18]

This story, as it was handled by the Western media, including CNN, provided a public relations coup for Nato. CNN reported the story intensively but uncritically. It never mentioned that the Serb action was carried out with TV and OSCE observers invited and present, who along with a French journalist were in and around the villages for many hours, but said nothing about a massacre before the presentation of the corpses in a gully the following day. The account of the incident by the two Associated Press TV reporters who filmed the operation, cited in both *Le Monde* and *Le Figaro*, contradicted the conclusions of William Walker and the KLA, but was never picked up by CNN.[19] CNN's one reporter who had the chance to see the bodies reported that they had been deliberately mutilated (Bill Neely, ITN correspondent, 16 January). But forensic tests by a Finnish investigating team as well as by Serb and Belorussian experts denied this and explained the damage as a result of animal bites (probably from packs of hungry stray dogs, numerous in Kosovo), contradictory evidence that went unreported by CNN (Johnstone, 1999:66). The Finnish experts were very cagey about releasing their report, and stories abound regarding the political pressure that was put on these experts right up to the date on which they announced their findings. 'The Americans in particular ... were hoping that [the Finnish experts] would accuse the Yugoslav authorities of a massacre to back up an initial judgment by the American head of the Western monitoring mission in Kosovo, William Walker', London's *Daily Telegraph* noted.[20] But this never happened. Belgrade forensic expert Branimir Aleksandric claimed that the Serb, Belorussian and Finnish studies all found that each of the dead bodies recovered from the villages had been killed by firearms used at a distance, adding that 37 of them had gunpowder residues on their hands, indicating that they were KLA fighters rather than civilians as claimed.[21] CNN, which initially followed William Walker and the KLA in asserting that all the victims 'appeared to have been shot at close ranges' (Juliette Terzieff, 16 January), never reported the conflicting findings by the forensic experts.

From beginning to end in reporting this story, CNN allowed itself to be led by the nose by the Walker-Nato hook. CNN never mentioned Walker's background as long-time Reagan administration official in Central America and apologist for government crimes in that area; its reporters never questioned the appropriateness of his appointment as head of the OSCE's observer mission, a fact that was resented by other OSCE officials and personnel; nor did they question the possibility that Walker was pursuing a war-preparation agenda.[22] Prominent European newspapers – among them *Le Figaro*, *Le Monde*, *Frankfurter Rundschau* and the *Berliner Zeitung* – raised questions about Walker's qualifications and agenda, about the possibility that the Racak 'massacre' was set up to be exploited by the war-making clique within Nato, and the peculiar facts of the massacre scene itself, but CNN ignored them, choosing instead to play the game precisely according to the rules of William Walker and Nato.

The Bombing of Serbian Broadcasting

Nato's threats to bomb Serbian Radio and Television began in early April, when Nato Supreme Commander Wesley Clark accused them of being 'an instrument of propaganda and repression of the Milosevic government', hence legitimate 'military' targets (*New York Times*, 9 April). A series of attacks followed, most notably on 21, 23 and 25 April – roughly the same period that Nato's 19 members gathered in Washington for its fiftieth anniversary celebration.

Little noticed and completely suppressed by CNN was the fact that through 20 April, just one day before the facilities were bombed, both CNN and other US broadcast networks had also occupied and made use of the building housing Serbian Radio and Television. *Washington Post* media critic Howard Kurtz reported that 'CNN and the US broadcast networks, which had been feeding videotape from the building, abandoned it after receiving private warnings from senior White House and Pentagon officials that Nato would soon hit the facility.'[23] In its coverage of the bombing, CNN never reported the fact that it had received private, high-level US official warnings to evacuate the building, and Kurtz himself failed to mention it when he co-hosted the CNN weekly programme *Reliable Sources* the same day that his report appeared in the *Washington Post* – a programme 'where we turn a critical eye on the media', in Kurtz's words (24 April).

Nor did CNN find newsworthy the ethical dilemma posed by its use of this knowledge to move its own employees out of harm's way, while failing to share this potentially life-saving information with its colleagues at Serbian Radio and Television. In deciding to bomb Serbian Radio and Television, Nato had clearly chosen to target a non-military facility occupied by civilians, with 16 people killed in the strikes that followed.[24] This is a violation of the rules of war that preclude deliberate attacks on non-military targets, which makes the attacks and deaths that followed a war crime. However, as Nato claimed that these were legitimate 'military' targets, that was enough for CNN. The issue was never addressed, and CNN's definitions of 'war crimes' were confined to those proclaimed by Nato and its war crimes tribunal adjunct at The Hague. Thus when the tribunal announced its indictments of Slobodan Milosevic and four members of his government on 27 May, CNN covered the event 'live', then followed it up with Christiane Amanpour's interview with then Chief Prosecutor Louise Arbour. Revealingly, although Amanpour remembered to ask Arbour whether the charge of 'genocide [could] be included in future indictments against these people', it never occurred to her to ask Arbour a single question about possible Nato violations of prohibitions against aggression, Chapters 2 and 7 of the UN Charter, Nato's own founding Treaty, or any of the 'laws and customs of war'.

Conclusions

Overall, CNN served as Nato's *de facto* public information arm during Operation Allied Force. Despite its pretensions to being a 'global' enterprise, its news-making was not significantly different from that of its US media rivals. Any effort at being 'open' and 'balanced' was overwhelmed by its reporters' internalised acceptance of Nato's aims, language, and frames of reference. Nato's basic truthfulness was assumed, and its spokespersons given command of the floor. Although immensely successful at reaching a large audience with 'breaking news', CNN broke the news that Nato wanted featured and rarely departed from Nato's perspective. From CNN's wartime coverage, one could never have anticipated the subsequent disclosures that estimates of Kosovo Albanian deaths had been grossly inflated by Nato in order to help justify the bombing; that Nato had engineered both the Western interpretation of the Racak 'massacre' and the entire Rambouillet 'peace process' to prevent a diplomatic solution to the Kosovo crisis (Øberg, 1999); and that since June 1999, Nato's military occupation of Kosovo has been accompanied by the 'ethnic cleansing' of *all* (non-Albanian) ethnic minorities.[25] CNN's post-war reporting has also thrown little light on these matters as the network has continued to serve as Nato's public information arm.

Notes

1. Time Warner *1999 Factbook*, Turner Entertainment section, p. 4; Time Warner Inc., *1998 Annual Report, passim*. These numbers reflect the global reach of the entire CNN News Group, within which there were twelve different divisions in 1999, including the flagship Cable News Network, CNN Headline News, and CNN International.

2. CNN's own research into audience demographics uses the term 'influentials' to describe their target audience, and a CNN official has said that 'there is no point in [determining viewership] in the bottom 50 percent of the socio-economic when they don't have access to CNN' (quoted in Flournoy and Stewart, 1997:197–8).

3. Boutros Boutros-Ghali, speaking before the CNN-hosted Fourth World Report Contributors Conference in Atlanta, May 1993, quoted in Brock (1993–94).

4. *1998 Annual Report*, pp. 5, 13, 37.

5. Nicholas Varchaver, 'CNN Takes Over the World', *Brill's Content*, June 1999.

6. This statement was made by Holbrooke at the annual awards dinner of the Overseas Press Club, cited by Norman Solomon, 'Media Toeing the Line', *Atlanta Journal Constitution*, 9 May 1999.

7. These last two cases are cited in Michael Massing, 'The Media's Own Kosovo Crisis', *The Nation*, 3 May 1999.

8. We are of course referring to the *Interim Agreement for Peace and Self-Government in Kosovo*, 'Appendix B: Status of Multi-National Military Implementation Force'. Space limitations prevent us from doing justice to the complete story here. For a good analysis of it, see the chapter by Seth Ackerman and Jim Naureckas in the present volume.

9. See George Kenney, 'Rolling Thunder: the Rerun', *The Nation*, 14 June 1999; and Robert Fisk, 'The Trojan horse that started a 79-day war', *Independent* (London), 26 November 1999.

10. This particular term can be found at Chapter 7, Article VIII, 'Operations and Authority of the KFOR', which is separate from and not identical with the terms of 'Appendix B'.

11. The relevant clause can be found at Chapter 8, Article I, paragraph 3. According to Eric Rouleau, 'Washington's real intentions are revealed by the argument that finally secured the KLA leader's agreement. The Americans explained to him in confidence that his signature would enable Nato to begin hostilities against Serbia without delay, since Serbia would then be seen as alone responsible for the deadlock.' 'French Diplomacy Adrift in Kosovo', *Le Monde diplomatique*, December 1999.

12. See 'Decisions and conclusions of the National Assembly of the Republic of Serbia, 23 March 1999', The National Assembly of the Republic of Serbia. This important document has been virtually ignored, by both CNN and the rest of the Western media. A copy of it can be found at both www.serbia-info.com and www.zmag.org under 'Kosovo'. See also Chomsky (1999:104–30).

13. Our summary here and the details that follow partly draw upon Johnstone (1999; 2000).

14. OSCE Office for Democratic Institutions and Human Rights, *Kosovo/Kosova: As Seen, As Told. An analysis of the human rights findings of the OSCE Kosovo Verification Mission*, October 1998 to June 1999, Ch. V, 'Stimlje/Shtime'.

15. Melissa Eddy, '15 Reported Killed in Kosovo', AP Online, 15 January 1999; Agence France Presse, 'At Least 15 Rebels Killed in Southern Kosovo', 15 January 1999.

16. We say 'a number of dead bodies' because the estimates that were circulating at the time of the number of dead bodies found in the gully (40–46) were later shown to be inaccurate. The OSCE puts the number of bodies found in the gully that day at 'more than 20'; the total number of dead in all the villages where fighting took place was between 40 and 45. The Finnish forensic team that performed autopsies on the remains claims the number of bodies recovered from the gully was 22. See OSCE Office for Democratic Institutions and Human Rights, *Kosovo/Kosova: As Seen, As Told*; and 'Racak Killings: Report says Victims were Unarmed Civilians', Deutsche Presse-Agentur, 17 March 1999.

17. Pierre Lhuillery, 'Forty-five Slain in Kosovo Massacre', Agence France Presse, 16 January 1999. Walker's accusations were carried internationally and parroted widely. For an illuminating treatment of William Walker's history of service to US government-sponsored state terror in El Salvador, see the report *A Year of Reckoning*, Americas Watch (Human Rights Watch), 1990.

18. Quoted by Don North, 'Irony at Racak: Tainted US Diplomat Condemns Massacre', *The Consortium*, 27 January 1999.

19. Christophe Chatelet, 'Les morts de Racak ont-ils vraiment été massacre froidement?', *Le Monde*, 21 January 1999; and Renaud Giraud, 'Kosovo: zones d'ombre sur un massacré', *Le Figaro*, 20 January 1999.

20. Julius Strauss, 'Kosovo Killings Inquiry Verdict Sparks Outrage', *Daily Telegraph*, 18 March 1999. Strauss also reports that at the news conference where the findings of the Finnish team were finally released, 'Mr Walker and his aides shook their heads to show their disapproval as [the Finnish team] refused to answer any question that would support Mr Walker's earlier claim that Racak amounted to a "crime against humanity".'

21. Johnstone (1999:67). See also 'Yugoslav Forensic Experts Say "No Massacre" in Kosovo', BBC Summary of World Broadcasts, 18 March 1999; 'Finnish Autopsies on Racak Massacre are Inconclusive: Report', Agence France Presse, 17 March 1999; 'Prosecutor Says No Reason to Charge Police Involved in Attack in Kosovo', BBC Summary of World Broadcasts, 12 March 1999; 'Serb Police Escape Legal Action over Racak Killings in Kosovo', Agence France Presse, 10 March 1999; 'Forensic Institute Says No Evidence Kosovo Albanians Massacred', BBC Summary of World Broadcasts, 18 February 1999.

22. On the possibility that Walker had a war agenda, see Johnstone (2000). As one Swiss member of the OSCE's Kosovo Verification Mission told the Italian journal *La Liberté*, 'We understood from the start that information gathered by OSCE patrols during our missions was destined to complete the information that Nato had gathered by satellite. We had the very sharp impression of doing espionage work for the Atlantic Alliance.' Quoted in '*Genève*' (a pseudonymous article), 22 April 1999.

23. 'Nato Hit on TV Station Draws Journalists' Fire', *Washington Post*, 24 April 1999. In personal communication with the authors, Kurtz insisted on the truth of this report and the reliability of his sources. See also Steven Erlanger, 'Nato Missiles Strike a Center Of State-Linked TV and Radio', *New York Times*, 21 April 1999.

24. We take this number from the 'Provisional Assessment of Destruction and Damages Caused by the Nato Aggression on the Federal Republic of Yugoslavia', published by the Yugoslav government, 1 July 1999.

25. See the OSCE report, *Kosovo/Kosova: As Seen, As Told. Part II*, which covers the period 14 June–31 October 1999; and Robert Fisk, 'Serbs Murdered by the Hundreds Since "Liberation"', *Independent* (London), 24 November 1999. A more fitting title for this OSCE report would be *The Triumph of Ethnic Hatred in Kosovo*. Under Nato's occupation, Kosovo has become virtually a monoethnic state.

11

Philip Hammond

Third Way War: New Labour, the British Media and Kosovo

The British Prime Minister, Tony Blair, was the most belligerent Nato leader in the Kosovo war. Following Nato's decision to escalate the bombing and hit civilian targets, for example, he proclaimed the military must do 'whatever is necessary to achieve our goals'. Warning there might soon be 'another Milosevic diplomatic ploy', Blair declared in advance: 'we should reject it' (*Sunday Telegraph*, 4 April). Paradoxically, such aggression was the product of the decent, caring image meticulously fostered by Blair and his government.

New Labour is renowned for its image-conscious political style, and it was no surprise to find this extended to the war against Yugoslavia. As the *Independent on Sunday* was told by one government 'insider': 'Policy and presentation go hand in hand ... It's very New Labour' (4 April). Similarly, the Prime Minister's Press Secretary, Alastair Campbell, later argued that 'the modern media has [*sic*] changed the demands of modern conflict', implying that policy may even have been led by presentation. Yet New Labour was not entirely happy with the reporting of Kosovo, frequently criticising both the overall coverage and individual journalists. As in other areas of government policy, the domestic political aim of bombing was to create a supposedly 'moral' consensus, and politicians wanted the news to become a fairytale in which a defenceless victim was saved from the clutches of an evil villain by a knight in shining armour. This is what Blair had in mind when he said Kosovo was 'no longer just a military conflict'. Instead, it was 'a battle between good and evil; between civilisation and barbarity; between democracy and dictatorship'. It was this simplistic moral framework which sanctioned the enthusiasm for war displayed by Blair and, notwithstanding his complaints, by many journalists too. Such self-righteousness meant that any escalation of the conflict was justified.

Below I offer a brief overview of how British newspapers and broadcasting responded to Nato's propaganda demands. I then examine in more detail the reporting of ethnic Albanian refugees and atrocity stories – two key components of the propaganda framework. As I aim to show, the nature of

123

the conflict was distorted by the simple-minded moralism demanded by political leaders.

The Press

Although every British newspaper except the *Independent on Sunday* took a pro-war line in its editorial column, there were, broadly speaking, two types of press support for the Nato attack. Politically conservative newspapers, such as *The Times*, *Telegraph*, *Express* and *Mail*, voiced their customary stout support for the British military. At the same time, however, these papers expressed a certain caution about the wisdom and goals of Nato action, particularly in the early days of the war. For the *Daily Mail*'s leader-writer, it surely came naturally to emphasise 'unequivocal support' for the British and Nato armed forces (25 March). Yet the *Mail* found it 'difficult to contemplate the way this conflict has lurched from threat and bluster to outright war with anything but the deepest unease'. Similarly, the *Telegraph*'s Tom Utley asked 'What are we fighting for?', while the paper's editorial column insisted 'We must have a war aim' (26 March). In familiar *Telegraph* style, Utley wrote that: 'When British Servicemen go to war, the first instinct and duty of every citizen must be to pray for their victory and safety. That I do with all my heart.' Nevertheless, he confessed to 'feeling very uneasy about the role that Nato has taken upon itself in the Balkans'.

By contrast, for the more liberal section of the press, particularly the *Guardian* and *Independent*, to whom a pro-military stance is not such a traditional reflex response, it was Nato's proclaimed moral mission which captured the imagination. The *Independent*'s editorialist welcomed the bombing as a thrilling personal triumph. Remembering with shame that Western troops in Bosnia had been 'forced ... to scuttle around in armoured personnel carriers, dealing out charity', the newspaper hoped: 'Now that humiliation may be over' (25 March). The *Guardian*'s Jonathan Freedland also recalled how in Bosnia 'the UN mandate was too weak', proclaiming unequivocally: 'This war is a just one' (26 March). Though not always clear-cut, there was a distinction between an old-fashioned militarist response and a newer, politically correct militarism. In a war fought for humanitarianism and 'values', rather than naked national interest, it was the liberal papers which were in tune with the times. As the *Guardian* put it in a 26 March editorial, Kosovo was 'a test for our generation'.

As these examples suggest, Kosovo was viewed by some as a fulfilment of hopes which had remained frustrated during most of the Bosnian conflict. Commenting on the 1990–91 Persian Gulf War, the *Guardian*'s Martin Woollacott described his paper as 'traditionally anti-imperialist' (Keeble, 1997:95). Yet in relation to Bosnia, liberal journalists frequently called for tougher Western intervention, and were enraptured by military action against Serbs. Woollacott wrote, for example, that the 1995 attack on the Krajina – in which some 2,500 Serb refugees were killed as nearly ten times that number fled under fire from US-trained Croatian forces – 'is to be welcomed' (*Guardian*, 5 August 1995), while the *Independent*'s leader-writer said it was 'tempting to feel euphoric' (7 August 1995). Today's liberal conscience demands more warfare, and has found its optimal expression in Blair's bellicose humanitarianism.

The Broadcasters

It is a time-honoured custom for governments to attack the BBC during wartime, as they did during the 1982 Falklands conflict (Harris, 1983:75) and the Gulf War (Keeble, 1997:168). The BBC's role in the ritual is to face both ways, simultaneously declaring its independence from, and loyalty to, the government. It was reported, for instance, that Downing Street offered the BBC an interview with Blair at the start of the war, but abruptly withdrew when the Prime Minister was scheduled to appear with Jeremy Paxman, who has a reputation as a hard-nosed interviewer. Blair's officials requested another interviewer, but the BBC refused because 'Downing Street simply can't tell us what to do' (*Express*, 26 March). This is the BBC's public face of robust independence. Its 'refusal' did not, however, prevent the BBC actually agreeing to Blair being interviewed by someone else – Tim Franks of BBC World.

As a public service broadcaster, the BBC has an obligation to be impartial, and sometimes its employees misguidedly take this seriously. John Reith, the first Director General of the BBC, understood the duplicity required. During the 1926 General Strike, Reith fought hard to prevent the government commandeering the organisation, but at the same time wrote in his diary that 'they know they can trust us not to be really impartial' (Lewis and Pearlman, 1986:69). Reith was knighted for his sound judgement that the trick is to appear impartial, whilst actually supporting the state. BBC balance operates within strict limits, and problems arise when reporters, who have the overt ethos of impartiality drummed into them, let this override the unspoken rule of loyalty to the establishment. Campbell and Blair were furious that broadcasters screened pictures which exposed Nato lies, such as the claim that Nato had not bombed civilian areas of Pristina or that the death of around 70 refugees in a convoy near Djakovica had been caused by the Serbs. Western correspondents on the spot later also countered the claim that 87 refugees killed by Nato at the village of Korisa on 13 May had been 'human shields' for a military target.

In response to such reports, politicians launched a series of personal attacks against individual journalists. BBC Radio's John Humphrys, for example, was pilloried for asking government ministers awkward questions about the success of Nato strategy. Humphrys rebuffed the criticism, saying 'we have a right to know what the Government is doing in our name and why' (*Sunday Telegraph*, 4 April). However, the editor of his programme was quick to emphasise that 'our line is not that we shouldn't be bombing'

(*Guardian*, 30 March). Similarly, the BBC's correspondent in Belgrade, John Simpson, was called a 'mouthpiece' for the Yugoslav authorities because he refused to ignore the evidence of his senses and repeat the government's absurd claim that ordinary Serbs were not opposed to Nato bombing. Simpson resented what he regarded as slander, but as a long-serving Corporation man he apparently understood his role:

> Why did ... public opinion stay rock-solid for the bombing, in spite of Nato's mistakes? Because they knew the war was right. Who gave them the information? The media. (Glass, 1999)

Channel Four's Alex Thompson struck the same bizarre pose of indignantly denouncing propaganda whilst simultaneously taking the credit for it: 'if you want to know why the public supported the war, thank a journalist, not the present government's propagandist-in-chief [Alastair Campbell]' (ibid.). Again, this is standard procedure: after the Falklands conflict broadcasters complained that the restrictions placed on them by the authorities had prevented them doing as good a job of bolstering morale as they would have liked (Glasgow University Media Group, 1985:18–19).

Refugees and Atrocities

In a 10 May speech, Blair complained that journalists were suffering from 'refugee fatigue', and Campbell voiced the same criticism after the war. The importance politicians attached to news reports of refugees should have made journalists wary, but it seems to have had the opposite effect. Commenting on coverage of refugees, Steven Barnett wrote in the *Guardian* (7 June): 'This, of course, was not propaganda but the cause of the war. It was precisely the evidence of ethnic cleansing and Serbian atrocity that we needed to convince us of the moral rectitude of this "humanitarian" war.' In fact the refugee crisis became Nato's strongest propaganda weapon, though logically it should have been viewed as a damning indictment of the bombing.

The mass exodus from Kosovo initially presented a public relations nightmare for Nato, since bombing had been explicitly justified as a measure to prevent refugees. US State Department spokesman James Rubin explained to the BBC on 25 March that if Nato had not acted, 'you would have had hundreds of thousands of people crossing the border'. In a special broadcast the following day, Blair told the nation: 'fail to act now ... and we would have to deal with ... hundreds of thousands of refugees'. As the refugees began to flee, Nato disclaimed all responsibility. Jamie Shea claimed bombing was 'the only positive thing' in the lives of refugees, who allegedly compared the roar of Nato jets to 'the sound of angels'. The British Foreign Secretary, Robin Cook, stated bluntly that, unlike every other bombing campaign in history, people were 'not fleeing Nato's airplanes'.[1] At least some undoubtedly were, of course. Channel Four News interviewed one of them on 26 March, a woman who said in Serbo-Croat: 'I survived the first air strikes. The Albanians are really pleased – finally the promise has been fulfilled.' Presumably she was interviewed by mistake, since the report did not mention she was speaking Serbian. If it was inconceivable that anyone would fear humanitarian missiles fired from democratic aircraft, there could be no Serb refugees.[2] The hundreds of thousands of Serbs who fled bombing were therefore determinedly ignored by British journalists, just as most of the killings, kidnappings, beatings and torture of Kosovo Serbs after the war were not deemed newsworthy. This was not unlike Bosnia, when, as veteran *New York Times* Balkans correspondent David Binder notes, a 'tyranny of victimology' meant that 'balanced journalism ... [went] out of the window' (Gowing, 1997:31).

More awkwardly, some ethnic Albanians told reporters they had not been forcibly expelled. A report in the *Sunday Times* (28 March), for example, noted that some refugees had fled 'the threat of Nato attacks', interviewing one woman who 'looked bewildered when asked if Serbian troops had driven her out. "There were no Serbs," she said. "We were frightened of the bombs."' Usually, however, journalists did their best to minimise such inconvenient information. The *Telegraph*, for example, reported that 'most residents [of Pristina] say they are fleeing of their own accord and are not being forced out at gunpoint' (1 April). This revelation was buried in the twenty-second paragraph of an article headed: 'Thousands expelled at gunpoint.' Similarly, the *Mail* (30 March) reported that 'while some spoke of atrocities others said they had fled before Serb forces arrived, after hearing rumours of attacks elsewhere', but put this in the twenty-seventh paragraph. The *Guardian* (30 March), in a report which emphasised 'systematic ethnic cleansing', revealed in the antepenultimate paragraph:

> many refugees said they had been able to keep identity documents and had faced violent conduct rather than a coordinated campaign of expulsion. 'Nobody told us to leave', said a Prizren man, 'but I did not want to wait for the police to come and tell me to go.'

The Times (3 April) carried a photo of a wounded refugee who, according to the caption, 'said his injury was caused by Nato bombing'. *The Times* ran no story about this picture, instead putting it next to an article alleging that Yugoslav MiGs had bombed refugees. No doubt refugees fled actual and rumoured violence by Serb paramilitaries, while many were expelled and deported. Yet it is also certain that many others fled from fighting between the KLA and Yugoslav forces, and from Nato bombing. In addition, as KLA soldier Lirak Qelaj admitted, 'it was KLA advice, rather than Serbian deportations, which led some of the hundreds of thousands of Albanians to leave Kosovo' (*Guardian*, 30 June). At the time this idea was dismissed as nonsense: it was only treated seriously three weeks after the bombing ended.

Although some commentators began to suggest intervention may only have made things worse, Nato turned the humanitarian disaster into a propaganda triumph by insisting the exodus would have happened anyway, since Milosevic had a plan for genocide all along. This still left the minor problem that, if Nato had expected refugees – as General Wesley Clark maintained – why had they not made any provision for them? British Development Secretary Clare Short replied that to have done so would have made the West 'complicit in ethnic cleansing', yet even when the refugees began to flow the West was in no hurry to help. General Clark dismissed aid drops as 'too dangerous a risk' (Swift, 1999:25), and one Brussels diplomat later described how 'the Nato countries hesitated: should we help them or not?' (*Le Nouvel Observateur*, 1 July). Just before the war, the *Guardian*'s Hugo Young wrote: 'This will be a television war. What will the people say, I heard policy-makers musing, when thousands of Kosovars are seen torched by Serbs? ... That's why we can't stand idly by' (23 March). Apparently New Labour planners were well aware of the propaganda value of refugees before the first bombs fell. As Swift commented, the refugees 'became more a symbol for continuing the war than real people'.

It seems likely that Nato expected the refugee exodus, but was surprised by its scale and wrong-footed by suggestions that round-the-clock bombing might cause people to flee. Yet Nato turned the situation to its advantage. As one senior Nato official later admitted:

> Following the fiasco of the lightning strikes, the refugees provided us with a new objective for the war. That was crucial. Without them, we would very quickly have cobbled together an agreement with Belgrade. (*Le Nouvel Observateur*, 1 July)

Campbell also later noted that 'justification was fairly easy when night after night refugees were telling their awful stories on TV'. No wonder he was concerned about the possibility of 'refugee fatigue'. In fact he need not have worried. The style of reporting on ethnic Albanian refugees was highly emotive, in contrast to the implacable lack of interest in Serbs fleeing Nato bombs. The BBC's Jeremy Bowen, for example, found he was 'running out of words to describe how these people have suffered, except to say that it's cruel, brutal, inhumane and criminal'. He went on to say: 'it's high time it stopped' (6 p.m., 16 April). After the war, journalists went to extraordinary lengths to praise Nato. Bowen explained: 'This is why Nato went to war: so the refugees could come back to Kosovo' (9 p.m., 16 June). Channel Four's Thompson crowed about 'the success of the US policy': 'after all, the President fought this war so that these people could go home in peace' (22 June). In their eagerness to prove Nato right, these reporters overlooked the fact there was no humanitarian disaster until the bombing started, and quietly forgot Nato's earlier promises to prevent a refugee crisis.

Nato's other main propaganda weapon was atrocity stories. Accounts told by refugees were routinely described by journalists as 'credible and consistent'. If so, it seems remarkable how seldom reporters managed to relay them in a consistent or credible way. On 2 April, for example, the *Mail*'s Paul Harris noted that 'every refugee had a horror story to tell'. Strange, then, that the only refugee to tell his story in Harris's report also told it – though with some important differences – to the *Mirror*'s Harry Arnold. Both reported the account of Etem Ramadani, an 'engineer' in the *Mirror*, but an 'Albanian resistance member' in the *Mail*. His horror story stretched credibility: it involved Serbs 'branding' a symbol onto the skin of ethnic Albanians with a 'red-hot iron'. No similar stories ever surfaced. Both papers reported that Ramadani had paid £1,000 to be smuggled out of Pristina in a lorry, but while the *Mail* gave the impression that the man had ended up in Macedonia talking to the press, the *Mirror* version revealed that Ramadani's destination had been Frankfurt. Since neither reporter was anywhere near Frankfurt, it seems unlikely that either had actually spoken to Ramadani directly. Many press accounts contained this strange mixture of inconsistencies and uniformity.

Atrocity stories also had the benefit of providing a retrospective justification for bombing. As Paul Wood put it on BBC *Newsnight* (14 June): 'for the Western allies, the steadily accumulating evidence of atrocities will be confirmation that this was a just war'. On entering Kosovo, Nato gave an 'official' figure of 10,000 people killed in massacres carried out by Serb forces, and the province's Western-appointed governor, Bernard Kouchner, promptly inflated the number to 11,000. Although he was later forced to retract this, Kouchner's willingness to exaggerate indicates that he is unlikely to prove an impartial administrator. The evidence did not, however, 'steadily accumulate': by November 1999 The Hague announced its investigators had found 2,108 bodies so far. When critics pointed out that the number of actual discoveries fell well short of the 10,000 estimate – let alone earlier claims of 100,000 or more dead – apologists for the war denied that Nato had ever produced exaggerated claims of 100,000 (though in fact it did), and clung to the 10,000 figure as one that was 'remarkably accurate' (*Guardian*, 3 November), suggesting that anyone questioning it had been 'bamboozled' (*Spectator*, 4 December).[3] We may never know the true number of people killed. But it seems reasonable to conclude that while people died in clashes between the KLA and Yugoslav forces, and paramilitaries committed crimes and atrocities, the picture painted by Nato – of a systematic campaign of Nazi-style 'genocide' carried out by Serbs – was pure invention.

In contrast to earlier coverage, the killings of Serbs in Kosovo after the bombing ended were either ignored or minimised by the British media. The story of graves near the village of Ugljare, for example, containing the bodies of around 14 Serbs who were shot, stabbed or clubbed to death after Nato entered the province, was carried by Reuters (15 September) and other international news agencies. Yet the interest of British journalists in this story was virtually zero. This attitude was quickly established after the war.[4] Philippe Biberson of Médecins Sans Frontières described the mass exodus of Serbs as 'voluntary ethnic cleansing', while Clare Short said lamely that 'no one can guarantee perfection'. Journalists took a similar line. One BBC correspondent said looting by ethnic Albanians was 'rough justice', which was 'to be expected' (15 June); another described Kosovo Serbs as 'a people now bent on mayhem and self-destruction' (17 June); and a third said they were leaving 'with their lips sealed, taking with them the dark secrets of ethnic hatred' (16 June). In the *Sunday Telegraph* (13 June), Philip Sherwell said the Serbs had 'chosen to "cleanse" themselves', calling them 'probably the world's least pitiable refugees'. Serbs affected by the war were literally treated less sympathetically than dogs. The *Mail* (20 August) devoted a double-page spread to the 'dogs of war': strays which had allegedly been 'victims of hate' at the hands of the Serbs. The paper expressed the maudlin hope that Kosovo would now have 'puppies of peace', but never thought to accord such attention and compassion to Serb victims of the conflict.

Conclusion

Three months after the war, Blair announced a 'new national moral purpose' for Britain. Its inculcation would be effected by measures such as the police and local authorities using new powers to deal with 'anti-social behaviour' by imposing curfews and court orders (*Observer*, 5 September). In fact the war itself was part of the moral consensus Blair hoped to create at home. In the media, the murder of a popular television personality, Jill Dando, and a series of nail-bomb attacks on ethnic minorities and homosexuals in April, were both linked, erroneously, to the Serbs. It was as if the Serbs became catch-all villains, responsible for killing girl-next-door TV presenters and 'ethnically cleansing' London as well as Kosovo. Such all-purpose hate figures are less easy to find in the domestic arena, and there is little doubt that militarism will continue to accompany the moralism. As Edgerton (1998:127) notes, Labour's 1998 Strategic Defence Review was underpinned by the assumption that Britain could maintain its disproportionate international influence 'by virtue of its military prowess'. High military spending, allied to 'a new moral imperialism' (ibid.:129), characterises New Labour's view of Britain's global role.

With the help of the media, Blair created a temporary 'national moral purpose' over Kosovo. Taking their cue from his talk of Good versus Evil, many journalists celebrated the bombing as a just war for victims of oppression, simplifying and distorting the reality of the conflict. As the Christian Crusades needed the Infidel, Blairite moral crusading requires anti-social barbarians who must be taught about tolerance, by violence if necessary. It was fitting that during Nato's fiftieth anniversary celebrations in April, Blair, Clinton, Schröder and others held a 'Third Way' summit in

Washington. New Labour's two strongest cards in the international arena today are its moral credentials, and its military clout. As the Serbs and others can testify, it is a lethal combination.

Notes

1. ITN, 6.30 p.m., 30 March. Refugees were only once said to be in danger from Nato bombs: when Yugoslav forces briefly closed the border (ITN, 6.30 p.m., 7 April).
2. The British Helsinki Human Rights Group, in a 22 May report, cited a Red Cross estimate that more than 1.2 million people were internally displaced in Serbia, 250,000 of them in Kosovo. We heard a lot about the 250,000 (a figure which Nato doubled), but almost nothing about more than three-quarters of a million refugees in the rest of Serbia. If hundreds of thousands had fled through 'fear of bombing', as the BHHRG suggested, why did it seem so implausible that people in Kosovo might be doing the same?
3. Francis Wheen (*Guardian*, 3 November), and Noel Malcolm (*Spectator*, 4 December) were responding to articles in the *Spectator* by John Laughland (30 October and 20 November). The debate also continued on the magazine's letters page (11 and 18/25 December).
4. Indeed, it reflected attitudes already established after the Croatian and Bosnian wars. In a letter to the *Independent* (1 December 1999), the Director General of the British Red Cross noted that even before the Kosovo crisis Yugoslavia had the largest number of refugees in Europe (over 500,000), but while over 300 humanitarian organisations operated in Bosnia, just 27 had a presence in Yugoslavia. Despite the fact that Yugoslavia's refugee population had increased by a further 230,000 following the Kosovo conflict, the country was still receiving 'very little media attention or funding'.

12

John Pilger

Censorship by Omission

(From the *New Statesman*, 19 April 1999)

At the height of the First World War the Prime Minister, David Lloyd George, confided to C. P. Scott, editor of the *Manchester Guardian*: 'If people knew the truth, the war would be stopped tomorrow. But they don't know and can't know.' Every day now, the suppression of truth and the organising of public ignorance shames journalism. It was shame enough eight years ago when the American-led attack on Iraq ended with newspaper editorials lauding the 'miraculously few casualties'. In truth, up to a quarter of a million people were killed or died in the immediate aftermath, many the very Kurdish and Shi'a minorities George Bush and John Major said they were 'protecting'.

Now Nato has bombed residential areas in the capital of Kosovo, terrorising and killing the people Clinton and Blair say they are protecting. The bombers were 'seduced off-target', said the press briefer in Brussels. The Americans are using A-10 'Warthog' aircraft, armed with depleted uranium missiles, over Kosovo. Depleted uranium was used in Southern Iraq where the level of leukaemia among children is now equal to that of Hiroshima. It is a form of nuclear warfare. Why are journalists mostly silent on this? On BBC news, the bombing of Kosovo was reported as 'the sound of angels'.

This is state propaganda, achieved by the repetition of received truths and by omission on a grand scale. The British public's primary source of information is television, yet according to a recent survey, programmes about international affairs account for just 3.4 per cent of peak-time viewing, almost all of it on the minority channels. 'I have recently found mountains of evidence', wrote the historian Mark Curtis, author of *The Great Deception*, 'pointing to a radically revised understanding of post-war British foreign policy, which has simply been sitting in the Public Record Office, apparently untouched.' He cited secret British backing for the denial of human rights in many countries, such as Indonesia, Turkey and Colombia, which are 'systematic and consistent' rather than evidence of 'double standards'. Neither the conservative nor liberal media betray much interest in exposing these topical realities.

Last week the Defence Secretary, George Robertson, claimed that all bombing targets were approved by him and Tony Blair. The Americans must have found this laughable. Why hasn't Robertson been challenged on such a critical issue? Who had the say of life or death over workers in the Zastava car factory? The people of the mining town of Aleksinac had nothing to do with Kosovo and they were bombed. We glimpsed the body of an old woman, her legs protruding from the rubble of her home. Who was responsible? Or was her life merely 'collateral'? And why did a Nato pilot fire his missiles at a railway bridge while a civilian train was crossing? Are these questions beyond journalists now? On the day the train was attacked, Kirsty Wark interviewed the Nato commander, General Clark, on *Newsnight* and failed to ask a single question about civilian casualties. Instead, she appeared to be egging him on to commit ground troops.

Supporters of the bombing are said to include 'the left', meaning liberals, chameleons like Roy Hattersley and Ken Livingstone and those who have simply lost their compass. The parallels with the American invasion of Vietnam are striking. When that began, the Hattersleys supported it; indeed, it was a liberal adventure, instigated by John Kennedy. The bombers of Clinton's New Democrats and Blair's New Labour are reminiscent of Kennedy's New Frontiersmen, who liked nothing better than to save people from themselves, even if it meant killing them.

Then, as now, the media played a central role in promoting public confusion. Stereotypes were important. The Vietnamese communists were 'Asian Prussians' guilty of 'internal aggression'. An entirely fictitious attack on American warships was used to fool Congress and the press, providing the excuse to begin the slaughter. Later, Hollywood transformed the aggressors into angst-ridden heroes and the Vietnamese to unpeople.

Today, the Serbs are the unpeople. They have no civilisation, no society, no poetry, no history. The savagery they suffered at the hands of the Nazis in the Second World War, exceeded only by the mass extermination of the Polish Jews, has been forgotten. Like the woman in the rubble, they are unworthy victims – unlike the Kosovo Albanians, who are worthy: until they seek asylum in Britain, of course.

'News' of the liberal mission in the Balkans comes largely from daily briefings in Brussels, which are conducted by a public relations man called Jamie and a military spin-doctor from the RAF. They remind me of the briefers at the Five O'Clock Follies in Saigon who, like Major Major in *Catch-22*, intoned their 'interdictions' and 'degradation' and 'collateral damage' with hardly anyone believing a word, yet almost everybody reporting it.

When the Vietnam war was over, I interviewed General Winant Sidle, the chief US spokesman. 'We sure took flak for not prosecuting the war efficiently', he said. 'But I don't recall anybody questioning our motives. That's a myth. I had two delegations of journalists, including the news bureau chiefs, call on me in 1968, asking me to please impose censorship. They wanted to know what they could and couldn't say.' In its retrospectives on Vietnam, the BBC invariably congratulates itself on having been 'more impartial' in its reporting than the American media. There is never reference to the BBC's blacklisting of reports by the cameraman Malcolm Aird and the journalist James Cameron on the bombing of civilian targets.

Little has changed. Since 25 March, I have tried unsuccessfully to have a piece published about the bombing. It has been used all over the world, but not in Britain. Radio, usually the freest medium, has cancelled four times. Friends in BBC current affairs, affronted by the notion of broadcasting as a government agency, describe how they must tread carefully. The real news is that the bombing has nothing to do with humanitarianism. 'President Milosevic', said Richard Holbrooke, the US envoy to the Balkans, last year, 'is a man we can do business with, a man who recognises the realities of life in former Yugoslavia.' So much for 'the butcher'. The man didn't obey orders, that's all. As a result, there is now a cataclysm that affords Clinton and Blair a special distinction among modern leaders: they share with a European tyrant the responsibility for virtually emptying a country, leaving its people to fester like the Palestinians, perhaps for generations. Blair also shares responsibility for destroying the democratic opposition in Serbia. 'The air strikes erased in one night', wrote Professor Vojan Dimitrijevic, the Serb former vice-chairman of the UN Commission on Human Rights, 'the results of ten years of hard work of groups of courageous people. The Kosovo problem will remain unsolved and the future of democracy in Serbia uncertain for many years.'

The real news is that the Americans are planning to 'degrade' Serbia with the same ferocity they destroyed Vietnam and now Iraq. The 'turkey shoots' are coming; and the future is to be militarised by Nato. Bored with the UN, the Americans want their own imperial posse. Congress has passed the 'Nato Participation' and 'Nato Facilitation' Acts, which allow the greatest expansion of American military influence since the Second World War. Clinton has ended a 20-year-old arms embargo to most of Latin America. In the current Nato Review, Argentina is welcomed as 'Nato's South Atlantic partner'. In Eastern Europe, a £22 billion bonanza beckons for American and British arms companies. This has passed virtually unreported in Britain.

At the same time, neutral or non-aligned states have been cajoled or bribed into joining Nato's 'Partnership for Peace'. Albania, Austria, Finland, Sweden, Switzerland, Macedonia and Slovenia have joined. Ireland is next. Nato describes this as 'the most intensive programme of military-to-military collaboration ever conceived'.

The threat to us all, and to our children's generation, is written on the bombs now falling on the Balkans. That is the real news.

(From the *Guardian*, 18 May 1999)

The room is filled with the bodies of children killed by Nato in Surdulica in Serbia. Several are recognisable only by their sneakers. A dead infant is cradled in the arms of his father. These picture and many others have not been shown in Britain; it will be said they are too horrific. But minimising the culpability of the British state when it is engaged in criminal action is normal; censorship is by omission and misuse of language. The media impression of a series of Nato 'blunders' is false. Anyone scrutinising the unpublished list of targets hit by Nato is left in little doubt that a deliberate terror campaign is being waged against the civilian population of Yugoslavia.

Eighteen hospitals and clinics and at least 200 nurseries, schools, colleges and students' dormitories have been destroyed or damaged, together with housing estates, hotels, libraries, youth centres, theatres, museums, churches and fourteenth-century monasteries on the World Heritage list. Farms have been bombed, their crops set on fire. As Friday's bombing of the Kosovo town of Korisa shows, there is no discrimination between Serbs and those being 'saved'. Every day, three times more civilians are killed by Nato than the daily estimate of deaths in Kosovo in the months prior to the bombing.

The British people are not being told about a policy designed largely by their government to cause such criminal carnage. The dissembling of politicians and the lies of 'spokesmen' set much of the news agenda. There is no sense of the revulsion felt throughout most of the world for this wholly illegal action, for the punishment of Milosevic's crime with a greater crime and for the bellicose antics of Blair, Cook and Robertson, who have made themselves into international caricatures.

'There was no need of censorship of our dispatches. We were our own censors', wrote Philip Gibbs, the *Times* correspondent in 1914–18. The silence is different now; there is the illusion of saturation coverage, but the reality is a sameness and repetition and, above all, political safety for the perpetrators.

A few days before the killing of make-up ladies and camera operators in the Yugoslav television building, Jamie Shea, Nato's man, wrote to the International Federation of Journalists: 'There is no policy to attack television and radio transmitters.' Where were the cries of disgust from among the famous names at the BBC, John Simpson apart? Who interrupted the mutual back-slapping at last week's Royal Television Society awards? Silence. The news from Shepherd's Bush is that BBC presenters are to wear pinks, lavender and blues which 'will allow us to be a bit more conversational in the way we discuss stories'.

Here is some of the news they leave out. The appendix pages of the Rambouillet 'accords', which have not been published in Britain, show Nato's agenda was to occupy not just Kosovo, but all of Yugoslavia. This was rejected, not just by Milosevic, but by the elected Yugoslav parliament, which proposed a UN force to monitor a peace settlement: a genuine alternative to bombing. Clinton and Blair ignored it.

Britain is attacking simultaneously two countries which offer no threat. Every day Iraq is bombed and almost none of it is news. Last week, 20 civilians were killed in Mosul, and a shepherd and his family were bombed. The sheep were bombed. In the last 18 months, the Blair government has dropped more bombs than the Tories dropped in 18 years.

Anti-bombing protests reverberate around the world: 100,000 people in the streets of Rome (including 182 members of the Italian parliament), thousands in Greece and Germany, protests taking place every night in colleges and town halls across Britain. Almost none of it is reported. Is it not extraordinary that no national opinion poll on the war has been published since 30 April?

'Normalisation', wrote the American essayist Edward Herman, depends on 'a division of labour in doing and rationalising the unthinkable, with the direct brutalising and killing done by one set of individuals ... [and] others working on improved technology (a better crematory gas, a longer burning and more adhesive Napalm). It is the function of experts and the mainstream media to normalise the unthinkable for the general public.'

This week, the unthinkable will again be normalised when Nato triples the bombing raids to 700 a day. This includes blanket bombing by B-52s. Blair and Clinton and the opaque-eyed General Clark, apologist for the My Lai massacre in Vietnam, are killing and maiming hundreds, perhaps thousands of innocent people in the Balkans. No contortion of intellect and morality, nor silence, will diminish the truth that these are acts of murder. And until there is a revolt among journalists and broadcasters, they will continue to get away with it. That is the news.

(From the *New Statesman*, 28 June 1999)

In *Newsweek* last week Tony Blair described the 'new moral crusade' that is to follow Nato's attack on Yugoslavia. 'We now have a chance to build a new internationalism based on values and the rule of law', he wrote. George Robertson was more blunt. The 'Rubicon has been crossed', he said, paving the way for the end of the UN charter that protects the sovereignty of nations. Robin Cook chimed in, making threats towards 'governments using aggression against their own people'. The warning did not apply to the government of Turkey, a Nato member, whose aggression against its own people has left 3,000 Kurdish villages ethnically cleansed, 30,000 people dead and three million refugees. Atrocities committed by the authorities in Indonesia, Israel, Colombia and other countries where Western 'interests' are in safe hands will also be exempt.

Those who recognise the standard hypocrisy will easily translate the euphemisms. In these days of political disorientation, translation is all important; for imperialism is not part of the modern lexicon in the West. In the best Stalinist tradition, it no longer exists. What Western power does is always benevolent. Blair can spout his breathtaking drivel about internationalism and morality while zealously enforcing genocidal sanctions that kill 4,000 Iraqi infants every month, and the connection is seldom made. Nato's aggressive expansion into Eastern Europe, the Balkans and the oil-rich Caucasus, attended by a $22 billion Anglo-American arms bazaar, is unworthy of mainstream discussion.

This is understandable. Since fascism expounded its notions of racial superiority, the imperial 'civilising mission' has had a bad name. Since the end of the Cold War, however, the economic and political crises in the developing world, precipitated by debt and the disarray of the liberation movements, have served as retrospective justification for imperialism. Although the word remains unspeakable, the old imperial project's return journey to respectability has begun. New brand names have been market tested. 'Humanitarian intervention' is the latest to satisfy the criterion of doing what you like where you like, as long as you are strong enough. The killing or maiming of 10,000 innocent civilians in Serbia and Kosovo by a bombing machine representing two-thirds of the world's military power and the clear provocation of the 'entirely predictable' Serb atrocities – all of it avoidable, since Slobodan Milosevic had agreed in effect to give up Kosovo six weeks before the bombing began – is called a 'moral victory'. George Orwell could not better it.

The ideological climate and disorientation among those on the liberal left, created by the Western powers' hijacking of 'human rights', is especially dangerous. The other day Mikhail Gorbachev sought to interrupt the victory celebrations with a speech in which he warned that Nato's assault on Yugoslavia had given impetus to a new global nuclear arms race. He said: 'Smaller countries – among them 31 "threshold" states capable of developing nuclear weapons – are looking to their own security with growing trepidation. They are thinking they must have absolute weapons to be able to defend themselves, or to retaliate if they are subjected to similar treatment.'

Under Blair's 'internationalism' any country can be declared a 'rogue state' and attacked by the US and Britain, with or without Nato. Read the Nato and US planning literature; it is all on the record. There is a Pentagon strategy called 'offensive counter-proliferation', which means that, if the Americans cannot prevent a 'rogue' country developing and building types of weapons of which they disapprove, they may well nuke it. North Korea is a likely candidate, allowing Washington to settle a historical score. The Russians fully understand the dangers. The defence ministry in Moscow has already announced plans to deploy new tactical nuclear weapons near Russia's Western border. Russia's National Security Council has quietly dropped its long-standing doctrine of 'no first use' of nuclear weapons. In the US, Clinton has sent to Congress a nuclear weapons rebuilding programme unmatched since the early Reagan years. If we are to speak of truly 'rogue' powers, the US leads the pack.

Blair's reference to the new 'rule of law' is quite obscene. One of the world's nuclear flashpoints is the Indian subcontinent, where India and Pakistan, both nuclear powers, are on the edge of all-out war over Kashmir. In the first year after coming to power, Blair and his government approved 500 licences for the export of weapons to the two countries – they also approved 92 licences for arms shipments to the Indonesian military, which is currently arming and training death squads to prevent East Timor achieving its independence.

New Labour's fake internationalism is part of 'economic globalisation', a project as old as gun-boats. The gathering assault on the principle of the sovereignty of nations, however, marks a new phase in the global war against democracy. Blair, essentially an opportunist, and his spinners trust that his Cold-War-style belligerence will invoke the Thatcher factor and ensure him a long reign. There are important differences. In the midst of the 1982 Falklands war, Thatcher did well in local elections. In striking contrast, Blair has just been crushed in the Euro elections by a lame-duck Tory leader. More significant, Labour voters stayed at home in record numbers, just as they did in the Scottish and Welsh devolutionary polls. They are not apathetic, as reported. They are on to him at last; and their growing awareness is crucial as he aspires to lead us across the Rubicon.

(From the *Guardian*, 19/20 May, and the *New Statesman*, 15 November 1999)

On 19 May, at the height of Nato's bombing of Yugoslavia, the pro-war *Guardian* attacked one of its own writers. Amidst much personal abuse, Ian Black, the Diplomatic Editor, accused me of misrepresenting the Rambouillet accords. He scoffed at my disclosure that the accords were a blueprint for the effective occupation of Yugoslavia, and were designed to be rejected by Belgrade. He described them as 'a standard ... status of forces agreement'. In fact, Rambouillet demanded that the Serbs give Nato rights of 'unrestricted passage and unimpeded access through the Federal Republic of Yugoslavia, including associated air space and territorial waters', and immunity 'from the legal process'.

Black also accused me of inventing a sentence in the Rambouillet document, which stipulated a free market economy for Kosovo as the ideological basis for Nato's occupation. 'The sentence does not exist', he wrote. Again, he was wrong. Chapter 4a, article 1, stated: 'The economy of Kosovo shall function in accordance with free market principles.' Although the *Guardian*'s chief reporter at the Rambouillet talks, Black admitted he had not read the accords. His reporting merely reflected Foreign Office briefings; he had been caught out.

The episode, which caused acute embarrassment in the pro-bombing group running Britain's oldest liberal newspaper, was important because it offered a glimpse of a virulent, though generally unrecognised form of media censorship. Voluntary and often subliminal, its effect is to minimise the culpability of Western power in acts of great violence and terrorism, such as the Nato assault. With the Serbs demonised in the British media, and Nato's 'humanitarian war' and Tony Blair's 'great moral crusade' embraced by most journalists, the real reasons and motives for the Nato bombing were obfuscated, at best, or simply left out.

Five months after the bombing, the expulsion and terrorising of 240,000 Serbs and other minorities from the province, now ruled by Nato, was not news. The Society for Endangered People reported that 90,000 Roma Gypsies had been forced to flee an ethnic-cleansing campaign conducted on a grand scale by the Kosovo Liberation Army. But who cared about Gypsies, let alone the demonised Serbs? The greatest non-news was the undermining of Nato's justification for killing and maiming several thousand civilians, both Serbs and Kosovo Albanians, and for devastating the environment and economic life of the region. This epic destruction was warranted, said Defence Secretary George Robertson in March, to stop 'a regime which is intent on genocide'. The 'G' word was repeated many times. Bill Clinton referred to 'deliberate, systematic efforts at ... genocide'.

The British press took their cue. 'Flight from Genocide', said a *Daily Mail* headline over a picture of Kosovo Albanian children in a truck. Both the *Sun* and the *Mirror* referred to 'echoes of the Holocaust'. The US Defense Secretary, William Cohen, said: 'We've now seen about 100,000 military-aged men missing ... They may have been murdered.'

Since the bombing, perhaps no place on earth has been as scrutinised by forensic investigators, not to mention 2,700 media people, yet no evidence of mass murder on the scale used to justify the bombing has been found. The head of the Spanish forensic team attached to the International Criminal Tribunal, Emilio Perez Pujol, estimated that as few as 2,500 were killed. In an interview with the Spanish newspaper *El Pais*, he said: 'I called my people together and said, "We're finished here". I informed my government and told them the real situation. We had found a total of 187 bodies.' He complained angrily that he and colleagues had become part of 'a semantic pirouette by the war propaganda machines, because we did not find one – not one – mass grave'.

The village of Ljubenic was believed to hold a mass grave of 350 bodies. Seven bodies were found. According to Carla del Ponte, the Swiss Chief Prosecutor in The Hague, five months of investigation had produced 2,108 bodies. One significant disclosure was that the Trepca lead and zinc mines contained no bodies. Trepca was central to the media drama of the aftermath of the bombing: the corpses of 700 murdered Albanians were presumed hidden there. On 7 July 1999, the *Mirror* reported that a former mineworker, Hakif Isufi, had seen dozens of trucks pull into the mine on the night of 4 June and heavy bundles unloaded. The *Mirror* was in no doubt:

What Hakif saw was one of the most despicable acts of Slobodan Milosevic's war – the mass dumping of executed corpses in a desperate bid to hide the evidence. War crimes investigators fear that up to 1,000 bodies were incinerated in the Auschwitz-style furnaces of the mine with its sprawling maze of deep shafts and tunnels.

All this was false.

This is not say that numerous bodies may yet materialise; perhaps by the time these words are published, the figure of the Kosovo Albanian dead may have edged closer to the figure of 10,000 claimed by the British government; less than half of the 'crime scenes' are still to be investigated. But this seems unlikely, as a pattern of truth versus propaganda emerges. The number of confirmed dead suggests that the Nato bombing provoked a wave of random brutality, murders and expulsions, a far cry from Robertson's claim that Nato's aim was to 'prevent a humanitarian catastrophe' and from his and the echoing media's charge of systematic extermination: genocide.

Other atrocities of particular media interest, such as 'rape camps', are turning out to be fiction. Dr Richard Munz, the doctor at the huge Stenkovac refugee camp, told *Die Welt*: 'The majority of media people I talked to came here and looked for a story ... which they had already ... the entire time we were here, we had no cases of rape. And we are responsible for 60,000 people.' He stressed that this did not mean that rape did not happen, but that it was not the media version. The same is true of the Milosevic regime. No one can doubt its cruelty and atrocities, but comparisons with the Third Reich are absurd.

These critical facts and the questions they raise have not been judged newsworthy. A data base search on 5 November revealed hardly a word in the news pages of the serious British national newspapers, with the exception of the *Sunday Times*. On 11 November, the *Guardian* broke its silence with a report headlined 'Graves in Kosovo put death toll in doubt.' Until then, it had published only a piece by its pro-bombing columnist, Francis Wheen, attacking the author of a *Spectator* article for suggesting that the death toll was indeed in doubt. Most of BBC News, at the time of writing, has had nothing to say on the subject.

This is understandable. With honourable exceptions, propagandists, not reporters, attended the Kosovo tragedy. Indeed, some journalists have been open in admitting that they, not Tony Blair's press secretary, deserve the credit for putting the government's case. The forbidden question was put on 5 November by a troubled Andrew Alexander in his column in the *Mail*. 'Could it turn out to be', he asked, 'that we killed more innocent civilians than the Serbs did?'

13

Diana Johnstone

The French Media and the Kosovo War

As post-modernism illustrates, ideology is one of France's luxury exports, alongside perfumes and wines. It goes to the head, for better or for worse. It is a field in which France leads its other partners in the 'international community', alias Nato, as they set out to make people good by bombing them. The closed Parisian circle of men and women of letters who form public opinion by books, articles, newspaper columns and multiple appearances on television talk shows have been fully mobilised throughout the 1990s to build a new conquering ideology of 'humanitarian intervention' on the ruins of Yugoslavia.

French media coverage of the Kosovo crisis was the continuation of a crusade begun over Bosnia, in which ideological suppositions excluded unwelcome facts and indignation silenced questioning. A vision of 'Bosnia' as a besieged Eden offered sentimental solace for a loss of political orientation. Passion for an idealised Bosnia increasingly took on the rigidity of dogma, and deviation was sacrilege.

Bosnia was already idealised. Likening Kosovo to Bosnia was a much greater idealisation still.

Mondialisation à la 'Monde'

The leading role in shaping the French attitude toward the Yugoslav conflicts has unquestionably been played by the newspaper *Le Monde* whose influence is perhaps without equivalent in any other country as the newspaper of the mandarins.[1] In France, an intellectual is sometimes defined as a person who reads *Le Monde*. In government ministries, universities, in all the places where 'public opinion' is developed, people read *Le Monde*, or *Libération*, and the weekly, *Le Nouvel Observateur*. And they watch television. All these media purvey the same centre-left apology for neoliberalism.

'*Le Monde*', observes Serge Halimi, whose widely unreviewed 1997 book criticising the French media elite nevertheless became a best-seller, 'is in the service of *mondialisation* and humanitarian wars.'[2] In France, 'globalisation' is '*mondialisation*' and *Le Monde* (the world) is its most effective voice.

In general, the post-Cold War 1990s were an era of such political uniformity (referred to as '*la pensée unique*') as to stifle any meaningful public debate about anything. The media were there to explain why, no matter what the voters meant to vote for, they were bound to get only another version of the same neoliberal policies. *Mondialisation oblige*. In France, precisely because popular resistance to neoliberalism is so deep-rooted and strong, the propaganda effort to sell it must be more subtle, relentless, elaborate and vehement. It is not enough to assail the public with dry statistics and economic pontificating (although there is plenty of that). There is also a perceived need for philosophy and idealism. Interpreted by the imaginative prophets of *mondialisation*, the conflicts in Yugoslavia proved to be a goldmine of symbols providing neoliberalism with something it totally lacked: human interest – or rather, in the current condescending jargon of the rich countries, 'humanitarian' interest.

Europe Meets Yugoslavia

In the early 1990s, the unification of Europe along neoliberal, monetarist lines met up with Yugoslavia, which was then falling apart under the blows of similar policies imposed by the International Monetary Fund. It was a fatal encounter.

In late 1991, in the midst of the delicate Maastricht negotiations, Chancellor Helmut Kohl's government surprised its partners by insisting they all immediately recognise the unnegotiated independence of Slovenia and Croatia, thereby condemning to an agonising death the existing nation of Yugoslavia. Diplomats – even German diplomats – saw the folly of this course. But for France, the common currency took precedence over the Balkans. Mitterrand's government wrote off Yugoslavia and the Serbs (traditional close allies of France) in favour of the all-important monetary partnership with Germany. This sordid deal was elevated into a triumph of the 'new Europe' in overcoming its old divisions: even though they may not quite have seen eye to eye, at least this time France and Germany had not gone to war over the Balkans.

The Treaty of European Union concluded in the Dutch city of Maastricht in December 1991 marked the decisive transformation of the European Union into a subdivision of the economic globalisation project promoted by the United States. The Maastricht Treaty introduced a monetary union tying the franc permanently to the Deutschemark, a project considered indispensable by French capital. The terms of the Treaty imposed economic policies unlikely to enchant citizens who actually examined the lengthy text. Faced with the peril of popular rejection in the referendum set for September 1992, the French media and political elite did not spare the rhetoric. Opposition to Maastricht was stigmatised as irrational, archaic, or, worse, 'populist' and 'nationalist'. The peril was real, because despite a media campaign leaving the impression that no sane person in France could oppose Maastricht, the Treaty squeaked through by only a slim majority of voters.

Meanwhile, the Yugoslav conflict had moved from Croatia to Bosnia, with Serb minorities in both Republics taking up arms to oppose secession from Yugoslavia that would reduce them to minority status on the very territories where Serbs had been victims of Croatian nationalist genocide in 1941. Although Serb fears were real, the danger of a return to 1941 persecution was surely less so. The fear was exploited by Serb nationalist leaders whose rise was ensured by the parallel rise of Croatian and Muslim nationalists. Motives on all sides were mixed and dubious, civil war was bound to be terrible. By actively promoting patient negotiations taking account of all factors, notably the genuine fears of the population, France, with the rest of Europe, should have been able to find solutions to stop the spiral of violence.

In the First World War, France salvaged the heroic remnants of the decimated Serbian army and used them to help reconquer the Balkans. In commemoration, the famous statue in Kalemegdan park in Belgrade bears the inscription, 'May we love France as France loved us, 1914–1918.' Over the years, a large diaspora of Serbian intellectuals and professionals have been drawn to France in part by such sentiments, which today have largely turned to bitter disappointment. In the early 1990s, this heritage suggested a danger: that the traditional (now considered 'archaic') Franco-Serb friendship could interfere with the new and infinitely more important Franco-German partnership. And this coincided with a related danger: that the French might read the fine print in the Maastricht Treaty and vote '*non*'. To prevent such disasters, the most effective precautionary measure was to combine the two issues, European Union and the Yugoslav crisis, in a Manichean dichotomy. On the one hand, the 'new Europe', built on recon-ciliation between the hereditary enemies, France and Germany, now united peacefully in eternal friendship and (hopefully) prosperity. On the other hand, the wicked 'old Europe', represented in miniature by Yugoslavia.

Not that this combination was the result of deliberate calculation. Rather, it seems to have sprung naturally from the juxtaposition of events and the mood of the times. Along these lines, a prominent journalist described the 1992 referendum as a choice between European integration and 'the logic of ethnic cleansing'.[3] Thus, thanks to Yugoslavia, Europe's new monetarist straitjacket was enhanced by a frightening antithesis: 'ethnic cleansing'. There was no middle ground, it was one or the other.

Bosnia and the *Furia Francese*

Meanwhile, from the ruins of the genuinely multinational, multicultural Yugoslav Federation, a previously (and still) non-existent harmonious 'Bosnia' had emerged as the symbol of idealised multicultural Europe. In a delirium of false analogies, this imaginary Bosnia became a 'little Europe' which must be saved from the evils of nationalism – Serbian nationalism – led by the 'new Hitler', Slobodan Milosevic.

This illusion was by no means exclusively French, it was the great Western myth of 1992–93. The French simply put more words and passion into it.

A main reason that the nasty territorial war in Bosnia-Herzegovina aroused far more outrage than the earlier war in Croatia was concern about assimilation of the large Muslim immigrant population in France. War reports from Sarajevo brought discovery, in dramatic circumstances, of a population of gentle blue-eyed Slavic Muslims, playing pianos and violins, who seemed to offer the ideal model for solving the problem. The 'lukewarm' Islam seen in Sarajevo seemed totally suitable for integration into any European country.

This imagined relevance to Western Europe's own 'Muslim problem' helps account for the vehement hostility that arose against the Bosnian Serbs, seen as rustic bigots destroying this ideal prototype of multicultural Europe out of pure barbarism. In another contribution to European Union, those same Serbs were retrospectively blamed for triggering the carnage of the First World War, and thus communism and fascism, thereby becoming the scapegoat for all the evils of the twentieth century at the moment of Europe's peaceful unification. A whole new version of twentieth-century history was found just in time to serve as its epitaph.

The fashionable writer Bernard-Henri Lévy was one of those who eagerly took up the cause of this ideal European Islam, to the point of acting as a virtual public relations agent for Bosnian President Alija Izetbegovic in France (Lévy, 1996:99, 165, 343). (The mistake, common at the time, was to identify idealised Sarajevo with Izetbegovic and his Democratic Action Party, whose ultimate goal was not the preservation of 'multicultural' society but an Islamic state. Izetbegovic not only did not represent the population of Bosnia-Herzegovina in all its religious diversity, he did not even represent the majority of Muslims before the war.)

BHL, Superstar

In the United States, a writer who comments on events in newspapers is called a columnist. In France, he (not she) is called a philosopher. Nobody better embodies this caste than Bernard-Henri Lévy, whimsically referred to by his initials BHL, by allusion to the Paris department store BHV. BHL could be seen as a sort of department store of ideas, prolific and shallow, well-displayed, fashionable and suited for mass consumption.

BHL is everywhere. The pages of practically all the leading dailies and weeklies are open to whatever he cares to write for them, he appears regularly on television, he is president of the supervisory board of the Franco-German TV channel Arte. He is an associate editorialist of Le Monde.

Bernard-Henri Lévy became famous as one of the 'New Philosophers' promoted in the mid-1970s by Le Nouvel Observateur and other media whose impassioned discovery, several decades after everybody else, of the crimes of Stalin as described by Solzhenitsyn, was used to discredit communism in particular, and the revolutionary left in general, as leading inexorably to barbarism. Having been coached by Marxist philosopher Louis Althusser during their elite student days, BHL and company established their lifetime credentials as left intellectuals whose disillusion had transformed them into infallible prophets of liberalism. The great contribution of the New Philosophers to public discussion was less the content than the style of their argumentation. Thanks to television, they were able to elevate hysterical moralising to the politically correct tone of debate. Any effort to establish the facts could be denounced as compromising with barbarism.

The cause of human rights provided a new ideal supposedly as inherently innocent as communism was inherently guilty. However, there is no ideal that cannot lose its innocence by association with war. It so happens that the New Philosophers adhered to 'human rights' as their new creed at precisely the moment when, in the United States, President Carter's National Security Adviser Zbigniew Brzezinski had adopted 'human rights' as the ideological half of his two-pronged offensive to destroy the Soviet Union. The more practical half, as he later explained, was to lure the Soviet Union into an unwinnable war against Islamic Mujahiddin in Afghanistan. BHL joined that half as well. In the early 1980s, Bernard-Henri Lévy had himself photographed in a stylish Mujahiddin turban somewhere among the rocks and rifles of Afghanistan. By the early 1990s, he was ducking behind walls for the benefit of photographers in Sarajevo. He was present, along with his protégé, President Izetbegovic, at American Ambassador Pamela Harriman's dinner in Paris in 1995 when Richard Holbrooke gave the go-ahead for Nato to bomb the Bosnian Serbs.

With communism gone, 'nationalism' has taken its place as the central 'barbarism'. This strikes a most responsive chord on the left, nostalgic for its lost internationalism. Among many others, BHL plays variations of the central ideological theme: nationalism – the root of all evil – must be drowned in internationalism. This theme happens to provide the best ideological justification for neoliberal globalisation. The trick is to make an exclusive identification of 'nationalism' with the political right and 'internationalism' with the political left. For this purpose, the presence of Jean-Marie Le Pen's National Front on the French political scene has rendered a great service to *mondialisation*. Instead of coming up with proposals and policies, it is enough to denounce Le Pen to merit the 'left' label. The fixation on Le Pen produces an unthinking left ready to grasp automatically whatever is presented as the opposite of Le Pen.

Confusion reigns between a progressive, political internationalism, and the capitalist seizure of global power. There is no reason why a progressive political internationalism need remove a country's ability to adopt economic policies benefiting the majority of the population. Economic globalisation is another matter: its dogma proclaims that the very survival of France depends on reducing government intervention in the economy to enable big business to compete successfully in the world market. 'The competition is fierce, the world is becoming a village and businesses which are the best adapted to fight and win are those which don't have to bear the weight and the constraints of the State', in the words of one of France's leading industrialists, Jean-Luc Lagardère, owner of the Matra-Hachette group whose properties stretch from high-tech armaments to mass media, including the radio station Radio 1 which broadcast these words of wisdom.

Lagardère is a friend of BHL. He helped finance BHL's film, *Le Jour et la Nuit*, perhaps the most rapid flop in French film history. Not that BHL needs money. His family made a huge fortune in wood, one of the business interests of another of his close friends, François Pinault, currently judged the richest man in France, who owns the multimedia retail chain FNAC, the Printemps department stores and other retail businesses as well as *Le Point*, where BHL publishes his columns as he chooses. Bernard-Henri Lévy is indeed the perfect 'organic intellectual' of the very rich, who expresses with untroubled conviction the ideas that are favourable to the interests of his highly privileged milieu.

To convince oneself, and perhaps others, that one is a genuine *intellectuel engagé* carrying on the tradition of Malraux and Sartre, a noble cause is required, preferably romantic and foreign, like the Spanish Civil War as reflected in films and novels. Bosnia was the 'Spain' of the yuppies, a consumer cause served on television. It is admittedly not always easy to be heroic, and even harder to get facts straight in the Balkans.

In May 1994, during television promotion of his film *Bosna!*, Bernard-Henri Lévy announced that to champion the Bosnian cause, a 'Sarajevo' list would run for election to the European Parliament. A number of personalities rushed to put their names on what was described as 'the intellectuals' list'. (BHL himself prudently bowed out.) Despite enormous publicity, the 'Sarajevo' list eventually scored an insignificant 1.56 per cent. In those days, the BHL crowd rallied to the slogan, 'Europe lives or dies in Sarajevo.' The rhetorical excess reached the point of actually likening (by its length), the 'siege of Sarajevo' to the incomparably more ghastly siege of Leningrad ... an indication of the zeal of the 'May '68 generation' in trying to render their own era more tragically dramatic than that of their parents.

Politically Correct, French-Style

'This is a generation', observes writer Régis Debray, 'that is profoundly anti-communist, for having been a little communist themselves.' Curiously, what many have retained are the Cold War dichotomies, now applied arbitrarily to Balkan conflicts. 'Criticism of the war is dismissed as "anti-Americanism" which is equated with communism, because the communists were anti-American', according to Debray. It even happens that objections to Nato's military attack on Yugoslavia give rise to accusations of 'campism' – that is, automatic defence of the 'Soviet camp', which no longer exists and to which Yugoslavia had not belonged for the past 50 years.

When it comes to the Balkans, the principal heritage of the '68 generation's brush with Marxism often seems to be its most abstract, obscure and useless sectarian polemics, a rehearsal for inquisitorial condemnation of whatever is not deemed 'politically correct'.

Thus, when in 1995 the Cannes film festival awarded its Palme d'Or to Yugoslav film-maker Emir Kusturica for *Underground*, *Le Monde* quickly published a column by the 'philosopher' Alain Finkielkraut excoriating the Bosnian-born (but persistently 'Yugoslav') cineaste as 'a servile and flashy illustrator of criminal clichés'.[4] Finkielkraut excoriated *Underground* as 'the rock, postmodern, hair-raising, hip, Americanised, and filmed-in-Belgrade version of the most senile and lying Serb propaganda'. The philosopher-reviewer accused Kusturica of 'capitalising on the suffering of Sarajevo', of 'symbolising tortured Bosnia' while taking the 'stereotyped arguments of those who are starving and besieging' it.

Someone who saw the movie might think, on the contrary, that this Fellini-esque fantasy was actually a condemnation of Tito's Yugoslavia for having kept the population 'underground' in an atmosphere of 'war communism' which eventually erupted in senseless and terrible civil war. A questionable thesis, but not exactly a reproduction of 'criminal clichés', and so on. However, the objective of *Le Monde* – which in another article suggested that even showing the film violated sanctions against Yugoslavia – was scarcely to encourage people to see *Underground* and judge for themselves. Why should they? Finkielkraut himself wrote his article without bothering to see the film.

When Serbia's leading novelist Dobrica Cosic visited Paris in December 1996 to sign his books at a Latin Quarter bookshop run by his Swiss publisher, L'Age d'Homme, *Le Monde*'s editors might, for instance, have sent somebody to interview Cosic, who after all had been President of Yugoslavia in 1992 and 1993 before being sacked by Milosevic. He might have had interesting things to say. Instead, *Le Monde* lent its columns to an obscure veteran of Sarajevo Internet editing to attack the bookstore for 'historical revisionism' – meaning it sold books presenting the Serbian side of the current conflicts.[5]

Such incidents abound. But the most spectacular thought policing by the media elite was reserved for a maverick from their own ranks, Régis Debray, who undertook to go see what was happening in Serbia, including Kosovo province, during the Nato bombing in May 1999. Debray reported that Nato bombs had struck civilian targets such as schools and factories; that Milosevic was an autocratic, manipulative leader without 'totalitarian' charisma, largely ignored by the population, and not the Hitlerian 'dictator' denounced by Nato; that Yugoslavia was a multiparty state without political prisoners and governed by a Constitution; that the Serbian exactions against Kosovo Albanians began with the Nato bombing and lasted three days; that ethnic Albanians had fled for a number of reasons, but that many had stayed behind or since returned; in short, that there was no 'genocide'; and that Nato was visibly not succeeding in destroying the Yugoslav army, which seemed to be in great shape. These reports were not dissimilar to other first-hand accounts by Western journalists, few in number at that time, notably those by Paul Watson, the Canadian correspondent for the *Los Angeles Times*, who stayed in Kosovo throughout the bombing and whom Debray interviewed and quoted.

In line with the French philosopher aspiration to counsel the prince, Debray wrote his main article as a 'letter of a traveller to the President of the Republic'. He warned President Jacques Chirac that the reality did not correspond to the official Nato version that Chirac himself was conveying. Debray closed with a reminder of what de Gaulle had said about Nato: 'an organisation imposed on the Atlantic Alliance and which is merely the military and political subordination of Western Europe to the United States of America'.[6] Still, on the whole Debray's article was unusually factual rather than rhetorical. *Le Monde* gave Debray the front page (13 May 1999).

Woe was he! Every elite pen in Paris was poised to stab the heretic. In the following days, *Le Monde* gave them free rein, *Libération* gave its own staff five full pages to attack Debray point by point, even the Communist daily *L'Humanité* treated Debray, not the war, as the matter 'under accusation', while the managing editor of *Le Monde*, Edwy Plenel, an ex-Trotskyist, even tossed off an entire book to denounce Debray as one of the ex-revolutionary generation who failed to pass 'the test' (*L'Epreuve*, the title of the book) of contemporary political correctness represented by Kosovo. Having hoped to stimulate debate about the war, what Debray stimulated was an uproar designed to ban dissent and close ranks around the official version.

Debray himself rather generously attributes this conformism on Yugoslavia to a 'Pétainist complex' on the part of a generation which, he says, was traumatised by the discovery of French collaboration with the Nazi occupation and passivity in the face of the Holocaust.[7] The collaboration plus communism gives them 'two things to expiate', suggests Debray.

Nato presented the ethnic Albanian refugee exodus as the result of a single cause: Serbian 'ethnic cleansing' or even 'genocide'. Television images of ethnic Albanians crowded onto trains leaving Kosovo were skilfully used to recall images of Jews being deported to Auschwitz. The significant difference between going to a slave-labour death camp and going to friendly shelter across the border was not visible in the all-important 'image'. An image may say 'more than a thousand words', precisely because it can be made to say almost anything.

In an era when everybody talks about 'identity', actually having one seems to pose problems. And thus there is a notable tendency to assume other identities: in play, in 'role games', and in politics, in striking poses mimed from earlier, more heroic moments of the twentieth century.

The favourite heroic roles for the 1990s were drawn from the 1930s and 1940s, in particular, the Spanish Civil War with its legendary International Brigades (especially the novelists), and of course the Second World War. Since nobody wants to play Hitler, his role is assigned to others, in this case to Yugoslav President Slobodan Milosevic. Around that role, all the others fall into place.

A Soul for Europe

In France in particular, a striking feature of the entire Yugoslav crisis up to and including the Kosovo war is the apparent power of the media to force their own policy agenda on governments, via the pressure of public opinion. This recalls the role of the press in promoting the imperialism of the nineteenth century, when private interests used their newspapers to popularise foreign expeditions, sometimes over the objections of better informed political leaders, by dramatising alleged atrocities committed by savages in need of the 'civilising mission'.

Remarkably, a large number of senior French officials acknowledge privately that they do not believe what the media says – or even what they themselves are obliged to say in public – about Kosovo. Rumour has it that scarcely anyone at the highest levels of the French government believes the official version of the Kosovo war. In particular, French Foreign Minister Hubert Védrine had previously demonstrated a lucidity he was obliged to hold in check during his role as co-host of the strange Rambouillet 'negotiations'. Describing the Yugoslav crisis in a book published scarcely three years earlier, Védrine noted that 'the media, soon followed by public opinion, lost no time in tacking onto this exceptionally complex conflict the simplistic Manichean ideology inherited from the Cold War' (1996:602–3). As in a 'Western', there had to be a bad guy. Thus, the Yugoslav Federation was 'suddenly turned into a detestable relic of communism that had to be destroyed. Within Yugoslavia itself, even before the start of the exactions, the adversary was the Serb.' The media version of the Yugoslav tragedy, in which Serbia, 'a detestable regime and people, communist and nationalist, invaded two neighbouring countries', Croatia and Bosnia, 'was only remotely related to the facts', said Védrine, but it persisted. 'Any other viewpoint was pro-Serb.' Warned by his own analysis, Védrine took care not to adopt any other viewpoint.

Why was there no serious public effort on the part of well-informed people like Védrine to counter this version 'only remotely related to the facts'? One can only speculate. In addition to fear of rocking the EU boat by clashing with Germany, there was the fear – once the United States began to champion the Bosnian Muslims – of arousing the wrath of Washington over an issue of minor importance. It is clear that United States media (not to mention the far more vicious British tabloids) are always ready to 'trash the French' when they get uppity. There are simply too many vital issues requiring France to stand up to US pressure, notably concerning trade and agriculture, to go looking for trouble in regard to issues considered secondary.

By an odd twist, François Mitterrand's reputation for being pro-Serb has contributed to Serbophobia in France. At the end of his life, which coincided with the end of his 14-year presidency, the various deceptions of the 'Florentine', as he was nicknamed for his mastery of the art of political subterfuge, had drastically thinned the ranks of his admirers. The balance sheet of his presidency is widely considered a moral calamity for the left. In foreign policy he is commonly judged to have done everything wrong. This general sense of disillusion has tended to fixate on the accusation that Mitterrand supported the Serbs out of an archaic attachment to old wartime allies. There is a grain of truth in this: it does seem that the only reasons Mitterrand perceived for *not* sacrificing Yugoslavia to the European common currency were old-fashioned reasons of French national interest in preserving its number one Balkan ally. And these reasons were not strong enough. Therefore, the ally was sacrificed.

Ambiguity was the hallmark of Mitterrand. His political success was built on his ability to seem to be everything and its opposite – the opposite of a didactic political leader who uses his office to try to advance public understanding of issues. His handling of the Yugoslav crisis was marked by obscure contradictions. He was capable on the one hand of expressing sympathy for Serbs as such, and on the other of lending his top jurist Robert Badinter to head a commission which invented ostensibly legalistic pretexts for the unprecedented act of recognising the unnegotiated secession of constituent parts of Yugoslavia, in total contradiction to existing practices and standards of international law, thus precipitating war. His mixed signals finally displeased everyone without advancing any solution. Overlooking the fact that at the crucial moment, Mitterrand in effect washed his hands of the Balkans in favour of the German partnership, for many intellectuals on the left, above all those who supported the unsuccessful 'Sarajevo list' in the 1994 European elections, vehement support for Bosnia was their 'revolt against the father', their repudiation of Mitterrand in favour of a supposedly pure idealism.

Thereafter, any challenge to a totally anti-Serb interpretation of events was tainted with suspicion not only of communism, nationalism and 'campism', but also of Mitterrandism.

Disapproval of the Nato bombing on the part of the French Interior Minister, Jean-Pierre Chevènement, is notorious but publicly mute. In 1991, Chevènement resigned as Defence Minister in disagreement over the Gulf War against Iraq. This time nobody resigned. France had major economic interests in Iraq. Nevertheless, France took part in the Gulf War against Iraq. A reason was cited at the time which no doubt goes far toward explaining the French role in the Kosovo war: only members of the club get to have a say in what is done. The price of influence is to follow the leader.

But there is another, more subtle factor at work. Yugoslavia has been the 'common enemy' needed to bring Europe and the United States together in a new missionary Nato. This new moralising Atlantic union obviously corresponds to US strategic interests. But European Nato leaders and media have bought into the demonising of the Serbs with equal enthusiasm, for a similar, yet potentially contrasting and more elusive reason.

The European Union is in need of a common identity more spiritual than a common currency. The 1994 slogan, 'Europe lives or dies at Sarajevo', was extravagant hyperbole. But it caught the need to associate 'Europe' with a dramatic cause, and the intellectuals feeling this need grasped onto a totally idealised 'Bosnia' as the symbol of this 'Europe' which, rather than being an economic powerhouse technocratically organised to take its place alongside the United States in world domination, was actually a tender bud of multi-ethnic civilisation in danger of being trampled to death by a new Hitler. Bosnia has since become an almost unmentionable morass of lies and corruption. The multicultural paradise is forgotten. Next fantasy: Kosovo.

Yugoslavia's disintegration was the first crisis to be poured whole into the mould of the ideological myth of the Second World War. This is a ritual for anthropologists to describe. Myth is built on history and transformed into a ceremony whose roles must be assumed by succeeding players on the stage of history. Finally, the scapegoat. Milosevic became 'Hitler', the Serbs became the new 'Nazis', and their adversaries were all victims of a potential new 'Holocaust'. Serbia bears all the sins of Europe's past, it represents everything Europe thinks it is not, or does not want to be.

By the time the 'Kosovo Liberation Army' began hostilities in Kosovo province in 1998, Serbia had already been condemned by the media to bear the heavy ideological responsibility of representing the total opposite of the paradise that European Union was supposed to achieve. The mass media project the chorus of the righteous myth. No deviation is allowed. The occasional intellectual who ventures to doubt – Peter Handke, Régis Debray – is pilloried by the chorus of right thinkers.

There are rewards for the politically correct. Bernard Kouchner, French cabinet minister and dashing media symbol of the 'French doctors' who cross national borders to bring the humanitarian skills of the rich countries to victims in the poor countries, was given the not altogether enviable post of United Nations administrator of the province of Kosovo, left in anarchy after Nato and its 'Kosovo Liberation Army' allies chased out the entire government administration. From his first concern for the hungry rebels of Biafra who were seeking to secede (with clandestine French encouragement) from Nigeria, to the Vietnamese 'boat people', whose briefly spotlighted plight helped tarnish Vietnam's hard-won victory, to Kosovo, Kouchner's most spectacular humanitarian impulses have more often than not coincided with more discreet political aims of governments. His wife, Christine Ockrent, is a fixture of the media elite, and was chosen by US television to present the French view of the Nato war, which was certainly authoritative, not to say official.

Side by side with the State Department's pet terrorist leader, Hasim Thaqi, Bernard Kouchner has taken on his job of creating a new Kosovo with apparent joy. 'Europe is born in Kosovo, the Europe of human rights, of brotherhood', Kouchner told *Le Monde* ecstatically, 'The Europe we love' (7 August 1999).

Ideology has triumphed over reality. But for how long?

Notes

1. *Le Monde* is not to be confused with *Le Monde diplomatique*, which belongs to the same group but whose editorial policy is altogether independent, and different, from that of *Le Monde*.
2. Halimi (1997). Remarks are from an interview with the author on 9 September 1999.
3. Jean-François Kahn, cited by Halimi (1997:29).
4. Alain Finkielkraut, 'L'imposture Kusturica', *Le Monde*, 2 June 1995.
5. Laurent B. Renard, 'Que fait Dobrica Cosic à Paris?', *Le Monde*, 6 December 1996. Renard is identified as editor in Sarajevo in 1995 and 1996 of the Internet service 'Sarajevo on line', not necessarily a gauge of objectivity.
6. Criticism of the Nato action as 'an Anglo-American-led war against Europe' tends to be separate from an analysis of the Yugoslav problem itself, leading only to the conclusion that 'Europe' in the form of the European Union should strengthen its own independent forces in order to be able to pursue 'humanitarian wars' without US meddling and to the benefit of European military industries. This is essentially the viewpoint of Alain Joxe, a strategic writer whose analyses carry influence in the French left. During the bombing, at a time when later reports indicate that the French government was reticent about US targeting of civilian installations in Serbia, Joxe advocated even more all-out war against the Serbs, in contrast to the German government which expressed open unwillingness to send ground troops into Kosovo to fight the Yugoslav army.
7. Conversation with Régis Debray, 22 September 1999.

14

Thomas Deichmann

From 'Never again War' to 'Never again Auschwitz': Dilemmas of German Media Policy in the War against Yugoslavia

> The German government has entered into a war consciously and with conviction. And in this situation the propaganda apparatus takes on a new quality. In all my experience I have never seen a Defence Minister appear before the press like Mr Scharping, armed with photos we were to describe in terms of what he saw in them. I have never seen a Defence Minister who allows no interruptions or questions during interviews. [It was] as if he had to convince himself of what he was saying.

This is how Albrecht Reinhard, head of the Foreign Section at Westdeutscher Rundfunk TV, described the new and problematic relationship between politics and media in Germany.[1] Characterising the new government propaganda as 'perhaps the most dangerous development for journalism', Reinhard pointed out that the media were entering uncharted territory in the Nato war against Yugoslavia: none of the country's journalists had experienced a war waged by their own government. Hermann Heym, head of the Association of German Journalists, criticised the quality of German war reporting, warning against emotionalising the conflict and noting that that 'there had been an anti-Serb tendency in the German media long before the onset of the war in Kosovo' (*Evangelische Kommentare*, July). The German Press Council, an independent agency which monitors compliance with professional standards, published a statement on 19 May arguing that 'military language' should not 'dominate the language of the media' and that 'euphemistic concepts like collateral damage' should be avoided.[2] The fact that the Press Council found it necessary to restate the most basic concepts of war reporting indicates there were major problems with the coverage.

German reporting on the Nato war was no better than elsewhere in the West. There were exceptional journalists who attempted to give a balanced picture, but they were scarcely heard. What people remembered afterwards was largely the one-sided condemnation of the Serbs. Although questions were raised about the devastating effects of Nato bombing, criticism was limited to the conduct of the war; its legitimacy was rarely called into question. For the most part, the media parroted official justifications of the war, and even offered arguments and rhetoric of their own to legitimise the air strikes. German politicians claimed Nato was not waging a war, but defending human rights and attempting to thwart a genocide Milosevic had long planned. Such claims were not only repeated uncritically, but actively promoted by journalists who were openly partisan.

As Heym's comments indicate, German reporting of Kosovo continued trends established since the beginning of the Yugoslav crisis in 1991. A new definition of international diplomacy, which evolved in the course of the conflicts smouldering in the Balkans for eight years, was sealed by the Nato war, and supported by the media. The central justification of Western policy today is the protection of human rights. The talk now is not of national interests, but of 'ethical foreign policy', and this strongly influenced reporting of Kosovo. After the end of the Cold War, the rhetoric of 'human rights' offers journalists, as well as politicians, a new moral mission. Many reporters now feel responsible for this moral agenda, and traditional journalistic principles such as distance and impartiality have faded into the background. In Germany, where the fall of the wall politically disoriented journalists, this trend is especially pronounced.

Below, I first set out the political context of the war for Germany, examining how problems were overcome by overblown rhetoric and comparisons with the Holocaust. I then go on to describe a paradigm shift in the German media and politics, whereby traditional conservatives were often the most critical, and liberals the most bellicose. Finally, I show how this shift ultimately led to the media's proclaimed democratic role being severely compromised, as editors bowed to political pressure.

Red–Green Acid Test

Reinhard noted that the Kosovo war was virgin territory for German politicians as well as reporters. Indeed, the war was a turning point for the political elite, who sent their military into battle for the first time since the Second World War. The post-war political culture of the Federal Republic had been decisively shaped by the moral and political renunciation of militarism, and it was not easy to 'normalise' sending German troops into action. Political and moral reservations had in fact largely been neutralised in recent years by the rhetoric of human rights, but actually gaining acceptance for war was still no routine event. The situation was further complicated by the fact that this rupture in Germany's political culture entailed violating both international law and the German constitution – which both have their roots in the reaction to the horrors of the Nazi era. In addition, the first battle orders for German soldiers since 1945 were issued by the Social Democratic Party (SPD) and the Greens, two parties who identified strongly with the liberal tradition of the Federal Republic. The task of explaining German participation in the war fell to Green Foreign Minister Joschka Fischer, who had spoken out during the Bosnian war, when he was in opposition, against sending German troops to the Balkans, recalling the fascist past.

The SPD, led by Chancellor Gerhard Schröder, had fewer problems with pacifist political baggage. Schröder himself, however, had another problem. In the 1998 election, the SPD had calculatingly and successfully imitated the 'modernising' politics of Tony Blair and Bill Clinton. Election strategists from Britain and the USA were consulted, and they turned once meaningful party conventions into shameless media opportunities for Schröder. With formulations devoid of content, the SPD sought to create the impression of accountability, playing up to the 'will of the people'. Significantly, they also substituted emotionalism for political argument. For example, after a harrowing train accident in the town of Eschede some weeks before the election, Schröder, campaigning for the chancellorship, announced that out of respect he would refrain from making a political speech at the coming SPD convention in Schleswig-Holstein (Reul, 1999). The rhetoric of 'ethical foreign policy' that is part of the New Labour platform in Britain was adopted too. The SPD campaign was highly effective, but it quickly became clear that this brand of politics was still in its infancy. Schröder often appeared awkward, like a bad copy of his model Blair, and the new ruling coalition suffered one embarrassment after another: suggestions for tax reform, energy and immigration policy were announced, only to be immediately criticised and sent back to committee for revision. The new government was not able, even for two months, to maintain the image of an innovative party of the 'New Centre'. The Red–Green 'modernisation crisis' reached a dramatic climax shortly before the Nato war, when SPD Finance Minister Oskar Lafontaine resigned from office and openly criticised the Chancellor's leadership style.

In the spring of 1999 the Red–Green coalition's legitimacy crisis was compounded by international pressure for an unambiguous vote in favour of the Nato war. In this situation they chose to take the bull by the horns. The war offered the opportunity to leave domestic political problems behind, to regroup and to remake the coalition's image. The combination of strategic problems and the first signs of decline of the new government, coupled with the need to work through remaining moral and political doubts concerning the justification of military engagement – especially in the Balkans where German fascism had wreaked havoc – led to sometimes hysterical overreactions. As in no other country, the vocabulary of the Holocaust was used in Germany by the political elite to lend moral legitimacy to the Nato war and the deployment of German troops. The use of this vocabulary was the result of profound uncertainty. The war could not simply be declared a punishment of Milosevic, because that would not have helped in the attempt to establish a moral consensus. Therefore moralising explanations for the war became prominent. Categories such as national or geopolitical interests played no part in the discussion. Instead, armed conflict was stylised into something holy, almost as if it were a matter of saving humanity from Satan. It is true that Western countries in general made use of the rhetoric of human rights as a primary justification of the war, but it was in Germany that this rhetoric bore the most questionable fruits.

The government complained of the burden it bore, giving the impression that the army found itself on a mission which had been forced upon it. The situation in Kosovo was equated with German fascism and the Serbs with Nazi henchmen. It was argued that to end the 'genocide', German participation in the war was an honourable and 'historic' duty that had to be fulfilled, especially by the present government with its commitment to the traditions of peace and anti-fascism. In an interview with ARD's *Panorama* programme (15 April), Foreign Minister Fischer justified his position on the war by stating he had 'not only learned the lesson "never again war", but also "never again Auschwitz"'. At the daily press conferences, SPD Defence Minister Scharping constantly drew new parallels between Serbia and the Third Reich. His horror stories about 'Serbian fascism' were calculated to shock and to lend a lofty, humanitarian justification to German participation in the war. Nato spokesman Jamie Shea seemed sober and self-possessed by comparison. Scharping reported on a Serbian concentration camp supposedly set up in a Pristina soccer stadium, adding: 'I use the term concentration camp consciously.' Daily, he sketched new images of heinous deeds, such as Serbs roasting foetuses ripped from the bellies of Albanian women. At the end of April, Scharping presented a photograph of dead bodies taken on 29 January close to the town of Rogova, as proof for his theory that the Serbs had been massacring and expelling Kosovo Albanians as early as January, and thus before the negotiations in Rambouillet. The photo was familiar to some reporters, however: OSCE experts had long since identified it as showing the aftermath of a battle between Yugoslav forces and the KLA. When journalist Ulrich Deppendorf questioned Scharping about this in an interview for ARD (30 April), he responded with outlandish speculation – the skulls of the corpses had been cracked open by 'baseball bats' – and rejected any criticism of his use of the picture. Furthermore, he continually challenged Deppendorf when he tried to raise further questions or stated there were serious doubts about the theory that 'ethnic cleansing' had begun in January.

Scharping's unprofessional conduct raised eyebrows in some media circles. Nevertheless, the vacillating German political elite employed highly irrational war propaganda to give the impression of unity, to quiet their own worries, and not least, to disqualify critics of the war at the outset. As Peter Scholl-Latour commented on *Panorama* (15 April):

> Concerning the leading politicians, I have the shocking suspicion that they must keep the attention of their followers, who are made up for the most part of peace-loving people, by means of grisly descriptions.

In an essay in *Novo*, the respected German commentator Cora Stephan also used sharp words to criticise the moral pose of politicians: 'Morality is, to overstate the point, the means of those who have no good arguments' (Stephan, 1999). Nevertheless, the new German government propaganda of moralising rhetoric and Nazi comparisons proved effective. For the most part, the media reported uncritically and news audiences had little sense of the contradictions and the extent of the manipulation. Indeed, Scharping became the second most popular government minister during the war, after Fischer.

Paradigm Shift

During the conflict, Germany experienced a rapid and definitive institution-alisation of 'ethical foreign policy', with all its attendant contradictions. To be sure, this kind of politics has long affected perceptions of international events in Germany, but now it was put to the test for the first time and this created difficulties for the media. The Red–Green coalition needed the war in order finally to jettison the last of its post-war ideological ballast. At times journalists criticised the resulting irrationality, but this had no meaningful influence on the situation as a whole. In fact there was a paradigm shift in the media landscape, accompanying the realignments in German politics.

Though one expects little from the yellow press, such as *Bild* and *Express*, or from most of the private TV channels, the respected dailies and weeklies and the public TV stations ARD and ZDF are a different matter.[3] As part of the liberal tradition of post-war Germany, public broadcasting and influential publications such as *Spiegel, Zeit, Woche, Stern, Süddeutsche Zeitung, Frankfurter Rundschau*, and *tageszeitung*, lean toward the social democratic/green end of the political spectrum. Yet the quality press and public broadcasters had two problems. First, their editorial boards had followed the mainstream in recent years, squandering creativity and quality to a large extent. Second, this was the government for which they had long yearned. Given the government's ongoing troubles in spring 1999, some publications may have decided to use the war to help strengthen Schröder, Scharping and Fischer, staving off the collapse of their government.

In this context it seems important to direct attention to those journalists who are traditionally not beholden to parties and from whom, in the past, an especially critical perspective on questions of war and peace could be expected. These are reporters who understood their investigative journalism and commentary also as a contribution to the hard work of democracy and thus questioned the foreign policy strategies of their own elites. However, during the Nato bombing – as during the war in Bosnia – it turned out that an independent investigative perspective was largely absent, or had often been turned on its head. On 30 April, for example, the green-oriented *tageszeitung* published three pictures of dead Kosovo Albanians accompanying an article headed: 'The dead from Djakovica'. The pictures were said to have been taken from a videotape showing 15 Kosovo Albanians massacred by Serb forces in early April. However, some readers recognised one of the shots from a 29 March *Spiegel* article about killings at Racak in January. A week later, the *tageszeitung* acknowledged the mistake but did not apologise. Instead, the paper compounded its error by asserting that the dead had been civilian victims of a massacre in Racak, presenting their 'correction' as further evidence of the crimes committed by Serb forces.[4] The highly motivated ministers who served in the Red–Green government with Scharping and Fischer, ministers who had been staunch advocates of peace and who now seemed really to believe what they said about 'defeating Serbian fascism', were not alone. In numerous publications, journalists who saw themselves as fulfilling this same mission were influential. There were, for instance, heartfelt arguments for the Nato war in the *tageszeitung*, whose writers relentlessly argued for ground troops, cautioned against accepting an early peace deal, blamed Milosevic for the war and sympathised with calls for him to be assassinated. The farther to the traditional liberal left journalists and editors stood, the more hawkish their commentaries, and the more disappointing the quality of their reporting.

Aside from a few exceptions on both sides, one could find more factual and more nuanced reporting in traditionally conservative papers. The *Frankfurter Allgemeine Zeitung* (*FAZ*), for example, which had been justifiably attacked for its anti-Serb bias since the beginning of the Yugoslav crisis in the early 1990s, did not change its basic position: but substantial criticisms of the war and Nato propaganda did appear, albeit primarily in its supplement section. *FAZ* writer Mark Siemons, for instance, was surprised that:

> leftists, of all people, who traditionally tended to approach political positions by investigating the underlying interests, in the process often falling prey to paranoid conspiracy theories, now identified uncritically with Nato as the representative of their interests. (15 April)

For the *FAZ*, a traditional organ of conservatism and the Christian Democratic Union (CDU), political opportunism may have played a role. Nonetheless, this and other articles made clear that conservative publications were critical of government policy, and condemned politicians for no longer attempting to justify the war rationally, much less to respond to critics factually. As a result, conservative editors defended principles of international law, the constitution and professional journalistic standards against the diffuse moral soup of the 'modernisers'. The conservative-leaning news magazine *Focus* provided an example of this paradigm shift in the German media, publishing a commentary by former Green Party member Jutta Ditfurth accusing Fischer of relativising the Nazi past:

> What could be better for Nato than a German Foreign Minister who misuses anti-fascist categories to glorify his own opportunism? Who pours

out buckets of mendacious morality on which former leftists and left-liberals slip and slide into a new fascination with war? (*Focus*, No. 17, p. 66)

In an ARD talk show (25 April), it was CDU representatives, including the Hessian Minister-President Roland Koch, who condemned the 'rhetoric against Mr Milosevic' and warned: 'We do not want total war, nor do we want a total defeat.'

The new closing of ranks[5] between 'modernisers' in politics and the media demonstrated more clearly than ever that those who were the loudest in their demands for the defence of human rights and democracy were the most absolute in their support of a total Nato war and their denunciation of criticism as Serbian propaganda. It also became clear that the very groups that most frequently used the terms 'concentration camp', 'Auschwitz', and 'genocide' contributed most effectively to the relativisation of Nazi atrocities and the ongoing rehabilitation of German militarism. While in the post-war era German history urged political and military restraint, this was now turned on its head under Red–Green auspices. A paradigm shift, apparent in Germany since the end of the Cold War, was thus sealed in the course of the Nato war against Yugoslavia.

Undermining Democracy

This paradigm shift brought a number of long-standing problems to the surface during the Nato war. Among other things, it became clear that German democracy has been undermined. The process of forming opinions in a democratic society depends on the multiplicity and reliability of the information made available. Thus the media, as key providers of information, play a central role. This role – which had never, of course, been fully realised – was revealed during the war as severely weakened. The most worrisome development was that publications with a left/liberal tradition began deliberately to sabotage the democratic process of forming opinions.

One important example of this was provided by the short-lived discussion about the Rambouillet negotiations. In Germany, the truth about Rambouillet remained hidden – including the provision, in an Annex to the draft 'Accord', for the termination of Yugoslavia's national sovereignty: 28,000 Nato soldiers stationed across the Federal Republic of Yugoslavia with the unlimited rights of a *de facto* occupying army. Not until two weeks into the war did the bomb explode here. On 6 April the *tageszeitung* first published extracts from the military Annex B of the Rambouillet treaty, and on 12 April carried a highly charged front-page article by Andreas Zumach, titled: 'The Rambouillet Lie: What did Joschka Fischer Know?' Zumach laid out the content of the treaty, calling earlier statements by Fischer into question. In the days that followed, it was revealed that on 23 February – the day the Rambouillet talks ended – the German government had tabled a motion in the Bundestag for sending 5,500 German soldiers to support the implementation of a possible peace plan.[6] The following day, Fischer briefed the parliamentary Foreign Affairs Committee on the negotiations and appeared confident that a peaceful resolution to the conflict would soon be reached. On 25 February, the Foreign Affairs, Defence and Budget committees met and voted for the participation of the German Army in implementing a Kosovo treaty.[7] Committee members, other Bundestag representatives, and even senior officials in Fischer's Foreign Office were largely uninformed about the Rambouillet negotiations and the military Annex of the treaty.

Zumach's revelations understandably caused alarm. Several members of parliament demanded an explanation and lamented the lack of information available to them before their vote. Even Green Party defence spokesperson Angelika Beer expressed her outrage in a public letter, and declared that had she known the text of the Rambouillet treaty she would not only have voted against the use of German troops but would have recommended an alternative strategy (*tageszeitung*, 13 April). Deeply disillusioned by the machinations of the Green Foreign Minister, journalist Stefan Reinecke commented:

> This appendix is a scandal. If the Federal Government was not informed about this passage, there is no hope. What is one to think about a government that has not read the failed treaty – and so does not know the details of why it is entering into a war. If the Federal Government in fact was informed about this appendix, and accepted its terms, it was a hair-raising political mistake. (*tageszeitung*, 13 April)

These events revealed how German reporters had earlier blithely accepted official press releases instead of verifying the truth of those statements through their own research.

Naturally, the Foreign Office attempted to limit the political damage. Fischer and his associates were not, however, able to bring the discussion to an end by themselves. This was only possible with the help of political and personal cronies on important editorial boards. The *tageszeitung* itself began the process. After they had kick-started the controversy with Zumach's 12 April article, they ended it on 15 April with the publication of a shameful interview with Fischer, titled 'It is a barbaric form of fascism.' Fischer tersely rejected the accusations against him, and pontificated about the Serbs' crimes and the honourable mission of the West. This interview brought the intense discussion of the events at Rambouillet to an abrupt close. According to Zumach, Fischer used his personal relationship with the publishers of the *tageszeitung*, closely connected to his party, to convince them to stop discussing the topic and give him the final word in the form of an interview. Fischer declined to meet Zumach or the *tageszeitung*'s then Bonn correspondent Bettina Gaus. The publishers agreed to his demands, and the interview was conducted by Dieter Rulff, a correspondent with no expertise in the subject. Zumach himself was angry that his professional reputation was jeopardised, since the interview gave the impression that the *tageszeitung* was apologising to Fischer for the earlier critical article (Zumach, 1999). German foreign policy was thus rescued from its first real test, by the *tageszeitung* bowing to political pressure over a matter of immense international importance.

Toward the end of the war, reporting was focused around Fischer's diplomatic efforts to resolve the conflict. Unimpressed, Nato meanwhile escalated the bombing day after day. In this respect, German coverage deviated from that in the US and Britain. While the German media stimulated hopes for an immediate end to the air war, CNN, for example, offered a more realistic analysis. Meetings between Fischer and Russian negotiators were much reported in Germany but were often not even worth mentioning in the American media. The spotlight on Fischer's diplomacy corresponded to a change in strategy in the German Foreign Office, which was reflected immediately in media reports. In the face of growing doubts about the war, worries that Germans would tire of refugees, and concern over Germany's lack of prominence in the international diplomatic scene, the new interest in Fischer's initiatives was very welcome: he became the most popular politician in the country. With the introduction of the G8 resolution, it was reported, Fischer had achieved the near-impossible: bringing the Russians on board and laying the foundations for peace with Yugoslavia. In the course of this cheerful discussion, doubts about the war and Germany's role disappeared once again.

A month after Fischer's *tageszeitung* interview, the publishers of the social democratic-oriented weekly *Die Zeit* similarly lent support to the government concerning Rambouillet, with a spectacularly advertised multipage dossier by Gunter Hofmann, 'How Germany got into the War' (12 May). Readers were informed that the editors had spoken with the German negotiators at Rambouillet and seen the Foreign Office's secret Kosovo files. The accusations made by Zumach were dealt with indirectly and meticulously stripped of their power. A soothing summary read: 'Germany meant well, was overtaxed, and was powerless in the end.' Unsuspecting readers were not told the dossier held only highly selective facts: the Foreign Office later replied to questions from journalists that 'foreign classified documents' were not made available to *Die Zeit*. There was no such qualification, however, in *Die Zeit*. The newspaper was clearly concerned to emphasise Yugoslav responsibility for the failure of the negotiations, and to underscore the moral rectitude of the German negotiating team under Foreign Minister Fischer. Furthermore, there were good reasons for the dossier appearing on 12 May: the day before the Green Party's special congress on the war began in Bielefeld. It was feared that delegates might withdraw support for Fischer, creating problems for the coalition government. The *Zeit* dossier did Fischer and his supporters the great favour of deflecting growing criticism of the war within the party. Only the *Frankfurter Allgemeine Zeitung* commented, initially, on the dereliction of journalistic principles described above: on 14 May Andreas Platthaus noted ironically that 'the German soul escapes without harm' since 'it is being judged by the notes of only one side'. The political writer Wolfgang Michal also later criticised the *Zeit* dossier:

> A press scoop? A tour de force? Investigative journalism? Hot air. A favour. Gunter Hofmann, Bonn correspondent for *Die Zeit* let himself be recruited by the Foreign Office ... Where they ought to be called into question, the arias of justification are being piously repeated. (Michal, 1999)

This dossier, in Germany's most important weekly newspaper, which sees itself as the democratic flagship of the nation, gave the impression, like the *tageszeitung* interview, of having been ordered by the Foreign Minister. It certainly belongs among the most inglorious moments in the history of the weekly (Deichmann, 1999).

Conclusion

The appallingly low journalistic standards of the *tageszeitung* and *Die Zeit* are prime examples of important changes in the liberal German media landscape. In other times, the revelations by Zumach might have led to calls for an independent commission of inquiry, and there might have been personal consequences for Fischer. Yet in today's emotionally charged climate, other rules came to bear, and with the active collusion of both papers an important discussion of government policy was assiduously swept under the carpet. Such conduct bodes ill for future discussions of the German military in wartime. The media, in collaboration with political decision-makers, abdicated responsibility for a fundamental element of any functioning democracy – the dissemination of information. Furthermore, the media contributed to a situation in which the duty of an elected government to justify its actions, especially on such an important issue as participation in a war, became a farce. This amounts to an abandonment of democracy. For the German media, the Nato war was a new experience, and a kind of test. By any reasonable standard, it is one they failed.

Translated by Scott Abbott

Notes

1. 'Wer kritische Fragen stellt, rechtfertigt den Kriegsgegner', *M – Menschen machen Medien*, July, pp. 16–18.
2. 'Kosovo-Krieg: Presserat mahnt zu besonderer Sorgfalt' (German Press Council press release), Bonn, 19 May [available at: http://www.presserat.de].
3. *Bild*, for example, carried a front-page photo of a refugee column with the caption: 'They are driving them into a concentration camp' (1 April). In fact the refugees were crossing the border into Macedonia.

4. For a refutation of Western claims over Racak, see Johnstone (1999).

5. In autumn 1998 alternative voices had still been audible. ARD's programme *Monitor* produced several background reports on the KLA and the secret political manoeuvres of the Western powers. There were, for instance, reports on the KLA's sources of funding in international drug-trafficking, and on the German Federal Intelligence Agency's covert support for the KLA. In addition, government documents were circulated which stated that there was no systematic expulsion or persecution of ethnic Albanians in Kosovo. Such information was quickly forgotten.

6. 'Rambouillet-Abkommen für das Kosovo militärisch umsetzen helfen (Antrag)', *Deutscher Bundestag – hib*, 23 February [available at: http://www.bundestag.de].

7. 'Möglichem Militäreinsatz im Kosovo mit großer Mehrheit zugestimmt', *Deutscher Bundestag – hib*, 25 February [available at: http://www.bundestag.de].

15

Karin Trandheim Røn

'Thank you God! Thank you Norway!' Norwegian Newspapers and the Kosovo War

Espen Barth Eide of the Norwegian Institute of Foreign Policy praised the Norwegian press for their varied coverage of the Kosovo conflict, but singled out two exceptions: '*VG* with its position in favour of bombing, and *Klassekampen* with its standpoint against the war' (*Aftenposten*, 29 April). In reality, every Norwegian newspaper took a pro-war stance in its editorial column, with the exception of the leftist *Klassekampen*, which has a circulation of only 6,500. Some dissident voices were heard: the writer Jostein Gaarder, for example, dismissed the 'humanitarian' justification for bombing as 'absurd'; and *Dagbladet* ran a regular diary column written by Ljubisa Rajic, a lecturer in Norwegian language at Belgrade University. Yet the vast majority of coverage excluded oppositional and pro-Serbian perspectives as not 'politically correct'. Furthermore, the press went to great lengths to emphasise Norway's role in the conflict, taking a strongly patriotic line despite the absence of any clear national interest. It is therefore perhaps not surprising that the majority of Norwegian public opinion supported the war.

Licensed to Bomb

For Norway, the decision to go to war was taken without written statements or formal resolutions, and with almost no debate in parliament (the Storting). As Norway's biggest-circulation broadsheet, *Aftenposten*, noted (17 April):

> In the Storting there are few who wish to say anything about the decision-making process behind the military action in the Balkans. Everything has its time. The conduct of war will not be confused by unnecessary noise.

Prime Minister Kjell Magne Bondevik, the Christian Democrat leader of Norway's coalition government, waved objections aside by remarking: 'We cannot run politics as a seminar' (*Aftenposten*, 18 April). Bondevik also maintained that the parliamentary committee dealing with foreign affairs had to operate in secret in order that 'our considerations are not exposed to the Serbian regime'. Yet it seems that Norwegian parliamentary representatives were also kept in the dark. As in other Nato countries, war was explained as a response to Serb intransigence at the Rambouillet negotiations. But a poll of politicians conducted by *Klassekampen* (7 April) revealed that most of them had no idea what was in the Rambouillet Accord. 'I have not read the agreement, I have read about it', was a common reply. The decision-making process will also remain a secret from the Norwegian public, since the deliberations of the foreign affairs committee are sealed for at least 30 years. Such conduct hardly supports Nato's claim to represent 'democracy'.

Despite their ignorance regarding the stated reasons for going to war, Norwegian politicians supported it with enthusiasm. Thorbjørn Jagland, leader of the largest parliamentary party, the Social Democrats, declared that Nato should 'Bomb Milosevic out of the presidential palace' (*VG*, 9 April). There were, however, reports that senior military personnel were sceptical of Nato strategy. The Norwegian Press Agency, NTB, reported on 29 April that Erik Ianke, head of the military's Press and Information Department, had said: 'This is a war initiated by the flower-children of '68 who have now come to power. This war is politically driven, and I believe it will be prolonged.' However, Ianke withdrew his comments later the same evening, emphasising that the military would loyally obey the decisions of its political masters. Similarly, Lieutenant-Colonel Arent Arntzen, second-in-command of the air force, professed: 'For my part, I have great trust in the Norwegian government and parliament when it comes to how we are used. I feel we are in safe hands' (*VG*, 24 March).

Us and Them

For their part, journalists were frustrated that official secrecy prevented them bringing more heart-warming stories to the folks back home. *Dagbladet* (28 March), for example, called Norway the 'world champion in secrecy', arguing that if soldiers could be ordered into war, 'they should also be ordered to say something to the Norwegian people. This is a question of the relationship between the Norwegian warriors and the country they represent.' Nevertheless, reporters made a valiant effort to provide a specifically Norwegian angle on the war. On 24 March, for example, *VG* featured a front-page photo of a bomber, with the headline: 'Ready for Nato attack: Norwegian pilots at war.' Three days later the paper described the safe return of 'the first plane to go into action since the Second World War': 'Colleagues on the ground are relieved, but their families sitting at home in Norway are also paying a high price.' *Aftenposten* (29 March) quoted a pilot's comment: 'The most important thing for us is that people at home appreciate what we are doing.'

As this indicates, coverage had a strong nationalist flavour. In line with Galtung and Ruge's (1973) argument that news choices are affected by ethnocentrism, *VG* reported on 27 March that 'Norwegian children fear the war.' The irony of reporting the alleged fears of Norwegian children rather than those of the victims of Nato bombing seemed to pass the paper by. Even when *VG* did report on the fears of Serbs, it did so through the perspective of the 'last Norwegian' in Belgrade (16 April). The paper also reported on Norwegian military preparations for revenge attacks by Russia (25 March), and on the 'fear of Serbian terrorism in Norway' (26 March). By contrast, the plight of ethnic Albanians featured prominently, but even here articles often adopted a patriotic angle. 'From Hell to Norway' proclaimed *VG*'s 6 April front page, reporting that a Kosovo Albanian boy had been given a sweater emblazoned with the Norwegian flag as he boarded a Norwegian plane in Macedonia. Similarly, *Dagbladet* (8 April) took as its headline the ecstatic words of one lucky refugee named Loshi: 'Thank you God! Thank you Norway! Thank you Knut Vollebæk!' Pictures showed Loshi hugging Foreign Minister Vollebæk, begging to be allowed to come to Norway, where he had family. On TV we also saw his relatives in Trondheim anxiously following the drama. In a blaze of good publicity, Vollebæk heard the case on the spot and allowed Loshi to come. The story unfortunately turned sour the following day when *Dagbladet*'s tabloid rival *VG* revealed that Loshi's brother was serving a six-year prison sentence in Norway for heroin dealing.

There were a number of negative reports on the activities of ethnic Albanian refugees in Norway – including the story of the manager of a Norwegian refugee centre who was assaulted by one Kosovo Albanian, furious that several Serbs had helped to prepare cottages for the refugees (*VG*, 9 April). Asked to comment on the high number of Kosovo Albanians involved in serious crime in Norway, Police Chief Arne Huuse said: 'I have my opinions about this, but because of the war I don't want to publish these. I don't want to add to the tragedy for the many refugees who are coming to Norway' (*Aftenposten*, 16 April).

When the bombing started, *Aftenposten* and *VG* both interviewed Serbs living in Norway, while *Klassekampen* reminded readers that Serbia had been a Second World War ally and that thousands of Yugoslavs had been sent to Norway as prisoners of war during the Nazi occupation. Yet sympathy for Serbs was generally seen as unacceptable. On 14 April *VG* ran a front-page story about Hans, Sverre and Else, three Norwegians who had volunteered to go to Yugoslavia to act as human shields. 'We will die for the Serbs', was the paper's headline. The following day, however, Sverre pointed out he was not 'pro-Serb', and was acting out of purely humanitarian motives. Nothing further was ever heard about the project.

After the bombing, when hundreds of thousands of Serbs were fleeing Kosovo, ethnic Albanians presented them as Europe's outcasts, but their comments went unchallenged by Norwegian journalists. On 3 July, for example, *VG* ran a feature on Rexhep, a naturalised Norwegian who had gone to fight with the KLA. Rexhep argued that 'the border between Kosovo and Serbia should be Europe's new Berlin wall. The border must be tight: no trading, no cultural exchange, no contact.' Similarly, on 5 August the paper interviewed another Norwegian Kosovo Albanian, who had enlisted as a sniper with the KLA. Asked how many Serbs he had killed, he replied:

> Only God knows ... I see myself as a farmer who watches his field. I can see the weeds threatening to destroy everything but choose to use poison to save the crop. This is what I have done, picking fascistic weed from the huge, European field.

These remarks drew no questioning or comment from Norwegian journalists. One may only imagine the reaction if similar sentiments had been voiced by Serbs.

Propaganda Techniques

Following the bombing of Yugoslav television, Ljubisa Rajic wrote sarcastically in his 'Diary from Belgrade' column: 'Only one voice should be heard: Nato's. This is to support "the free flow of information"' (*Dagbladet*, 2 May). There were also a number of authoritative critics of Norwegian media coverage, including Rune Ottosen of the Oslo School of Journalism, who commented: 'It is very strange that Norwegian journalists did not show a greater degree of empathy with colleagues killed at work in the television building in Belgrade, or in the Chinese Embassy, where two of the victims were journalists' (*Dagbladet*, 23 June). The General Secretary of the Norwegian Press Union, Per Edgar Kokkvold, called Nato's attempt to silence Serbian television 'fundamental stupidity' (*Klassekampen*, 27 April), and argued that: 'In a war situation one cannot trust anybody, neither Slobodan Milosevic's propaganda-machine, nor the Nato briefings in Brussels' (*Aftenposten*, 26 March). For the most part, however, Norwegian journalists dismissed Yugoslav claims as 'Serb propaganda' and uncritically adopted Nato's definition of reality. *VG*'s 24 March explanation for the war was typical: 'We are not at war with the Yugoslav people. We are at war with President Milosevic. He, and he alone, is to blame for this.' With the exception of *Klassekampen*, all sections of the press swallowed Nato's 'humanitarian' justification for bombing. Headlines such as 'Only Nato can save them' (*VG*, 14 April) were common. Similarly, *Aftenposten*'s Website offered a guide to on-line sources, characterising *Kosova Press* as 'the Kosovo Liberation Army's press service [which] puts new information on the Net continually, with a focus on the Albanians in Kosovo'. *Serbia Info*, by contrast, was described as 'very pro-Serb'.

There was a tendency to indulge in overblown rhetoric, often on the basis of flimsy and questionable evidence. Reports would mention that stories were 'unconfirmed' but repeat them anyway, in the most lurid detail. *VG*, for example, reported on 28 March that 'Unconfirmed rumours tell of Serb paramilitary units committing the most bestial atrocities. More and more, refugees are telling of murders and rapes, and according to some, masked men have blinded and chopped fingers off women and children.' The following day, the paper reported that refugees from Pristina had seen 'several corpses' in the streets: 'This is information that cannot be confirmed, but Nato claims that the orgies of killing have run completely out of control.' 'Unconfirmed' information did not prevent the use of emotive terms such as 'orgies of killing'. *Dagbladet* adopted a similar policy, when it tried to contact several Kosovo Albanians by phone and received the answer, in Serbian and English, that the line was unavailable. 'Murdered or on the run', the paper concluded (28 March). When Nato bombed a refugee convoy near Djakovica, *Dagbladet* headlined its report 'Massacre', with the sub-headings: 'The Serbs ... Mutilated corpses ... Awful' (15 April). The newspaper explained that: 'Tonight it was still not clear if the bloodshed was caused by Nato planes which had mistaken military vehicles for those of Kosovo Albanians desperately on the run, or if Serb forces had cold-bloodedly caused these scenes of mass murder.' The choice of language prejudged the issue, and when Nato later admitted it had bombed the convoy, there were no headlines about 'massacres' or 'mass murder', only some mild criticism of Nato misinformation.

If Serb victims of the war were reported at all, they were usually represented by a number, whilst reports on ethnic Albanian victims were heart-breaking stories of individual destinies. Attacks on Serbs after the end of the bombing were presented as no more than they deserved. *Dagbladet* reported on 28 August:

> Extensive reprisals have been carried out against Serbs still left in Kosovo after the Serbian military and police withdrew in June. The reprisals have triggered a mass escape, and the UN now estimate that less than 30,000 Serbians are left in the province of around 200,000 who lived there.

Even after the war, the emphasis was on the suffering of Kosovo Albanians: *VG* wondered if they would 'take revenge' for 'the terrible atrocities committed against their people' (13 June). This time, of course, there was no outcry about 'ethnic cleansing'.

The Norwegian Red Cross wrote to the Prime Minister and the President of the Storting, raising questions about the legality and morality of the Nato bombing. Bondevik characteristically brushed his critics aside, claiming Nato's achievements were 'positive', and that the 'limited military action' had been 'worth the prize' (*Dagbladet*, 11 June). With Kosovo and the rest of Yugoslavia in ruins, thousands dead and hundreds of thousands more made homeless, one wonders just what this 'prize' might be? Such questions remain unasked: Prime Minister Bondevik enjoyed the support of the Storting during the war, and the bombing helped increase his, and his government's, popularity. Norwegian participation in a war against a country with which past relations had been only friendly raised almost no political or public discussion.

16

Nikos Raptis

The Greek 'Participation' in Kosovo

In the twentieth century the Greek people have experienced the 'influence' of various foreign powers. A fascist dictatorship by a British-supported king (1936–41) was followed by Nazi occupation (1941–44). A few weeks after the Nazis left, the British occupied the country until 1947. That year the US snatched the baton and American 'influence' in Greece began. From 1967 to 1974 this took the form of a brutal dictatorship, but US influence continues still. Perhaps this long experience explains why most Greeks could not accept Nato's 'humanitarian' justification for bombing Yugoslavia. Two surveys conducted 25 days into the air war showed that Greeks were 96 per cent to 98.6 per cent against the bombing and 1.3 per cent in favour.[1] Even highly conservative sectors of Greek society condemned the bombing. For example, 20 judges from the Supreme Administrative Court declared it was not only 'an affront to ... ethical principles ... but also to the fundamental precepts of international law'.[2] Though they did not support the regime of President Slobodan Milosevic, most Greeks opposed the bombing as immoral and thought a diplomatic solution to the crisis should have been sought.

Throughout the bombing there were almost daily demonstrations all over the country and by all kinds of people. The basic slogan shouted was the '*Foniades*' ('murderers') slogan.[3] The resistance at the port of Salonica, where the Nato forces landed on their way to Macedonia, was tremendous and effective. Almost daily the port was besieged by demonstrators who sometimes invaded the fenced-off dock area, overturning the fence or the gates. One wealthy young woman stopped her Mercedes in front of some Nato trucks on their way to Macedonia, while in another incident a young man on a motorbike used his helmet to smash the window of a Nato jeep containing two German soldiers (*Eleftherotypia*, 5 May). The policy of the Greek government and Nato was to try to sneak through the port at night when the city was asleep, but demonstrations and vigils then started to be held during the night. The resistance was not confined to Salonica: at least one convoy of Nato trucks, which had sneaked out of the port, was forced back at the Greek–Macedonian border.

Another focal point was the US embassy in Athens. Observers were left speechless when policemen marched in front of the embassy shouting the

'*Foniades*' slogan while their colleagues stood in front of the building's fortified fence, protecting the US Ambassador, Nicholas Burns (*Eleftherotypia*, 15 May). In the first of several such requests, Burns visited the Minister of Public Order shortly after the bombing started and asked that 'all measures should be taken to protect the embassy' (*Eleftherotypia*, 27 March). In April the Prefect of Hania, in Crete, declared Burns *persona non grata*, and the prefecture's General Assembly said that 'US soldiers are unwanted persons' and that 'their physical safety cannot be guaranteed' (*Eleftherotypia*, 28 April). These statements were 'strongly condemned' by the Greek government, but by 11 May Burns was reportedly 'very annoyed "with the anti-Americanism of the Greeks"' (*Eleftherotypia*, 11 May).

Two days before the bombing began President Bill Clinton expressed fears that continued 'Serbian aggression' could create a large-scale refugee crisis and destabilise the region, suggesting that 'even two [Nato] members, Greece and Turkey, could be dragged into a wider conflict' (*International Herald Tribune*, 25 March). The reaction of the Greek elite was predictably mild: Prime Minister Constantine Simitis simply said that Kosovo was 'a special case and it does not touch on the Greek-Turkish relationship' (*Eleftherotypia*, 26 March). However, the reaction of Turkey, America's local policeman, was quite in tune with Clinton's perspective. Turkish Foreign Minister Ismail Cem said: 'A war can only be possible between Turkey and Greece over Kosovo if Greece leaves Nato and begins fighting Nato, having joined ranks with the Serbs' (*Kathimerini* (English edition), 26 March). The threat was heeded by the Greek elite and the stage was set for their drama. They had to be part of the US (Nato) aggression, while trying to persuade a very angry population that they were not 'participating' in the immorality of the aggressors.

Before the Bombing

Before the bombing began the situation in Kosovo was reported almost daily in the Greek media, but this was largely based on stories from Western news agencies. Editorial opinion, which was rather infrequent, tended to be fairly even-handed. *Eleftherotypia*, for example, kept an almost equal distance from the KLA, which it considered as bearing 'a great part of the responsibility for the conflict', and from the 'atrocities by the Serbs'.[4] However, most editorials argued that ethnic Albanians were intensifying the conflict in order to 'invite' Nato into Kosovo. As Takis Diamandis put it in *Eleftherotypia* (27 February): 'It is obvious that the aim of the Albanians is ... to "coerce" an immediate intervention by the international community and especially Nato.' Fears were also frequently expressed that secession by Kosovo Albanians would destabilise the Balkans and lead to the emergence of a 'Greater Albania'.[5]

The media reflected wider suspicion of US aims in the Balkans, tending to regard the EU and Nato as mere tools of American policy. Since access to Kosovo, for geographic reasons, was easiest through Greek ports, there were ample opportunities for the population and the media to protest against the

US intervention. On 5 January *Eleftherotypia* revealed that on New Year's Eve Salonica's port authorities had confiscated 18 containers of heavy armaments, characterised as 'American Aid to Macedonia', on the Honduran freighter *Sea Pioneer*, because there were no accompanying documents for the cargo. Local organisations protested against the preparation for war in the Balkans, but the Greek government remained almost silent and the US embassy blamed the shipping agent for not furnishing the documents in time. The Ministry of Justice returned the containers to the Americans during the bombing.

The beach at Litohoro, about 90 kilometres (55 miles) south of Salonica, is the ideal place for landing craft to unload military equipment. On 23 February the Greek army installed nine sentry-box-like chemical toilets on Litohoro beach, for the Nato troops that were to land there. The toilets were of blue and white plastic, in the colours of the national flag. By night they were guarded by Greek soldiers and in the mornings were inspected by a colonel and a brigadier. For days, this absurd scene was ridiculed and protested by the media, reflecting the sentiments of the Greek public. Demonstrators painted the name '*SS Simitis*' on the side of one Nato landing craft, linking Prime Minister Simitis to the Nazi SS. Two weeks later, on 10 March, newspapers and TV carried pictures of a German Nato tank on which protestors had painted 'Yankees Go Home'. Both *Eleftherotypia* and *Kathimerini* (English edition) titled the story: 'The Germans passed by once more ...', referring to the German invasion of 1941.

Eleftherotypia's 14 March comment that what the 'international community presented at Rambouillet was an ultimatum' was typical of editorial opinion on the build-up to the conflict. As the paper further explained on 21 March, the Rambouillet terms were designed to provoke the bombing since Milosevic could not accept 'what in reality was a US occupation force'. Nato claims about 'humanitarianism' were dismissed as blatantly hypocritical. As Christos Yiannaras pointed out in *Kathimerini* (7 March): 'the Albanians of Kosovo are a "freedom movement" that should be vindicated, the Kurds ... are "terrorists"'. On 22 March *Eleftherotypia*'s correspondent in Macedonia reported an unofficial estimate that there were over 16,000 refugees in Macedonia, but journalists also reported predictions that Nato bombing would cause a huge wave of refugees and a violent reaction on the part of Serbs.[6]

During the Bombing

Greek journalists considered Western media coverage suspiciously inadequate. As *Kathimerini*'s Antonis Karkagianis noted: 'CNN broadcasts often cause anger and guffaws among all the correspondents, without exception, up there in Belgrade. The same holds for most of the "big" Western papers' (reprinted in *Eleftherotypia*, 15 April). Similarly, articles in *Eleftherotypia* on 4 and 5 May criticised the *International Herald Tribune* for not reporting Nato 'mistakes' which killed and injured civilians in Kosovo. The establishment newspaper *Vima*, owned by the Lambrakis Organisation,[7] reprinted articles from the *New York Times*, *Washington Post* and *Le Monde*, thereby simply reproducing the views of the mainstream US (and other) media. But most Greek news organisations aimed at much more comprehensive coverage. *Eleftherotypia*, for example, carried extensive material from international newswire agencies, including reports on the refugee situation which were supplemented by continuous dispatches from correspondents in Macedonia and Albania, a few hundred miles away. On 19 April, for example, the paper reported the discovery of an ethnic Albanian woman frozen in the snow of a mountain pass clutching her frozen child while trying to flee from Kosovo. At the same time, *Eleftherotypia* also gave prominence to non-mainstream views, such as a double-page article by Noam Chomsky on 1 April, and like other Greek papers it had its own correspondents in Kosovo and Serbia. There were also five Greek TV crews in Kosovo, and five to seven elsewhere in Yugoslavia.

Most journalists opposed the bombing and emphatically refused to accept Nato's 'humanitarian' justifications. *Eleftherotypia*'s 15 April front-page headline, for example, stated: 'the saviours [are] murderers'; and a 23 April report noted that Nato had 'already forgotten' the refugees, who 'live under horrible conditions in Albania'. Nevertheless, Nato had some fanatical supporters in Greece. Of the 1.3 per cent of the population that supported the bombing, the most prominent were five persons: a former Minister, a journalist, a teacher, an author (of books on Albania) and an Albanian syndicalist (representing Albanian immigrants in Greece). During the first weeks of the bombing these five were all over the TV channels, almost daily, as apologists for the Nato war. Perhaps these pundits were promoted by the TV channels in an effort to increase ratings through generating controversy, but the five were denounced in *Eleftherotypia* (5 May) by Nikos Kiaos, president of the Journalists' Union, as suspiciously supportive of the government and the US. This aggravated popular anger against the five, who suddenly disappeared from the TV screens.

There were very few other dissenting voices. The most important (and instructive) cases were those of Andreas Andrianopoulos, a former Minister in conservative governments, and Rihardos Someritis, a senior journalist with *Vima*. Andrianopoulos, a Thatcherite neoliberal, published an article headed: 'Nato's odd man out' in *The Wall Street Journal Europe* (14 April). Of course, the 'odd man out' in the 'humanitarian' enterprise was the Greek population. The anger and ridicule against Andrianopoulos was immediate, extensive, and very strong.[8] Someritis wrote in his 11 April *Vima* column: 'the great mistake of the [Nato] Alliance was not the bombing, but the much delayed start of the bombing ... and that the allies, without any reason, declared from the beginning that they excluded the possible use of ground forces'. Someritis was not only ridiculed, but was attacked for playing a suspicious role. The Communist Party newspaper, *Rizospastis*, said 'it is of little consequence whether he is a paid or unpaid agent of the USA ... he should have the ... contempt of the Greek people' (14 April).

The (not so strange) fact that in relation to the bombing, the Greek population morally was 'the odd man out' in Europe, inevitably created a negative climate against the Greeks. One easily available target was Greek TV coverage of Kosovo, which some – such as the five TV pundits discussed above – accused of being biased in favour of the Serbs and of ignoring the plight of the refugees. Elsewhere in Europe, there was even some doubt that Greek TV crews could get into Kosovo, or suspicion that their reporting must be entirely controlled by the Yugoslav authorities. However, Nicholas Vafiadis, a war correspondent for the Antenna TV Channel who was continuously in Kosovo from 15 March to 20 June, said he had 'access to many areas, especially to those that had been bombed by Nato planes, and almost anywhere else'.[9] He did not feel he had 'less freedom of movement than during the Gulf War or any other wars' he had covered. Vafiadis also described the war as 'a conspiracy of silence'. The Americans wanted to hide the fact that the bombing 'gave the upper hand' to extreme nationalists in Serbian politics, and was a 'licence to kill' the Albanians. At the same time, he argued, the bombing 'silenced moderate Albanian voices', instead favouring the KLA, and finally led 'not only to thousands of victims and refugees but to the ethnic cleansing of the Serb minority'.

Similarly, George Georgiadis, a prominent war correspondent with 20 years' experience, who covered Yugoslavia for the relatively independent Star TV Channel, said that: 'reporting from Yugoslavia presented no more or no less difficulties than those I experienced in Baghdad before the Gulf war, or in Iraq during the Gulf war, or in Israel during the Intifada, or elsewhere. Even if there was some inspection of visual material for military reasons, journalists were free to communicate to their home channels anything they wished by voice.' George Philippakis, who also reported from Kosovo for Star TV, maintained that: 'TV crews were free to go anywhere in Kosovo that they wished and to report anything they wished.' Most Greek journalists would agree with these views, including the president of the Journalists' Union, Nikos Kiaos, who visited Kosovo and Serbia. The respected Greek activist, author and psychiatrist, Kleanthis Grivas, who visited Yugoslavia from 3 April to 22 May 1999 testified that 'all the Greek journalists ... [did] their duty with self-sacrifice and with honesty'.

There was, however, a dissenting voice among Greek journalists who reported from Yugoslavia, that of Christos Telidis. Telidis was in Kosovo for about 48 hours, on the basis of which he wrote an article titled 'The Lies of a Dirty War' in *Klik* magazine (May). Telidis said he visited the offices of the Albanian paper *Koha Pitore* in Pristina, where he saw that 'everything was broken and shattered and there was blood all over the floor and the walls', which he photographed. After that, he was warned by colleagues and others that his life was in danger and decided to leave. At the border the Serbs confiscated all his material after 'turning [his] car inside out'. Teldis was also present at a meeting of what one might call the 'Someritis Team': the Eighth Pan-Hellenic Journalists' Conference, held on the island of Samothraki in early July. Predictably, the dominant view at the conference was that Greek journalists in Kosovo had been biased in favour of the Serbs. Equally predictable, however, was the reaction to such criticism, by journalists and others. Giorgos Votsis, political editor of *Eleftherotypia*, clearly had Someritis in mind when he wrote that 'war is the culmination of irrationality, which explains some isolated cases of paranoia' (24 May). Dr Maria Arvaniti-Sotiropoulou, an author and the president of the Greek chapter of International Physicians for the Prevention of Nuclear War, pointed out that if the few journalists at Samothraki did not like the relatively objective coverage available in the Greek media, 'they could always turn to CNN', whereas most Western news audiences did not have the 'luxury' of such a choice (*Eleftherotypia*, 5 August). On 13 October, the Mayor of Athens awarded the Medal of Honour and of Moral Acts to 24 Greek reporters who had covered Nato's war against Yugoslavia.

In reporting the Kosovo crisis, Greek journalists had the implicit assistance of the Greek population, who were not duped by Nato's 'humanitarianism' into classifying the Albanians as the 'good guys' and the Serbs as the 'bad guys'. Although, as expected, the Greek government complied with the wishes of the US, the 'participation' of the Greek population in the Kosovo crisis can be found in their resistance to the US/Nato intervention. As in some other cases – such as the abduction and arrest of the Kurdish leader Abdullah Ocalan – the Greek media reflected public sentiment and dared to side with the population, not with media owners or the government. In this, all sections of the Greek media did emphasise the barbarity of the bombing, but also, almost daily, presented the drama of the Albanian refugee crisis, unanimously considered to be a predictable consequence of Nato bombing. Headlines such as *Eleftherotypia*'s 'Nato Über Alles' (18 April), and 'How Many "Euros" to the "30 Pieces of Silver"?' (19 April), were like protest slogans, encapsulating the attitude of the Greek media and the Greek people.

Notes

1. *Eleftherotypia*, 19 April. All dates refer to 1999.
2. *Eleftherotypia*, 29 April. An English translation of the complete statement is available at: http://www.lbbs.org/judges.htm.
3. The colloquial Greek word '*fonias*' (plural: '*foniades*') means 'murderer', and 'specifically implies stealth and motive and premeditation and therefore full moral responsibility', according to *Webster's* 10th. The slogan '*Foniades ton laon Americanoi*' means 'The murderers of peoples (are) the Americans', the uncomfortable syntax being necessary to attain the proper (musical) rhythm when the slogan is shouted. This slogan has been heard with remarkable frequency on Greek streets since the early 1960s.
4. *Eleftherotypia*, 3 January. *Eleftherotypia* was started as a collective effort by a group of progressive journalists in the mid-1970s, during a long strike of people working in the Greek press. It is considered an independent paper.

5. See, for example, *Kathimerini* (English edition), 4 February; and *Eleftherotypia*, 21 February. *Kathimerini*, established in the early 1930s by the Vlachos family, is considered a 'serious' conservative paper and is now owned by a wealthy engineer.

6. See, for example, *Eleftherotypia*, 18 March, reporting a meeting between the Minister of Defence and the Minister of Foreign Affairs about the problems likely to be caused by Nato's war.

7. The Lambrakis family (father Demetrios and son Christos), have been the 'king makers' *par excellence* in Greece since the late 1930s.

8. See Aristidis Terzis, 'The War, the Media and the Greek People', *Utopia*, No. 34, March–April 1999, pp. 37–42.

9. This, and other quotations from journalists, are from interviews conducted by the author unless otherwise stated. Antenna, one of Greece's most important TV channels, is politically conservative, owned by a shipping magnate.

17

Philip Hammond, Lilia Nizamova and Irina Savelieva

Consensus and Conflict in the Russian Press

On the evening of 24 March 1999 Russian state television interrupted its usual programming with the announcement that Nato had started bombing Yugoslavia. The terse style of the newsflash was reminiscent of Soviet Inform-Bureau bulletins during the Great Patriotic War. Yet despite talk – both in Russia and the West – of a Third World War, or at least a new Cold War, the reaction of the Russian media was not monolithic; and neither did opposition to Nato come only from those who wished to turn back the political clock. The impact of the war on Russian political and public opinion stemmed largely from the perception that the attack on Yugoslavia had far-reaching implications for Russia's loss of international status and her own future relationship with the West. While some sections of the press embodied this reaction, however, others commented ironically on how the war had revealed Russia's 'power complex'. Descriptions ranged from neutral terms such as 'military operation' or 'Kosovo crisis', to more loaded phrases such as 'aggression against a sovereign state'. While some papers defended President Slobodan Milosevic, others condemned him.

This chapter is based on a study of eight newspapers, covering a broad political spectrum: the state-owned *Rossiyskaya Gazeta*; the Communist weeklies *Pravda Rossii* and *Zavtra*; and the privately owned *Argumenty i Fakty*, *Kommersant Daily*, *Izvestiya*, *Komsomolskaya Pravda* and *Nezavisimaya Gazeta*. The privately owned titles all favour market reform and are relatively liberal in political outlook, though there are important differences between them. Patterns of ownership and control in the Russian press are obscure, and details tend only to leak out as a result of conflicts between media owners. *Izvestiya* and *Komsomolskaya Pravda* are both controlled by the Oneksim financial group, while *Kommersant Daily* and *Nezavisimaya Gazeta* are controlled by the mogul Boris Berezovsky. Figures such as Berezovsky, or Oneksim's Vladimir Potanin, also wield considerable political influence. *Argumenty i Fakty* is one of the very few titles that appears to be genuinely independent, owned by the paper's journalists and without corporate or political sponsors.

All sections of the media opposed Nato bombing, but disagreed over several aspects of the conflict. This chapter explores three key areas of divergence: the perceived significance of the war for Russia's position in the New World Order; the notion of Slavic fellow-feeling, often seen in the West as the explanation for Russia's angry response to the Nato campaign; and the issue of propaganda. The common thread running throughout is that perceptions of the Kosovo war were coloured by domestic and international political considerations, and it is this which largely explains both the divergences in coverage and the shared opposition to Nato.

Russia in the New World Order

In a 27 March editorial, *Izvestiya* remarked that no other external political event in the history of the New Russia had so roused the population. It was that rare case when indignation grew from the bottom up, rather than being orchestrated. Why did this distant war appear so close and disturbing? As far as *Izvestiya* was concerned, it was the first time Russians had felt 'the possibility of direct aggression against our country too, for not behaving obsequiously to Nato' (30 March). Similarly, *Komsomolskaya Pravda* said uneasily: 'The operation in Kosovo is a war. A war against sovereign Yugoslavia. War in Europe. War on our doorstep' (27 March). The cooling of relations with the US/Nato prompted 'patriotic' authors to adopt a hawkish tone, but the implications of the war for international relations was a key theme of commentaries in all sections of the press. Expressions of anxiety and indignation were accompanied by ironic remarks about 'democratic' bombs, falling 'with the best intentions'. As one comment piece in *Argumenty i Fakty* put it: 'The humanitarian bomb is very likely to be the most effective weapon in the democratic arsenal of Nato. Whoever gets it will never need any other kind of help' (No. 16, April).

The destabilisation of the existing world order, Nato's pretensions as an international policeman and disregard for the UN were central issues for Russian journalists. Covering Nato's fiftieth anniversary celebrations in April, for example, Yuri Chubchenko and Boris Volkhonsky wrote in *Kommersant* that 'the Washington summit writes off hopes for the Yalta world order' (27 April). Similarly, *Izvestiya*'s political correspondent, the former diplomat Alexander Bovin, saw Kosovo as a part of a wider 'strategy for the twenty-first century', whereby Nato was seeking to 'modernise' international law (14 April). Bovin conceded that since 'the UN was created more than half a century ago', under different historical circumstances, the process of 'adaptation to the present-day world' was unavoidable and difficult. 'But', he concluded, 'Nato's arbitrariness will hardly help this.' The Soviet-era dissident Alexander Solzhenitsyn, writing in *Argumenty i Fakty* (No. 15, April), condemned Nato for 'flinging the United Nations aside, trampling its Charter'. For Solzhenitsyn, shocked that 'civilised governments' could applaud as 'a wonderful European country is annihilated', Nato action was based only on 'the law of the jungle: the powerful are absolutely right'.

The decision, at the start of the war, by Prime Minister Yevgeny Primakov – *en route* to talks in Washington about credit for Russia – to turn round in mid-air and return to Moscow, won applause from *Izvestiya*'s Alexander Bovin, who objected that 'prestige is more expensive than money': 'Primakov did right. The Americans have become too impudent ... The attack against Yugoslavia is a slap in Russia's face' (25 March). Yet Russia was in the delicate situation of, on one hand, sharply condemning Nato bombing as an unjust war, but on the other discussing the possibility of getting credit from the 'aggressors'. An opinion poll in April showed three-quarters of Russians believed the country should rely on its own potential rather than the help of Western creditors, and that the intervention of the International Monetary Fund would only do Russia harm (*Izvestiya*, 3 April).

Advocates of market reform viewed this and similar surveys with some alarm, since they revealed important internal political consequences of the Balkans war. Noting the enormous growth of 'patriotic passions' and 'anti-Nato hysteria', journalists in the privately owned media concluded that Nato action had anti-reform consequences. It could become a pretext for 'rolling back' the economic reform process, increasing state control, and lead to political and financial isolation. As *Kommersant*'s 26 March editorial put it: 'the greatness of the country is not in sabre-rattling. It is in the ability to build a democratic society and create a normal economy, providing the life its citizens deserve after 70 years of a totalitarian regime.' For their part, nationalists and Communists sought to raise opposition to Nato to the status of a uniting 'national idea'. The Communist leader Gennady Zouganov, for example, declared 'the absolute failure' of the reform process in Russia, and called for the creation, 'on the ruins of Yeltsinism', of a new patriotic climate (*Zavtra*, No. 13, March–April).

The Limits of 'Brotherhood'

The nationalistic response to Nato bombing prompted much talk of brotherhood between Russians and Serbs, based on shared Orthodox religion and a common Slavic identity. As Zouganov exclaimed: 'Brother Serbs, we are with you! Russians and Serbs are two hundred million!' (*Pravda Rossii*, No. 13, March–April). Zouganov's Communists, Vladimir Zhirinovsky's nationalist Liberal Democratic Party (LDP), and some regional and military leaders called for Russia to break off all agreements with Nato, to renounce UN sanctions against Yugoslavia (and also against Iraq, Libya and Iran), and to organise military aid to Yugoslavia. A further proposal was to send detachments of volunteers to Yugoslavia: the Communists promised 13,000 and the LDP 5,000 'true patriots', ready to fight for 'brother Serbs'. Volunteer registration, starting from the end of March, became an important part of the nationalist campaign, although ultimately its significance perhaps lay not so much in volunteers actually going to Yugoslavia, as in the personal expression of patriotism and solidarity which attending one of the registration centres represented.

Although some did not hesitate to declare Russia a Slavic state, in reality it is a multicultural, multiconfessional state, with 20 million Muslims. The so-called 'Muslim Republics', such as Tatarstan or Bashkortostan, found themselves in a delicate position. In the Republic of Tatarstan two opposing sides both declared their intention to send volunteers: LDP members willing fight for Slavs against Nato, and supporters of the Tatar Public Centre wishing to help Kosovo Muslims. This raised the possibility that volunteers from Tatarstan – all citizens of the Russian Federation – could find themselves on different sides of the barricades. Again, the war had domestic political implications: the potential danger of inter-ethnic and inter-confessional conflict in Russia. For this reason, Tatarstan's President and State Council ruled no volunteers from Tatarstan should go to Yugoslavia, and avoided taking sides between Russian and Tatar volunteers by describing them all as mercenaries who would pose a threat to social order when they returned home (*Argumenty i Fakty*, No. 15, April, Regional Supplement). The Russian federal authorities took a similar line, and the Ministry of Justice issued an official warning against organising illegal military groups and recruiting mercenaries (*Kommersant*, 14 April).

The liberal press took a much cooler view of the volunteers issue. Interestingly, *Argumenty i Fakty* understood 'brotherhood' not as a question of blood or shared religion, for example, but as a political and ideological relationship rooted in the communist past and in some cases preserved in the present. The paper included Poles, Hungarians, Bulgarians, Czechs and Slovaks as 'former brother-Slavs', since all had been allies of the USSR (No. 13, March). *Nezavisimaya Gazeta* said it did not make sense to speak of Slavic brotherhood, since it does not really exist. Instead, policy should be a matter of an 'utterly concrete and absolutely pragmatic geo-political decision, dictated ... by the strategic and historical national interests of Russia' (25 March). On 16 April the State Duma adopted a resolution 'On the Federal Republic of Yugoslavia joining the Union of Byelorussia and Russia', with 293 deputies voting for and 54 against. Public opinion, however, seemed to take the opposite view, with one survey indicating that 72 per cent thought the situation in Russia would become worse or would not change if Yugoslavia joined the union (*Kommersant*, 13 April). Again, liberal papers took a wary stance. *Izvestiya*'s Alexander Sadchikov, for example, dismissed the initiative as mere posturing, and warned that: 'the consequences of this process which seems inoffensive at first glance could be very sudden' (17 April).

While Communists and nationalists supported the Yugoslav government, liberal writers tended to distinguish between Milosevic's regime and ordinary Serbs who found themselves under Nato bombing. As noted above, Milosevic was roundly condemned in the liberal media, *Kommersant*'s Maria Golovanivskaya calling him the 'Saddam of Yugoslavia' and an 'inveterate communist-nationalist' (15 April). Compassion for the Serb people, and the charm of being loved just for being Russian – a long-forgotten feeling – did not outweigh a rational sense of self-preservation and a desire to understand what was really happening. Boris Muradov and Igor Popov, who reported from Belgrade for *Argumenty i Fakty*, wrote:

> The most important thing we understood after staying a week in Yugoslavia is that a very strange war is going on there ... [Both Yugoslavia and Nato] admit the possibility of the Balkan conflict developing into a Third World War and are ready to fling themselves into its whirlpool. Colossal slaughter that may wipe half of Europe off the face of the earth does not frighten them. (No. 14, April)

In an earlier article they noted how 'ordinary Belgrade citizens almost do not notice' the war, just as the conflict in Chechnya had little impact on 'the everyday life of calm and satisfied Moscow' (No. 13, March). Memories of Afghanistan and Chechnya consolidated the idea that it would be impossible for Russia to intervene militarily. In the liberal press, it was proposed that 'brother Serbs' should receive humanitarian, but not military, aid. Liberal journalists also paid more attention to the plight of Kosovo Albanian refugees, though, as discussed below, they often criticised the one-sided coverage of Western media. Over time the tone of coverage shifted, and by mid-April there were more reports on the refugees and less use of terms such as 'Albanian separatists' and 'Muslim guerrillas'. Most of the Russian celebrities replying to a questionnaire in *Kommersant* which asked 'Who do we need to help?', gave answers such as: 'all Kosovo refugees', or 'all who feel bad here and there' (7 April).

The Propaganda War and the Russian Media

The debate within the Russian media about the proper response to the war led to contradictions, inconsistencies and mutual recriminations. Much of the discussion was focused around Western reporting and Nato propaganda. While the Western media presented ethnic Albanian refugees as obvious victims of Serb atrocities and 'ethnic cleansing', describing the exodus as a 'humanitarian catastrophe', Russian journalists pointed out that people were fleeing from Nato bombing, and that air raids supposedly designed to protect the Kosovo Albanians had only made their situation worse. Genrikh Trofimenko wrote in *Zavtra* (No. 15, April) that Nato 'all the time lie, and lie, and lie, accusing Milosevic of every mortal sin and denying the fact that the American bombing of Serbia itself led to the colossal humanitarian catastrophe in Kosovo'. Even those liberal journalists who acknowledged the suffering of Kosovo Albanians, also recognised that this was being manipulated by Nato. Muradov and Popov, for instance, noted that:

Western TV channels have been showing Kosovo refugees every day. It is impossible not to feel for worn out old men, women, mothers with babes in arms ... Nevertheless, the tragic fate of Albanian refugees is just half the truth. Western journalists do not show Serb refugees at all. (*Argumenty i Fakty*, No. 19, May)

Similarly, *Komsomolskaya Pravda*'s 10 April editorial remarked that the 'propagandistic cover of the bombings' had served its purpose, producing TV reports about Albanian refugees from Kosovo, while Vladimir Katin, writing in *Nezavisimaya Gazeta*, accused Nato of 'frantically manipulating public opinion and juggling with the facts' (14 April).

The Russian press argued the Western media were fighting a propaganda war on the side of their own governments, targeting domestic public opinion and Yugoslavia itself. Western journalists were censured by their Russian counterparts for their one-sided reporting, and Nato's conduct of a 'ruthless' propaganda war was frequently criticised (for example, *Rossiyskaya Gazeta*, 26 March; *Komsomolskaya Pravda*, 31 March). Former Defence Minister General Igor Rodionov, writing in *Komsomolskaya Pravda* (14 April), argued that:

> The Third World War has already raged on our planet for a very long time. It started when the USA lost its monopoly on nuclear weapons, and the name for that fight is a propaganda war. The average mind does not grasp the character of a propaganda war, although its goals are the same as in normal wars.

It was said that real information reached Western TV screens only with great difficulty. Nato losses were concealed, for example, so that 'Washington learnt about the shot down F-117 when the whole world had already viewed the broken wings and burning fuselage of the stealth aircraft on Yugoslav TV' (*Komsomolskaya Pravda*, 3 April). At the same time, however, the privately owned press also published opinions outside the mainstream – which in the Communist media would have been seen as pro-Nato views – including some praise for Western reporting. In *Izvestiya*, for example, Andrei Kolesnikov argued that: 'Western newspapers are trying to understand events. They publish different, sometimes diametrically-opposed opinions' (17 April). Similarly, Vladimir Kozlovsky noted in *Argumenty i Fakty* (No. 16, April): 'Serbian representatives are willingly invited onto American TV, and every day one channel broadcasts ... news from Belgrade, where Nato is branded a "fascist organization" and its bombs and aircraft are called no less than "villainous".'

Kozlovsky went on to note that 'ponderous Yugoslav propaganda is completely neutralised by reports about Serbian atrocities and the suffering of refugees from Kosovo'. However, Yugoslav propaganda proved a divisive issue among Russian journalists. Communist papers believed the Serbs won the information war. In *Zavtra* (No. 16, April), for example, Vladislav Shurygin and Denis Tukmakov interpreted the demonisation of Milosevic and appeals by Nato leaders to the Serbian people as tacit acknowledgement that Nato was losing the propaganda war, and Mikhail Bouyny hailed the Internet as an 'effective weapon of struggle against liberals, Atlanticism and Americanism', since it was relatively free from Western control (*Zavtra*, No. 14, April).

Another frequent argument was that Belgrade owed its propaganda success to strict control of the media. In their article quoted above, Shurygin and Tukmakov wrote approvingly of how the expulsion of many Western journalists meant 'the Americans lost their faithful "fifth column"', and welcomed the lack of US TV footage from Yugoslavia since this could no longer be 'prepared, perverted, [and] flavoured with misinformation' before being broadcast. In *Pravda Rossii* (No. 13, March–April), Zouganov tried to turn the popular anti-Americanism provoked by the bombings into domestic political capital, denouncing the 'pro-American group' and 'party of treachery' which govern Russia; while in *Zavtra* (No. 15, April) Genrikh Trofimenko condemned the 'pro-American Russian mass media', suggesting 'almost all of them are pro-American here'. Such arguments were often underpinned by conspiracy theories, sometimes with anti-Semitic overtones. Vladislav Smolentsev (*Zavtra*, No 14, April) argued that it was even mistaken to allow Russian journalists into Serbia since 'these "Russians" work for the West'. Clearly, such writers favoured similarly censorious policies in Russia, and both in the press and in the State Duma Communists argued that the NTV, ORT and RTR television channels were too pro-Nato – a suggestion rebutted by broadcasters.

The arguments of papers such as *Pravda Rossii* and *Zavtra* posed a challenge to the reform-oriented media. Whilst conceding that 'the Communists and their allies have gained powerful and forcible arguments against the democrats' pro-Western orientation', *Komsomolskaya Pravda*'s Yevgeny Anisimov condemned the 'patriotic hysteria' whipped up by the nationalist press (6 April). However, although liberal papers disagreed with the Communists' positive assessment of Belgrade's authoritarian media policy, they interpreted this as the reason Yugoslavia was losing the propaganda war. Whilst they agreed the Western media were biased, liberal commentators noted regretfully that, as in the Croatian and Bosnian conflicts, Serbian propaganda remained ineffective, uninventive, and saturated with ideological clichés. *Izvestiya*, for example, blamed Milosevic, saying he behaved like an 'ordinary apparatchik', able only 'to forbid, to deport, to close down' (27 March). Russian journalists frequently bemoaned the way the Yugoslav authorities missed easy opportunities to correct the largely black-and-white picture drawn by the Western media. 'We can't see the Serbs' grief because the Serbian leadership do not want to show it', complained Igor Kots in *Komsomolskaya Pravda* (6 April).

Reactions to Nato's 23 April attack on the Belgrade TV building provided a microcosm of the debate within the Russian political class and media. When the Communist chairman of the State Duma proposed that Russia should fund the rebuilding work, *Kommersant* (19 May) warned that such a move would be seen as supporting the Milosevic regime and undermining the Serbian opposition. Yet *Izvestiya* saw the attack as the beginning of a 'war without rules', deliberately targeting the civilian population (24 April). Despite complaints from some journalists about the professional difficulties they faced in reporting from Yugoslavia, the TV station bombing was severely condemned by all sections of the Russian media. And despite the way that domestic political considerations coloured the response of different newspapers to the war, all generally agreed with the fact that Western reporting on Kosovo was incomplete, biased and inadequate.

Conclusion

International events sometimes afford an insight into a country's internal situation, revealing divisions and clarifying problems which had been little discussed. The Kosovo war acted as a prism, refracting domestic political views and prompting a re-evaluation of Russia's role in the world. Virtually all the Russian media were concerned by the role assigned to Russia in the conflict – or more precisely, the lack of a role. As seen from Russia, there were two main stages to the conflict: 'without Russia's participation' and 'with Russia's presence'. This was reflected in media coverage, which at the start of the crisis featured sharp disapproval of 'Nato aggression' and support for 'sovereign Yugoslavia'. Yet after the 'role of Russia' was recognised, most newspapers adopted a more neutral tone, carrying more articles about the Albanian refugees and the excesses of the Milosevic regime, and fewer reports on 'brother Serbs'.

The media's evaluation of Moscow's participation in brokering a peace deal was undoubtedly positive. Vladimir Lapsky, writing in *Rossiyskaya Gazeta* (1 April), observed with satisfaction that 'the intermediary role of Russia was highly appreciated in the world'; and *Izvestiya*'s Taras Lariokhin enthused that 'Russia really has become a participant in the peace-making process' (8 May). Nonetheless, curtseys from the West were also viewed more cynically, as an attempt to solve a complicated and difficult problem 'by Russian hands'. The rapprochement with the West facilitated by Russia's diplomatic role perhaps helped to heal the sense of wounded national pride felt by both the authorities and the population. The West followed its own goals, but did not mind if Russia helped Nato to shed its uncomfortable image as an aggressor and to repair what Primakov called its 'tragic mistake' in the Balkans.

18

India

HOW INDIA SEES THROUGH WESTERN REPORTS
Raju G.C. Thomas

Until the *Times of India* sent one of its senior journalists, Siddharth Varadarajan, to Yugoslavia while it was under attack by Nato, the Indian media and its attentive public saw events in Yugoslavia through the eyes of the Western media. India's main sources of information about the crisis were Agence France Presse (AFP), Reuters, Associated Press (AP), CNN, BBC, Sky News, and *Time* and *Newsweek* magazines. Most of the leading Indian newspapers, such as the *Times of India*, *Hindustan Times*, the *Hindu*, *Indian Express* and the *Statesman* subscribe to AFP, AP and Reuters Wire Services, often amalgamating them together with the by-line, 'From the Wire Services'. India's own two newswire services, the Press Trust of India (PTI) and the United News of India (UNI), have no representation in the Yugoslav crisis area, or indeed, in most parts of the world. They serve essentially as news sources on India for the rest of the world.[1]

International television networks such as CNN, BBC and Sky News are now standard channels available on Indian TV. Likewise, BBC Radio, Voice of America and Sky Radio are easily accessible in India. However, before economic liberalisation and open markets were introduced in 1991, the only television available to the Indian public was the state owned *Doordarshan*, and its radio counterparts, All India Radio (in English) and *Akashvani* (in Hindi). *Doordarshan* and All India Radio are the Indian equivalents of BBC television and radio. Liberalisation has brought in cable television with several foreign channels, including Pakistan Television (PTV), and domestic private channels. The American news magazines *Time* and *Newsweek* are available at most newsstands in the major Indian cities but they are overwhelmed by a flood of Indian counterparts that include *India Today* (an independent magazine), *Frontline* and *Sunday*. *The International Herald Tribune* that essentially reproduces reports and editorials from the *New York Times*, *Washington Post* and the *Los Angeles Times*, is available in select book and magazine stores in Delhi, Bombay, Madras, Calcutta and Bangalore.

Under these circumstances, where the information flow is mainly from Western media sources, the perspective of the Indian press on the Yugoslav crisis ought not to be different from that projected in the United States. However, analysis and assessments by the Indian media based on these Western reports projected mainly, though not exclusively, an opposing viewpoint of the crisis. An Indian editorial during Nato's attack even claimed that the real victims (the Serbs) were being portrayed as the villains, and the real villains (Nato and the US in particular) were being projected as honest interventionists.

The Clinton administration's spokesman, David Leavy, attributed this phenomenon to the fact that 'President Milosevic has an extensive propaganda machine. We've worked very hard to try to counteract that propaganda machine' (AP, 8 August 1999). The White House spokesman claimed that Kosovo was the best recent example of how the United States needs to fight a propaganda war in concert with military strikes. Accordingly, a new International Public Information Agency has been set up to prevent (presumably) countries like India from coming to conclusions that support the Serbian point of view. Likewise in Britain, Downing Street was locked in an extraordinary battle with the British media on the issue of fair reporting. Prime Minister Tony Blair's spokesman, Alastair Campbell, accused British journalists of being duped by the Serb 'lie machine' and of being too lazy to cover the Kosovo conflict properly (*The Times* (London), 10 July 1999).

Given eight years of international sanctions on Serbia and Serbs, and the bankruptcy caused by war and economic sanctions, clearly this massive and well-financed worldwide propaganda machinery of President Milosevic – as alleged by the Clinton and Blair governments – could not possibly exist. On the contrary, in India and elsewhere in Asia and Africa, the well-financed and well-equipped Western propaganda machine was the only source of information through much of the crisis. The American politicians' and media's ability to 'spin' the facts are well-known to the sceptical and critical Indian media. The United States is not just the sole superpower, but also deploys the most powerful media and public relations firms, and the most well-funded overseas governmental operations. Its ability to portray the American version of events in the former Yugoslavia is not in doubt, especially in a situation where the propaganda machinery of the demonic Serbian 'enemy' is non-existent.

Retired Vice-Admiral Ashok Chopra wrote in 1998 that it was plain to the enlightened Indian elite interested in these events, that the reports on CNN and BBC were nothing more than selective and manipulated propaganda, with the same tragic scenes being recycled when presenting new events of Serbian atrocities (1998:475). However, retired Major-General Vinod Saighal observed that Indian foreign and security policies were always conditioned by the need to avoid 'annoying' the United States, China and the Muslim world, and especially the Arab world (1998:456–7). The Indian media may also be affected by this self-limitation.

M.D. Nalapat, a senior editor at the *Times of India*, referred to the dishonesty underlying the reporting during Vietnam (4 May 1999):

> There were dozens of My Lais in Vietnam, but no honest correspondent to cover it. Watching the likes of Christiane Amanpour and her BBC counterparts, one is reminded of Stalin's USSR, when lies were first believed thoroughly and then uttered. To these 'unbiased' commentators, there is no connection between the Nato bombing and the refugee floods. There is no harm in killing Serbian media persons, or in bombing away at a country in a manner reminiscent of Hitler's war against Republican Spain in the 1930s.

The reaction of the mainstream Indian English-language press that includes the *Times of India*, the *Economic Times*, the *Hindu*, the *Hindustan Times*, *Indian Express*, *Statesman*, the *Pioneer*, the *Telegraph* and *Asian Age*, has been one of condemnation of Western actions against the remnant Yugoslavia, but there has sometimes been a withholding response, or even a mild endorsement of Western policy to avoid 'annoying' the US. One senior Indian journalist informed me in November 1998 that from a pragmatic perspective, Western attention on Serbia because of its repressive measures in Bosnia and Kosovo, diverted attention from India's problems in Kashmir, Punjab and elsewhere. Following economic liberalisation in India and the collapse of the Soviet Union, India's economic dependence on the US had also increased several fold. More than half of India's trade and investments are with the US, whereas India accounts for less than 3 per cent of US external trade and investments. Thus, whether conscious or subconscious, the Indian media's condemnation of US policies, as also that of the Ministry of External Affairs, has been modified by pragmatism, a dilemma that is not unique to India alone.

As regards the relevance and balance of the Indian media's coverage, foreign press reports on the Yugoslav crises in its various stages were rarely front page news in Indian newspapers, or headline news on Indian TV networks. The exception might have been the initial phase of the 78-day Nato assault from 24 March to 10 June. However, with the eruption of the 'Kargil' crisis in Kashmir from mid-May 1999 onwards (where Pakistan forces infiltrated and captured a strategic sector on the Indian side of the Line of Control in Kashmir), these foreign news reports declined, and the anti-Western editorials and op-ed pieces on Nato's military actions against Serbia almost disappeared. Beyond the need to focus on an issue of vital Indian national security interest, the Clinton and Blair government's support for the Indian position on the Kargil crisis may have also contributed to the change.

While the Indian government's and media's reactions to Western political and military policies against Serbia were mainly in opposition, it is important to note that *these protests and condemnations were completely ignored in the Western and especially American media*. While some attention was given to Russian and Chinese opposition to Nato actions, official and unofficial Indian views did not count as far as the US government was concerned, and never happened as far as the American media was concerned.

How Representative is the English-Language Press?

The English-language press reaches perhaps 2 per cent of the Indian population of nearly one billion, and therefore the question could be raised as to how representative of the general Indian public are these Indian press analyses. Note that 2 per cent of India constitutes 20 million readers, which is a significant absolute number when compared to the number of newspaper readers in Britain or France. About 40 per cent of the Indian population is illiterate. More significantly, however, as far as the print media are concerned, about 60 per cent are literate which translates into some 600 million people. The measure of literacy in India is based on whether a person can read and understand a simple newspaper. This does not, of course, mean that most of them care to read newspapers, especially in the villages where 70 per cent of the Indian population resides.

I have not followed the press in the several regional languages of India, but my assumption is that they do not have the resources to translate all Western reports on the Yugoslav situation, unlike the English-language press that simply reprint them. Much of the billion literate and illiterate Indian population's source of information in the regional languages are local and national TV and radio news reports. These are provided by the government-owned national network stations of *Doordarshan* television and *Akashvani* radio that may occasionally re-transmit footage, or re-broadcast news from BBC TV and radio, and CNN television news, with appropriate commentaries in the Indian languages alongside. These Indian commentaries, if any, most likely are translations of BBC and CNN reports.

It is possible that the Urdu-language press in India (the language of north-central Indian Muslims) showed greater interest in the plight of Bosnian and Albanian Muslims and Nato's use of massive force against the Serbs. Their reactions may be similar to that of the government and people of Pakistan and Bangladesh who supported Nato's attack on Serbia. When the Russian Federation introduced a draft resolution in the UN Commission on Human Rights on 23 April to stop Nato's attack, it was supported by China, India and Sri Lanka. Pakistan and Bangladesh joined the US to oppose the end of Nato attacks. However, the largest Muslim state in the world, Indonesia, abstained.[2] In general, however, the average Indian has either rejected or shown no interest in the Western version of the crisis in Europe.

Although reaching between 1 and 2 per cent of the Indian readership, the English-language press in India is disproportionately more powerful than the much larger, disparate and varied vernacular press that reaches the ethnically diverse masses speaking some 35 different main languages. The English-language media have a nation-wide readership, with regional editions, all of which links the Indian elite and middle classes speaking a variety of regional languages into a common national public audience. This audience takes a greater interest in events in the rest of the world and has considerable political clout in the capital and main cities of India. English remains the main link language in India and has become even more important with the enormous growth of the computer software industry in India. The views of the English-speaking elites matter more in international issues and foreign policy-making than the regional vernacular press, which are more focused on domestic and local news. Besides, most of the regional language newspapers and magazines are owned by the main English-language presses.

Thus, the Indian situation was rather unusual. Western information was disseminated in India about events in Yugoslavia, and then contradicted by Indian editorials, commentaries, op-eds, and letters to the editor. Unlike the United States, where the media and government appeared as unabashed collaborators and conspirators feeding and supporting each other in their virulent anti-Serbian views and official policy, there was no collusion or complicity between the media and the government in India, despite seeing eye-to-eye in opposing Western policy in the former Yugoslavia. Official and unofficial Indian assessments and proclamations of the crisis in Yugoslavia coincided, especially during Nato's assault from 24 March to 10 June. Condemnations of Nato's 'unprovoked aggression' – the standard term used in India to describe what the Western media and governments called 'humanitarian intervention' – were widespread.

The Nature of Indian Media Reports and Analyses

During Nato's assault on Serbia over Kosovo, Indian media criticisms revolved around the following issues: (a) the sources and causes of the conflict; (b) violations of international law and the UN Charter; (c) consequences for the future of the United Nations; (d) the rationale for the existence of Nato itself; (e) the ineffectiveness and failure of Russia to protect Serbia; (f) the sheer physical, human and ecological destruction inflicted on a small country by an unopposed massive military machine; and (g) the lessons for India and the rest of the world.

There were five categories of reports carried by the Indian press: (1) condemnations of Nato's actions by the current and previous Indian prime ministers, Atal Beharee Vajpayee of the Bharatiya Janata Party, and Inder Kumar Gujral of the United Front, and by the current Defence Minister George Fernandes, a Socialist Party member of the BJP coalition government;

(2) severely critical opinion articles by former Foreign and Defence Secretaries and retired high-ranking officers of the Indian military; (3) opinion columns by the newspapers' columnists and op-ed contributors; (4) editorials; and (5) letters to the editor. Although reports of the war in Yugoslavia coming from Western sources provided a radically different perspective, the Indian media were near unanimous in rejecting Western accounts and in denouncing Western policies. A few extracts from the flood of anti-Nato and usually pro-Serb reports from the Indian press are provided below.

T.V. Rajeshwar stated the basic problem unambiguously in the *Hindustan Times* on 1 May 1999: 'The war unleashed by the North Atlantic Treaty Organisation (Nato) on the sovereign nation of Serbia on March 24 was a clear case of aggression.' Former Foreign Secretary of India, A.P. Venkateswaran, wrote:

> The aerial attacks launched by Nato against Yugoslavia once again establishes the truth of the axiom, 'Power tends to corrupt, and absolute power tends to corrupt absolutely.' There is no legal sanction whatsoever for this unilateral action by Nato carried out at the behest of the US, following the failure of the talks on Kosovo. (*Hindustan Times*, 1 April)

Another former Foreign Secretary of India, Mukchund Dubey, referred to the 'Nato Juggernaut', condemning its unmitigated act of aggression against Serbia, and declared that Nato's actions had justified India's decision to acquire a strong nuclear deterrent to avoid Western nuclear monopoly and Western pressures during times of crisis that affect the Indian national interest.[3] The permanent representative of India to the UN Security Council declared on 24 March that Nato's attack on Yugoslavia was in violation of Article 53 of the UN Charter and was not authorised by the Council, acting under Chapter VII.

> What Nato has tried to do is to intimidate a government through the threat of attack, and now through direct and unprovoked aggression, to accept foreign military forces on its territory ... There are several traditional descriptions for this kind of coercion; peacekeeping is not one of them.[4]

K. Subrahmanyam's views are perhaps the most incisive and relevant since he is a former Secretary for Defence Production and Director of the Institute for Defence Studies and Analysis, the leading security studies scholar in India, the Foreign Editor of the *Economic Times*, and currently the Chairman of India's National Security Advisory Board. He wrote a series of articles in the *Times of India* analysing the strategic consequences of Nato's actions for the rest of the world and for India in particular. In his 3 May article, entitled 'Clear and Present Danger: US Path to Unipolar Hegemony', Subrahmanyam observed that Nato's illegal attack on a sovereign state further justified India's decision to acquire a nuclear deterrent and declared that 'it must be clear to everyone that the present international security environment is the worst since the end of World War II'.[5] According to Subrahmanyam:

> [The] UN has been rendered redundant since there is no balance of power in the world and the entire industrial world, barring a ramshackle Russia, is under US overlordship. If this is not a dangerous international security environment, what is? It is not accidental that the only countries voicing strong protests against the bombing in Yugoslavia happen to be Russia, China and India, all nuclear weapon powers.

Perhaps the most significant assessments of the broader Indian media perspective were provided by Siddharth Varadarajan, one of the senior editors of the *Times of India* (who later became the only Indian correspondent reporting out of Belgrade during Nato attacks); and Prem Shankar Jha, the former editor of the *Economic Times* and later the *Hindustan Times*. Their views conformed with the official statements of the Indian Prime Minister and Defence Minister, A.B. Vajpayee and George Fernandes, and India's representative at the UN. In one of his articles, entitled 'Nato on a Dangerous and Illegal Course' (29 March), Varadarajan observed that Nato had revealed itself as 'an aggressive military alliance dedicated to the projection and promotion of US power in Europe, and even beyond'. He noted the indisputable nature of Nato's aggression on a sovereign state that had not attacked any other state, let alone a Nato member. Yugoslavia, a one time member of the Non-Aligned Movement, was made to pay a very heavy price for defying Washington and refusing to become part of the US-dominated post-Cold War security framework. According to Varadarajan, the Security Council had not authorised the attack.

> Its last major resolution on the Kosovo crisis was 1199, passed in September 1998 with one abstention (China). That resolution called on the Yugoslav government to end its offensive against Kosovar Albanian militants but did not sanction the use of force; indeed, it explicitly stated that the Security Council would meet again to decide what steps to take in the event of Yugoslav non-compliance.

However, knowing that Russia and China would veto any resolution authorising force, the US then decided to bypass the Security Council to proceed with the bombing.

Prem Shankar Jha published a series of four articles in the *Hindustan Times* at the end of April 1999. These articles were then consolidated into a single article published in the journal *World Affairs* (New Delhi). Jha traced the origins of the struggle to the KLA which the State Department had previously branded a terrorist organisation. He pointed out that migrations and divergent population growth rates may change the composition of ethnic distribution but this does not give new regional majorities the right to secede. He pointed out that 'despite strict immigration controls, in the past four decades, Mexicans and other Hispanics have drastically altered the population composition of the southern states of the US, and are close to forming a majority in California'. He then went to on declare that Nato's bombing of Serbia was 'unprecedented': 'Even Hitler, when he decided to invade Poland, claimed that Poland had attacked Germany first' (Jha, 1999:112).

A similar view was expressed by Thomas Abraham, a columnist of the *Hindu*, reporting from London in his article, 'Is the Nato attack justified?' (28 March). The strategic and military correspondent of the *Hindu*, C. Raja Mohan, in an article on 6 April entitled 'Kosovo: The Liberal's War', asked:

> Where have all the Western liberals gone? Nearly two weeks into Nato's war against Serbia, there is barely a whimper of protest in either Europe or North America. But then you can't expect Western peaceniks to protest against a war they themselves are waging.

In 1991, the Democrats had threatened to refuse support for President George Bush's war against Saddam Hussein's Iraq. 'But now it is a Democrat in the White House who is pursuing an open-ended war in the Balkans.' A similar switch from peaceniks into warmongers prevailed in Britain under the New Labour Prime Minister, Tony Blair, the most virulent hawk on Kosovo; and also among liberals in Germany, 'where the ruling alliance of Social Democrats and pacifist Greens has ordered the German bombers into combat for the first time since the end of Second World War'.

The following are some of the main points raised in the editorials of India's three leading newspapers, the *Times of India*, the *Hindu*, and the *Hindustan Times*.

1. A dangerous new American-dominated world has come about at the turn of this century, with the American development of new missile defence systems, the legitimisation of wars of intervention abroad on self-determined moral grounds, and the ability to fight them with very few or no casualties to Americans because of the new high-tech weapon systems (see *Times of India*, editorial, 3 April).
2. The United Nations was in danger of going the way of the League of Nations. 'The decline of the League of Nations started with its condoning the aggression of Japan against China, and that of Italy against Ethiopia.' When the Security Council voted down the Russian resolution demanding cessation of Nato's aerial aggression against Yugoslavia by a vote of twelve to three, it was an indication that this body had lost its political and moral authority (*Times of India*, editorial, 3 April). A senior editor of the *Times of India*, M.D. Nalapat, referred to

Nato as 'the hijackers of the United Nations', and the UN Secretary General as a mere 'deputy undersecretary of State' under Madeleine Albright (4 May).

3. The inability of Russia, China and the rest of the world, to counter US dominance and the unrestrained use of massive conventional force by Nato could provoke other states who are threatened in similar fashion to acquire a nuclear deterrent capability, and if that is not possible, to adopt the strategy of terrorism (*Times of India*, 4 May).

4. There were several endorsements of Yevgeny Primakov's call for a counter-alliance among Russia, China and India. According to Nalapat (*Times of India*, 4 May):

> Nato's new policy of intervention anywhere, has all the ingredients for a new world war, one that will pit Nato against Russia, China and India ... The *Panchatantra* says that there can only be friendship between equals. This implies that either the Nato countries accept India, China and Russia as equals, or they are in danger of being treated in a way that will make them enemies. Kosovo has shown the need for Indian power, and the need for diplomacy that can bring the three giants of Asia together, not to begin a world war but to stop the Nato planners from igniting one with their racist arrogance.

> Endorsing the prospect of a Moscow–Beijing–New Delhi trilateral security relationship, an editorial in the *Hindustan Times* (31 May), noted that: 'Nato's ruthless action in Yugoslavia may bring India and Russia (and possibly China) even closer together as they realise the danger of a world with only one superpower.' India should consider raising the level of the Indo-Russian relationship 'to the level of what the Russian Defence Minister recently called "real strategic partnership"'.

5. Nato's indiscriminate bombing of civilian and industrial sites, especially chemical plants, amounted to ecocide and therefore long-term fatal health hazards for the entire civilian population of Yugoslavia (*Times of India*, editorial, 21 April).

6. The new strategic concept and 'hegemonic intent' adopted during Nato's fiftieth anniversary was cause for concern. According to one *Times of India* editorial (29 April):

> The callousness displayed towards civilian lives in Yugoslavia, the Orwellian language used to justify this, and the deliberate bombing of Serbian TV stations in an attempt to censor the broadcast of scenes of destruction caused by 'smart bombs' also raise disturbing questions about the robustness of the organisation's democratic credentials ... If Nato's aggression against Yugoslavia is allowed to prevail, the alliance will eventually turn its destructive attention to

other 'out of area' operations ... The Kosovo adventure shows how wrong the world was to be optimistic about Nato reforming itself. Irrationality and hubris continue to dominate the Nato mindset.

7. US and Nato actions against Yugoslavia had undermined the effectiveness and credibility of international law (*Times of India*, editorial, 5 June).
8. Nato's decision to launch the bombing by bypassing the UN had caused the catastrophe it was supposed to prevent. 'Innocent civilians are paying for the gross miscalculation of the Western military alliance as the war being waged in the Balkans with the ostensible purpose of saving them goes into a second fortnight' (*Hindu*, editorial, 10 April).
9. The war conducted by Nato was futile and the claim that the war was being conducted to prevent an even greater tragedy was unconvincing. A lengthy commentary in the *Hindustan Times* (15 June) declared that the 'participation in a human rights mission on foreign soil not conducted at the negotiation table but by air strikes and media blitzes', is not sufficient argument to counteract ethnic cleansing:

> The result is the destruction of lifelines which have so far served the 'cleaners' and those to be swept out. Is the life of a Kosovar worth more than that of a Serb? Is one destruction a suitable and justifiable means to mitigate another? Will this attitude of the ends justifying the means not create a chain-reaction of hate?

10. The use of Nato air power where no American or Western lives or interests were at stake had ushered in an era of 'overlording from above', blackmailing entire nations into 'subjugation', and a new form of terrorism based on a 'demonstration of raw bullying power' (*Hindustan Times*, 15 June).

An Explanation of the Indian Media's Reaction

The explanation for the adverse Indian media (and official Indian government) reaction against Western policies and Nato's actions is quite simple. India is the former Yugoslavia writ large. It is a country professing seven major religions, where some 35 major languages are spoken of which 18 (including English) are recognised official languages. India is divided by five major caste groups, over 3,000 subcastes, and several tribal groups along its fringes. Perhaps it could be argued that more than 50 years of democratic liberalism and a centuries-old tradition of indigenous cultural tolerance may make such a violent unravelling effect less likely in India. However, the bloody carving out of Pakistan from India in 1947, and the separation of Bangladesh from Pakistan in 1971, that led to nearly a million deaths and millions of refugees in each case, suggest a far worse outcome than that of Yugoslavia if India were to disintegrate. The political situation in Buddhist Sri Lanka has not been fundamentally different from that found in India. Majority Buddhist Sinhalese have been combating a violent separatist movement by its minority Hindu Tamils, despite the fact that in the previous 2,500 years of their history on the island, Sinhalese and Tamils had lived peacefully side by side (Little, 1994).

The experience in Europe in the 1990s suggests that South Asia could meet the same fate. Indeed, Kashmiri separatists pointed out that the secessions of the Baltic states from the Soviet Union in 1991 on the grounds that they were wrongfully annexed by Stalin in 1939, was not fundamentally different from their claim of wrongful annexation of Kashmir by Nehru in 1947. Similarly, Sikh separatists seeking a separate Khalistan out of Indian Punjab pointed out in the early 1990s that their objective was no different from the successful secessions and recognition of Slovenia and Croatia from Yugoslavia. Indians will disagree with these comparisons and parallels, but disagreement alone may not deter Western military interventions in the future. Writing in the *Hindustan Times*, Prem Shankar Jha noted on 5 November 1999:

> two days ago, the Congress of the United States began a hearing on human rights. It was not an enquiry into the state of human rights in America but in Kashmir, in a country that did not elect them, over which it does not have the remotest jurisdiction, and where even the most calamitous events would not affect America's political or economic well-being.

Thus, an element of national self-interest and preservation pervades the reaction of the Indian media broadly reflecting the views of the Indian attentive public.

General Satish Nambiar, the first UNPROFOR Commander in the former Yugoslavia, expressed a pervasive Indian sentiment regarding Western policies towards the Serbs (1999:17):

> if what is being done by Nato forces to the people of Yugoslavia reflects the combined will of the 'civilised world' (which is what the developed world unfailingly calls itself), I would much prefer to remain in 'uncivilised' societies like India where we at least continue to have some traditional values and genuine respect for human life and dignity.

The Indian press disagreed with the Western perspective and performance during the Yugoslav crisis, as did much of the rest of the world that encompassed Russia, China, the Orthodox Christian countries, most of Latin America harbouring long memories of American imperialism and military interventions over the last century, and Africa with its memories of white colonial oppression. But the American and Western media and their governments continue to languish in the bliss that the United States is the sole superpower with a monopoly on wisdom and morality, that Nato is the protector of the world, and the West is the 'international community'.

AN INDIAN VIEW OF THE WESTERN MEDIA FROM IRAQ TO YUGOSLAVIA
Siddharth Varadarajan

Western reporting of wars generally falls into two categories. When covering other peoples' conflicts, the focus is on the savagery and futility of violence. Blame is freely apportioned to both parties, even if their subterranean links to the West are passed over in silence. But when it is the West which is fighting and killing, the emphasis is on the aesthetics of pure violence unsullied by base motives. The use of force becomes at once destructive and purificatory, a rite sanctified by the morality of purpose. 'Sometimes', said Nato spokesman Jamie Shea two days after the US-led alliance acknowledged that it had 'mistakenly' bombed an Albanian refugee column near Djakovica, 'one has to risk the lives of the few to save the lives of the many.' 'The pilot', he stressed, had 'dropped his bomb in good faith. As you would expect of a trained pilot from a democratic country.'[6]

In the New World Order, the accusation of crimes against humanity is at once a marker of barbarism – defined not so much in terms of race but political transgression – and a license for intervention by Jamie Shea's 'trained pilots' from 'democratic countries'. Cosmology has always played a crucial role in the construction of knowledge and information. Often, the question and the manner of its framing help to predetermine – and then rigidly fix – the parameters within which a problem is looked at. And that in turn conditions the texture of news flows. When Nato's bombardment of Yugoslavia began on 24 March 1999, the first question 'experts' on CNN and BBC were asked was not whether the action was legal but whether the attacks would, in fact, compel Slobodan Milosevic to surrender. Nato's action was taken as morally and legally justified and the entire body of news coverage erected over this flawed foundation. In India, on the other hand, the first media questions tended to revolve around the issue of legality. The editorial consensus was that Nato's actions were not just illegal but also immoral and dangerous. But, at least at the initial stages, news coverage in India tended to reflect the Western discourse. Even though the country prides itself on its independent world view, most media organisations rely heavily on Western news agencies for basic inputs. The only permanent foreign correspondents most leading Indian newspapers have today outside South Asia are in Washington – a far cry from the golden era of the 1970s and 1980s, when Russia, Europe and the Middle East were well-covered.

In the case of the *Times of India*, editorial dissatisfaction about the quality of Western news agency reports prompted the newspaper to send its own correspondent to both Iraq and Yugoslavia. Reporting from Iraq in February and March 1998, and from Yugoslavia in May and June 1999, provided me with a first-hand insight into the multilayered manner in which consent for US policies is manufactured by the Western media. This can occur at the stage of news gathering, when reporters choose to do only certain kinds of stories, ignoring others which do not conform to the set pattern. In case reporters file stories that challenge the dominant paradigm, editors in the head office can filter what appears. Finally, manipulation is achieved by defining and locating, at the outset, the central points through which information is to be manufactured, processed and disseminated, the panopticon from which the entire 'story' can be best observed and in relation to which other theatres are secondary and peripheral. In the case of Yugoslavia, the central observation post was located in Brussels, in the briefing room of Nato itself, with auxiliary locations being the Pentagon and State Department in Washington and the MoD in London. The daily press conferences held at these locations became the primary reference point for coverage of Nato's war, while the pathetic camps in Macedonia and Albania – where Kosovo's unfortunate refugees fled once Nato's operations began – provided footage of an appropriate visual and aural texture.

In comparison, the daily press conferences held by the Yugoslav authorities, in which senior officials would provide details of the effects of Nato's bombardment on civilians, hardly received much attention from the Western media. CNN and BBC did not telecast these press conferences live; indeed, many of the Western journalists based in Belgrade did not even bother to attend them. To an Indian reporter based in Yugoslavia during the war, the manner in which Nato's bombing was affecting ordinary people was the big story. Indeed, it was frustrating to see Nato spokesmen claiming that civilians were not being targeted when all the evidence around me showed that the aim of the US-led alliance was precisely to wear down the population by attacks on the electricity system and to terrorise them by occasionally targeting hospitals, apartments, roads and other facilities used by civilians. Despite this, most Western reporters – except, of course, the Greeks and a handful of others – treated Nato attacks on civilian structures as 'aberrations' and consciously attempted to play down the human tragedy that Nato bombing was causing. Western reporters who visited sites where such 'aberrations' had occurred were usually deeply sceptical of the hard evidence they saw. At the Dragisa Misovic hospital in Belgrade, which took a direct hit by a US bomb on the night of 19 May, two US reporters got excited when they found the casing of a bullet on a road near the destroyed maternity ward. This, they said, suggested that the hospital might not have been a hospital but some kind of military installation.

In Iraq during the 1998 crisis over United Nations Special Commission (UNSCOM) weapons inspectors' access to Iraqi presidential sites, many of the Western journalists who flew in to Baghdad anticipating US air strikes were little more than cheerleaders for the Pentagon. With rare and honourable exceptions, they had little time to probe some of the more important stories crying out for media attention – the appalling condition of Iraqi children after nearly a decade of sanctions, the state of Iraq's hospitals, schools and sanitation system, and the tension between the UNSCOM inspectors and the UN's humanitarian workers. (The latter called the former 'UNSCUM'; the former called the latter 'bunnyhuggers'.) When I met the representative of the Food and Agriculture Organisation in Baghdad for a detailed briefing about the terrible state of Iraq's agriculture, he expressed his frustration at the fact that no other journalists had come to see him to find out how sanctions were affecting the country's ability to feed itself.[7]

Perhaps the most revealing incident during this period was the press conference held by Staffan di Mistura, an urbane Swedish diplomat sent by UN Secretary-General Kofi Annan to measure the precise area of the presidential sites to which UNSCOM was being denied access. Di Mistura and his team worked with modern measuring systems and were given unhindered access to all sites. At his press conference – apparently authorised by Annan as a means of disproving the claim made by President Bill Clinton that 'just one of these sites is as big as the whole of Washington DC' – di Mistura revealed that the entire area of all eight presidential sites was only twelve square miles. Half of this consisted of bodies of water like lakes. Given that President Clinton was all set to go to war over these sites, di Mistura's press conference was extremely well attended. Once they heard what he had to say, however, the Anglo-American press corps fell upon him like a pack of wolves. Di Mistura was repeatedly asked to confirm that there were no weapons of mass destruction hidden in these complexes and several reporters openly mocked his supposed naiveté at having confirmed Iraqi claims about the size and nature of the disputed sites. Two US reporters told me after the press conference that they thought di Mistura was 'a fool' and that they did not intend to highlight his findings. Others said they would report what he had said but only after 'balancing' his statements with appropriate responses from UNSCOM and the State Department. One Washington-based reporter who phoned his newspaper all excited was told by his editor to calm down and remember the 'bigger picture'. Not surprisingly, a story that I (and fellow journalists from Japan, China, Russia and even France) considered truly sensational did not receive the sort of play it deserved in the British and US press, or on BBC and CNN.

Several months after the dispute over access to the presidential sites was successfully resolved, the US and UK went ahead and bombed Iraq anyway. Washington had earlier instructed UN weapons inspectors to pull out and the purpose of the bombing was in fact to provoke the Iraqis into ending all co-operation with UNSCOM so that sanctions could continue to remain firmly in place. On 10 January 1999, virtually every English-language Indian newspaper carried an AP despatch out of UN headquarters which contained the following glaring misrepresentation: 'The US, which has led bombing raids to ensure that (UN weapons) inspectors can carry out their work ... .' No newspaper bothered to clarify that the US *claimed* to have bombed Iraq in order to ensure the inspectors could carry out their work. No amount of counter-editorialising can insulate a newspaper from such distortions. In fact, there is really no alternative to newspapers from the non-Western world having their own correspondents on the ground.

Notes

1. A large variety of English and Indian language newspapers are accessible at http://www.samachar.com/
2. UN Press Release, HR/CN/99/54, 23 April 1999.
3. *Times of India*, 8 April 1999. See also A.P. Venkataswaran, 'The Arrogance of Power', *Hindustan Times*, 1 April; Siddharth Varadarajan, 'Nato on a Dangerous and Illegal Course', and 'Ruses for War: Nato's New Strategic Concept', *Times of India*, 29 March and 10 May; C. Raja Mohan, 'Kosovo: The Liberals' War', *Hindu*, 6 April; and Nambiar (1999).
4. Quoted in A.P. Venkataswaran, 'The Arrogance of Power', *Hindustan Times*, 1 April 1999.
5. See also K. Subrahmanyam, 'Nato's Sham Concern Hides Many Truths', and 'Covering Up a Blunder: Nato's Hegemonism and Irrationality', *Times of India*, 3 April and 20 April 1999.
6. BBC Online, 15 April 1999.
   [http://news.bbc.co.uk/hi/english/world/europe/newsid_320000/320204.stm].
7. My despatches from Baghdad and Belgrade may be accessed at http://mail.indiatimes.com/indiatimes/users/svaradarajan.

Conclusions

Philip Hammond and Edward S. Herman

First Casualty and Beyond

The mainstream media of most countries have regularly jumped aboard a patriotic bandwagon when their governments have gone to war, and have very commonly helped stoke war fever. Truth is the 'first casualty' in this process (Knightley, 1989), though this is rarely recognised in the heat of battle, when the seemingly obvious justice of the home cause overwhelms the capacity for objective evaluation. Even in war's aftermath the media are not inclined to rigorous self-examination, although doubts and qualifications on specific matters may seep into the public domain. The media continue to support the 'home team', and the retrospective exposure of journalists' role in perpetuating misinformation and propaganda during the last war would not only reflect badly on the media as objective and independent providers of news, but may also hurt the home team's ongoing and future endeavours.[1]

The mainstream media of the dominant Nato powers did not break this tradition of bandwagon support in their coverage of the Kosovo crisis and war (see the chapters on Britain, France, Germany, the United States and CNN). It is noteworthy that in a marginal Nato country such as Greece, where the population has had painful experiences with the leading Nato powers in the recent past – the United States, Britain and Germany each imposed and/or supported oppressive right-wing regimes in Greece in the years 1935–70 – public hostility to the Nato bombing of Yugoslavia was so general and intense that the mainstream media expressed serious doubts about the Nato policy followed by the Greek government (Raptis, Chapter 16). Outside of Nato, there was widespread public, government, and media hostility to Nato policy, as reflected in India (Thomas and Varadarajan, Chapter 18), and of course in Russia (Hammond, Nizamova and Savelieva, Chapter 17). Within Nato, however, with the partial exception of Greece, the media provided a solid and uncritical phalanx of support for war.

If the pro-Nato policy bias of the Western mainstream media follows the long tradition of truth being the first casualty, that does not make it any less worthy of close attention and analysis today. The media still claim to be objective and truthful servants of democracy, contributing to informed public debate rather than helping to engineer consent to policies decided from above. If they fail in this regard and join the leadership in promoting and selling a war, they are *de facto* enemies of democracy, and servants of the policy-making elite. This demands reiteration, even if it represents no departure from a sorry tradition.

Furthermore, there are always distinctive features in war coverage, which are important in helping us to trace the changing forms of media work and propaganda service. During the war against Yugoslavia, the insistence of the media in the major Nato countries on the alleged 'humanitarian' concerns of Western governments – even in the face of policies with highly destructive results – and the complementary support of a war crimes 'tribunal' operating in coordination with Nato during the war itself, stand out. So too does the extent to which liberal and even left reporters and intellectuals supported the new 'ethical' foreign policy displayed in the bombing of Yugoslavia and occupation of Kosovo.

Another outstanding feature of coverage of the Kosovo crisis was the growing scale and speed of media operations. The media of the dominant Nato powers more than ever reached across the globe, seeking to influence people and governments outside their own borders. CNN notably has a global clientele whom it claims to be providing with objective news. But during the Kosovo war CNN was not objective (nor were other Western media with a global reach, including the BBC): it was virtually in partnership with Nato, serving as its *de facto* public information arm (Herman and Peterson, Chapter 10). Furthermore, even in India, while editorial opinion was highly critical of Nato, the power and reach of Western sources was so great that much of the news reaching the public was pro-Nato, in accord with the news choices and framing of the Western media.

Rewriting History

To a remarkable degree the media of the leading Nato countries helped build the agenda for war by oversimplifying and distorting history. There was little or no recognition of the role of the Nato powers in encouraging the earlier break-up of the Yugoslav federation (Chandler, Chapter 2). The Nato powers had domestic and international political goals in their Balkan policies which brought them into conflict with the Republic of Serbia and the interests of Serb minorities in the other republics, and the policy biases of Nato leaders encouraged warfare rather than negotiated settlements. Yet this was almost entirely ignored by the Nato bloc media, whose members generally accepted that these powers were simply pursuing humanitarian aims and wanted to ensure 'stability' (Johnstone, Chapter 1). Nato's policy in Bosnia has involved the imposition of an undemocratic external authority on groups which are allowed no self-government, offering no apparent route to reconciliation. Yet this too is ignored in the mainstream media, despite its relevance to Nato's Kosovo 'solution' (Chandler, Chapter 2).

The mainstream media not only failed to analyse the West's role in encouraging the splintering off of Slovenia and Croatia, they also ignored the support which the US and other Nato powers gave to the August 1995 Croatian attack on Serbs in Krajina, despite the fact that it caused the largest single refugee crisis of the Yugoslav wars prior to 1999.[2] Instead, the selective reporting of Western journalists ensured that the phrase 'ethnic cleansing' became overwhelmingly associated with actions by Serbs.

Ironically, in the early 1980s the terms 'ethnic cleansing' or 'ethnic purification' were used almost exclusively to describe the long and successful ethnic Albanian efforts to push out non-Albanians and 'purify' Kosovo (Ackerman and Naureckas, Chapter 9). This, of course, was conveniently forgotten, as was the role of Germany, Austria, Albania and the United States in arming the Kosovo Liberation Army, contrary to international agreement and law, inevitably eliciting a military response from the Yugoslav government.[3] As late as February 1998, US special envoy Robert Gelbard described the KLA as a 'terrorist organisation', saying of it on 22 February: 'it is the strong and firm policy of the US to fully oppose all terrorist actions and all terrorist organisations'. But once Nato had decided to occupy Kosovo and teach Serbia a lesson, word usage and frames shifted drastically, and the KLA became 'freedom fighters', whose interest in provoking the Serbs in order to expedite the desired Nato attacks was barely noticed.

Misrepresenting the Rambouillet Conference

The Nato bloc media's treatment of the Rambouillet conference and associated diplomatic impasse was dramatic evidence of their propaganda service and failure to report truthful news of public importance. Journalists and junior politicians in Nato countries maintained a wilful ignorance about the terms and conduct of the Rambouillet 'negotiations'. The decision for war taken by the '19 democratic nations' of Nato was not reached on the basis of informed public discussion, but was accompanied by obfuscation and a total lack of debate (see Pilger, Chapter 12; Deichmann, Chapter 14, and Røn, Chapter 15). Following Nato's lead, the mainstream media portrayed the diplomatic process as one of a reasonable Nato interested in a negotiated settlement confronting an evasive and unreasonable enemy. The fact that the 'talks' were actually about convincing the parties to accept a preordained Western proposal was not reported critically; nor was the fact that it was deemed unnecessary to allow the parties to meet. There was no criticism of the initial deadline of one week to complete the agreement, nor of the later short extensions. The media generally failed to see that Nato was delivering an ultimatum that required Yugoslavia to accept Nato occupation of Kosovo and the effective termination of Yugoslav sovereignty in the territory.[4] They buried the fact of Serb acceptance of non-Nato observers and substantial moves toward Kosovo autonomy. And although 'rafts of journalists' were told by a senior State Department official at Rambouillet that Nato had deliberately 'raised the bar too high for the Serbs to comply',[5] ending the diplomatic process by inserting an Appendix B requirement allowing it to occupy all of Yugoslavia, the media failed to report this important fact (see Ackerman and Naureckas, Chapter 9, and Herman and Peterson, Chapter 10).[6]

The failure properly to assess the nature of Nato's ultimatum and refusal to negotiate, while making Yugoslavia the delinquent, exactly paralleled the media's conduct during the Persian Gulf War, when they refused to report and analyse the meaning of the unwillingness of the United States and its allies to accept anything but abject and total surrender (Chomsky, 1992). That Yugoslavia regarded the 'negotiations' as a set-up, and the 78-day bombing campaign as warfare on behalf of the KLA, escaped the notice of Western reporters.[7] Similarly, Nato's post-war failure to disarm the KLA and protect Serbs, Roma and dissident Albanians, in accord with UN resolution 1244, from the widespread KLA violence which has occurred under Nato auspices, has also been given low-key treatment in the Western media. During the bombing, as Robert Fisk of the (London) *Independent* notes, 'No Brussels reporter asked what protection Nato intended to give the Serb minority in Kosovo, post-war' (17 January 2000).

Demonisation and Atrocities Management

For Nato and its mainstream media, the conflict in Kosovo resulted from unprovoked Serb misbehaviour, and the special villainy of President Slobodan Milosevic. The demonisation of Milosevic followed the same pattern as that of Iraq's Saddam Hussein, but in the European context Milosevic and the Serbs were compared with the Nazis, just as they had been during the Bosnian war (Hume, Chapter 6). The fact that Serbia has an elected government, no political prisoners or torture chambers, and the most ethnically diverse population in the region, was of no interest to Western journalists; nor was the fact that the killings and expulsions in Yugoslavia were carried out on all sides in a process encouraged by Western policy and Western discrimination within the Balkans (Chandler, Chapter 2). As in earlier conflicts, a complex civil war was portrayed as a one-sided aggression, and Western interference as disinterested humanitarianism.

Nato wanted the media to focus on Serb atrocities and the media obliged, with gusto and gullibility. There surely were Serb atrocities committed before Nato's bombing assault began on 24 March, but there was a civil war in Kosovo being stoked from the outside, and the atrocities were neither unprovoked nor of proportions to support any allegations of 'genocide'. Jacques Prod'homme, a member of the Organisation for Security and Co-operation in Europe's Kosovo Verification Mission, testified that 'in the month leading up to the war, during which he moved freely throughout the Pec region, neither he nor his colleagues observed anything that could be described as systematic persecution, either collective or individual murders, burning of houses or deportations'.[8] Interestingly, the post-war assessments issued by the US State Department, the International Criminal Tribunal for Former Yugoslavia (ICTY), and the OSCE, as well as the selection of KVM reports now available, all corroborate Prod'homme's statement and fail to support the claim of large-scale Serb violence against civilians before the Nato bombing began on 24 March.[9] By ignoring the context, the provocations (including KLA atrocities), and the Nato–KLA stake in publicising Serb atrocities, the media became instruments of the war party. In the case of the killings at Racak on 15 January, the possibility that this was a slaughter of KLA fighters, converted into a 'massacre of civilians' by the KLA and US–OSCE official William Walker, was given serious attention in the French and German press, but not in the British or US media (Herman and Peterson, Chapter 10). Indeed, Renaud Girard, one of the French reporters who questioned the official version of what had happened at Racak, found that his honest reporting angered his Anglo-American colleagues, who complained to him: 'You're killing our story.'[10]

During the air war that followed the Rambouillet conference, the media focused intently on the abuse, killing and exodus of the Kosovo Albanians, described in detail, deplored with passion, and frequently referred to as a 'holocaust' and 'genocide'. Nato's role in this humanitarian disaster was denied or played down, on the ground that the Serbs were planning on doing this anyway, a claim of Nato officials and apologists which they had never mentioned prior to the bombing. It was (and remains) standard US language to say that the Nato bombing was in 'retaliation' to the Serb onslaught, rather than precipitating it. Official Nato claims of ongoing Serb mass killing, with figures of 100,000 and more given by State Department spokesman James Rubin and others, were unchallenged, and the atrocities-genocide claims helped justify the intensifying bombing raids on Serbia.

As reporters accompanied Nato troops into Kosovo immediately after the bombing, it was confidently predicted that evidence of genocide and atrocities would vindicate Nato's actions. Indeed, many reports claimed the situation in Kosovo had been 'even worse' than Nato had suspected. Gradually, however, a different picture began to emerge. 'The killing of ethnic Albanian civilians appears to be orders of magnitude below the claims of Nato, alliance governments and early media reports', said the US research organisation Stratfor.[11] A Reuters dispatch from Kosovo on 13 October reported: 'Absolutely No Bodies Found in Supposed Mine Shaft Mass Grave in Kosovo.' These revelations followed a report by a Spanish forensic team sent to investigate allegedly major killing fields, where instead of the predicted thousands the pathologists found 187 bodies. Five months after the end of the war, the ICTY itself reported having found the remains of 2,108 bodies, without distinguishing between civilian and military casualties, nor between Albanians and Serbs. It is clear that Nato engaged in serious propaganda inflation, helped along by Nato and media reliance on KLA and refugee sources treated uncritically (see Hammond, Chapter 11; Hume, Chapter 6, and Pilger, Chapter 12).

In contrast to the intense and emotive focus on Serbian violence in Kosovo, Nato bombing was treated very matter-of-factly. Journalists displayed minimal interest or indignation over 'collateral damage', over the refugees generated by the bombing (both in Kosovo and in the rest of Yugoslavia), or over the morality and legality of Nato's shift from military targets to bombing the civilian infrastructure of Serbia. Nato's use of cluster bombs and depleted uranium weaponry was also of little interest, and reporters treated Nato 'errors' with patriotic credulity. Much media 'debate' concerning the air campaign was dominated by banal technicalities – would bad weather hamper Nato's efforts? – while 'criticism' was largely confined to questioning Nato's reluctance to launch a ground invasion. Robert Fisk was amazed and outraged when, on the day Nato killed at least 87 ethnic Albanian refugees in the village of Korisa and injured a hundred more, the Nato spokesman said the alliance had had 'another effective day', on which operations 'again went very well', and no reporter questioned this (*Independent*, 15 May). A veteran war correspondent, Fisk was so dismayed at the obsequiousness of his fellow reporters he dismissed them as 'sheep'.

The cosy relationship between official spokespersons and mainstream journalists is one that has been carefully fostered by a Western military keen to 'work with' the media in order to get its message across (Skoco and Woodger, Chapter 7). When Nato bombed a passenger train on 12 April, killing between 14 (Nato) and 55 (Yugoslavia) civilians, reporters were shown a videotape as 'proof' that the train had been travelling too fast for the trajectory of the missiles to be altered. A BBC reporter noted that 'there hasn't been public uproar in Nato countries', and suggested this would 'embolden' Nato to hit more, similar, targets (*Newsnight*, 13 April), apparently unaware that a likely reason for the lack of uproar was the media's treatment of the story. Meanwhile, Nato's denunciations of the Yugoslav media as 'Milosevic's lie machine' were dutifully repeated and amplified by most mainstream journalists, seemingly unconscious of their own propaganda service. Perhaps again 'emboldened' by the media's response, Nato bombed Serbian broadcasting, knowing civilians would die (see Pilger, Chapter 12; Gocic, Chapter 8, and Herman and Peterson, Chapter 10). Still Western journalists failed to question Nato's actions; in Britain, it was left to Harold Pinter to accuse Nato of murder over the attack. Months after the war, it was revealed that the videotape of the 12 April train bombing had been played at three times its normal speed, but even this was given minimal attention in the Anglo-American media, prompting little reflection on media gullibility in the face of Nato disinformation. It still seems not to have occurred to the vast majority of mainstream reporters that 'lie machines' exist much closer to home.

The ICTY as an Arm of Nato

The role played by the International Criminal Tribunal for Former Yugoslavia was a unique feature of the Kosovo war. Although by its charter it is supposedly funded by the UN and 'independent' of individual states, much of its funding has come from Nato power sources, and in its choice of personnel and actions it has served as an arm of Nato. Its processes have consistently violated legal norms considered elemental in the leading Nato states, yet the Western media have unfailingly treated the Tribunal's actions as those of an independent and apolitical judicial institution (Skoco and Woodger, Chapter 3). The ICTY has depended on Nato for documentation and enforcement, and in exchange has pursued war crimes as defined by Nato interests. Most notably, in the midst of the Nato bombing campaign, on 27 May 1999, ICTY Chief Prosecutor Louise Arbour issued an indictment against Slobodan Milosevic. In contrast, although Tribunal investigators identified three Croatian generals as indictable for war crimes over the 1995 attack on the Krajina, in which a great many Serbs were executed and disappeared, no indictments have been forthcoming. This is because the United States supported that earlier instance of 'ethnic cleansing', disapproved of any Tribunal action in the case, and withheld requested information on the attack (*New York Times*, 21 March 1999).

Astonishingly, many news reports presented the indictment of Milosevic in the midst of the Kosovo war as proof of the Tribunal's independence from Nato, on the ground that the indictment would undermine any peace negotiations. Having misrepresented Nato's conduct at Rambouillet and failed to report the deliberate 'raising of the bar' to permit military action, journalists continued to pretend that Nato's core leaders were interested in negotiations and failed to recognise their commitment to victory through bombing (Gowan, Chapter 4). In reality, the indictment of Milosevic served to legitimate Nato's war, giving it the stamp of judicial approval. As Nato publicists themselves were quick to point out, the ICTY's decision 'justifies in the clearest possible way what we have been doing' (James Rubin) and 'will enable us to keep moving all these processes [including bombing] forward' (Madeleine Albright). Since Nato was at that very time greatly intensifying its attacks on Serbia's civilian infrastructure – targeting not 'justified by military necessity' as demanded by international law – the highly politicised Tribunal was actually helping to facilitate the commission of war crimes.

Carla del Ponte, appointed as the ICTY's Chief Prosecutor in September 1999, considered a dossier accusing Nato of committing war crimes during the bombing. Yet she was eager to emphasise that 'it's not my priority, because I have inquiries about genocide, about bodies in mass graves' (*Observer*, 26 December). The reporter to whom del Ponte made this admission nevertheless portrayed her as tough and independent (as well as 'blonde and energetic'), and some US officials were reportedly angry that del Ponte had even countenanced the allegations. Yet Nato officials said the prosecutor had assured them 'she would not carry this exercise far', emphasising that 'Nobody seriously thinks del Ponte will even try to make a case against [General Wesley] Clark or [Javier] Solana' (*Washington Post*, 20 January 2000).

The Media's Role: A 'CNN Effect'?

The mainstream media of the leading Nato powers supported the war against Yugoslavia with almost uniform and uncritical enthusiasm. They accepted without question the justice of the Nato cause, their position in this regard bolstered by the fact that many liberals and leftists, including those in journalism itself, also strongly supported Nato's policy. Many had been nurtured in reporting on the Bosnian war, where they had been sold on the special evil and misdeeds of the Serbs; and their own sense of moral obligation meshed well with the fulminations of Madeleine Albright and Robin Cook. Crusading journalists contributed readily to the demonisation process, eagerly endorsing claims that this was a 'just war'. In this fetid atmosphere of sanctimony, the hugely biased reporting which characterised the Kosovo conflict flourished (for example, coverage of the Rambouillet process, of the source and extent of the pre-war atrocities, of the alleged Serb 'genocide' in Kosovo, of the scope and effects of Nato's bombing policies, and of the work of the supposedly 'independent' Tribunal).

The media's aggressive support and promotion of recent wars and interventions, including the Nato attack on Yugoslavia, has led some analysts to claim that news organisations have become an independent source of conflict generation, pressing political leaders to do what they would otherwise not do, or would do with less precipitousness. This process has been labelled the 'CNN effect', reflecting the global role of CNN and its facility in quickly getting on-the-scene material before the public that may arouse it and force politicians to respond. In our view, however, the mainstream media rarely, if ever, press themes that the dominant political and economic leaders of their respective countries do not favour (although there may be divisions of opinion, with some sectors of the elite unhappy with the publicity and pressures).

In the case of Bosnia, it may often have appeared that partisan journalists were intent on goading reluctant politicians into action. Yet the sort of 'criticism' to which such reporters and commentators subjected their political leaders must have been wholly welcome, since it presupposed that the West had a right, indeed a duty, to interfere around the globe. The liberal media's self-image as moral crusaders in Bosnia perhaps helps to account for the enthusiasm with which they embraced the idea that Nato's attack on Yugoslavia represented the new dawn of an 'ethical' foreign policy, and the alacrity with which mainstream journalists adapted to a virtual party line handed down by the US and its allied Nato leaders in support of violent policies.

Rather than a 'CNN effect', the main problem, as evidenced by the record of media performance during the Kosovo crisis and war, is that instead of providing reasonably objective information that would contribute to public debate, the media quickly move to promoting war, featuring enemy evil and intransigence, and pressing for violent action to maintain 'credibility'. And if truth continues to be the first casualty in situations like Kosovo, it follows that the mainstream media of the 'democratic' West are failing to meet the informational needs of a genuinely democratic order.

Notes

1. The Anglo-American media's poor performance during the 1990–91 Persian Gulf War is a case in point. If more serious attention had been paid to the US–British refusal to negotiate and insistence on war, and to the West's prior support of Saddam Hussein, this would have weakened their ability to impose harsh sanctions on Iraq for the next decade, and might have made their refusal to negotiate and insistence on war with Yugoslavia harder to carry out. On the US–British refusal to negotiate and the media's failure to report this during the Persian Gulf War, see Chomsky (1992).

2. Agim Cheku, a leading planner of the 1995 Croat offensive, was appointed military leader of the KLA during the Kosovo air war. Asked about this at Nato's 14 May briefing, spokesman Jamie Shea said he had 'no comment', though he nevertheless suggested that any violence by the KLA or Croatian army should ultimately be blamed on Milosevic.

3. For details of foreign support of the KLA see Erich Schmidt-Eenboom and Klaus Eichner, 'Wem gehoert die UCK? Die Rolle der Geheimdienste bei Vorbereitung und Durchfuehrung des Nato-Krieges', *Junge Welt*, 17 January 2000.

4. Even when Nato policy was described as an 'ultimatum', this was not accompanied by any critical analysis of its content. Thus the *Daily Telegraph*'s front-page headline on 30 January 1999 was 'Nato Ultimatum in Kosovo Crisis', but two days later the paper felt able to report this same ultimatum as the 'delicate task of persuading the two warring sides in Kosovo to accept peace'. The paper mentioned no questioning of the threat of force until 14 February, when Tony Benn's criticisms were reported in an article by John Simpson.

5. The story of 'the bar' was related to former State Department official George Kenney. In a personal communication with the authors, Kenney notes that the State Department has never denied the story.

6. The very first mention of 'Appendix B' in the global media for which the Nexis database has a record did not occur until 26 April, when a reporter asked Jamie Shea a specific question about it in a news conference which CNN carried live. Crucially, no mention of this Appendix ever surfaced in the news media when public knowledge of its existence might have made a difference – prior to the start of the bombing.

7. Belatedly, the *Wall Street Journal* (31 December 1999) acknowledged that some human rights researchers 'now say ... the Serbs were trying to clear out areas of KLA support, using selective terror, robberies and sporadic killings', and cited a Serb strategic planner as saying 'We believed Nato was using the KLA as its invasion force.'

8. Eric Rouleau, 'French diplomacy adrift in Kosovo', *Le Monde diplomatique*, December 1999.

9. Noam Chomsky, 'In Retrospect', *Z Magazine*, April/May 2000 (forthcoming).

10. Interview with Diana Johnstone, 25 January 2000.

11. Stratfor, 'Where Are Kosovo's Killing Fields?', 20 October 1999 [http://www.stratfor.com/crisis/kosovo/genocide.htm].

Notes on Contributors

Seth Ackerman is a media analyst at Fairness and Accuracy in Reporting, based in New York City, and is a contributor to *The Kosovo News and Propaganda War* (International Press Institute, 1999).

David Chandler is a Research Fellow at the Policy Research Institute, Leeds Metropolitan University. He has written widely on aspects of international relations, globalisation and the war in Bosnia, and is author of *Bosnia: Faking Democracy After Dayton* (Pluto Press, 1999).

Thomas Deichmann is a freelance journalist based in Frankfurt. He is editor of *Novo* magazine, co-editor with Klaus Bittermann of *How Dr. Joseph Fischer Learned to Love Bombs: The Greens, the SPD, Nato and the Balkans War* (Tiamat, 1999), and editor of *Once More for Yugoslavia: Peter Handke* (Suhrkamp Verlag, 1999). Deichmann provoked an international discussion about war reporting with his article 'The picture that fooled the world', published widely in Europe and the US. He can be contacted at: Thomas.Deichmann@t-online.de.

Goran Gocic is a freelance journalist from Belgrade. A regular contributor to several major newspapers and magazines at home and abroad, he was formerly features editor on the independent daily *Dnevni telegraf*. He is author of *Andy Warhol and the Strategies of Pop* (Prometej, 1997), and a contributor to seven other books. He has recently completed an MSc in Media and Communications at the London School of Economics, and is currently working on a monograph about film director Emir Kusturica.

Peter Gowan is Principal Lecturer in European Politics at the University of North London and a member of the editorial boards of *New Left Review* and *Labour Focus on Eastern Europe*. Recent publications include *The Global Gamble* (Verso, 1999), *The Twisted Road to Kosovo* (Labour Focus on Eastern Europe, 1999), and *The Question of Europe* (Verso, 1997), jointly edited with Perry Anderson. He is currently working on a book dealing with the transformations in Europe during the 1990s.

Philip Hammond is Senior Lecturer in Media at South Bank University, London [email: hammonpb@sbu.ac.uk]. During the Kosovo conflict his analyses of the media coverage were carried in the *Independent*, *The Times* and *Broadcast*, as well as numerous on-line publications, and he worked as a consultant on BBC 2's *Counterblast: Against the War* (May 1999).

Edward S. Herman is Professor Emeritus of Finance, Wharton School, University of Pennsylvania. He has written extensively on economics, political economy and the media. Among his books are *The Global Media* (with Robert McChesney) (Cassell, 1997), *Manufacturing Consent* (with Noam Chomsky) (Pantheon, 1988), and most recently *The Myth of the Liberal Media: An Edward Herman Reader* (Peter Lang, 1999).

Mick Hume is editor of *LM* magazine, and author of *Whose War is it Anyway?* (Informinc, 1997).

Diana Johnstone is a Minnesota-born independent journalist who lives in Paris and writes on European politics. Her publications include *The Politics of Euromissiles: Europe in America's World* (Verso, 1984).

Richard Keeble is director of the Journalism degree course at City University, London. He is author of *The Newspapers Handbook* (Routledge, 1998), and *Secret State, Silent Press: New Militarism, the Gulf and the Modern Image of Warfare* (John Libbey, 1998).

Jim Naureckas has worked as an investigative reporter for the newspaper *In These Times*, where he covered the Iran-Contra scandal, and was managing editor of the *Washington Report on the Hemisphere*, a newsletter on Latin America. Since 1990, he has been the editor of *Extra!*, the bimonthly journal of media criticism published by Fairness and Accuracy in Reporting. He is the co-author of *The Way Things Aren't: Rush Limbaugh's Reign of Error* (New Press, 1995), and co-editor of *The FAIR Reader* (Westview Press, 1996).

Lilia Nizamova is a lecturer in Sociology at the Centre for the Sociology of Culture, Kazan State University, Tatarstan, Russian Federation.

David Peterson is an independent journalist and researcher based in the United States.

John Pilger, war correspondent, film-maker and author, has won numerous awards for his journalism, notably his reporting from Southeast Asia. His latest book, *Hidden Agendas* (Vintage, 1997), examines the power and myths of the media.

Nikos Raptis worked as a professional engineer up to his retirement in 1992. Since the late 1960s he has been writing on political and social matters for papers, magazines and journals. He is the author of *Let Us Talk about Earthquakes* (Topos Press, 1981), and *The Nightmare of the Nukes* (Carre, 1986), and translated the Greek editions of Noam Chomsky's *Year 501* and *Rethinking Camelot*.

Karin Trandheim Røn has recently completed an MA in Media Studies at the University of Oslo, and works as a PR consultant.

Irena Savelieva is a postgraduate student at the Centre for the Sociology of Culture, Kazan State University, Tatarstan, Russian Federation.

Mirjana Skoco was a journalist at Sarajevo Television up until the first months of the war in Bosnia. She is currently completing an MSc in Media and Communications at the London School of Economics, and teaches at South Bank University, London. She researches war reporting for the LIRE Media Group.

Raju G.C. Thomas is Professor of Political Science at Marquette University in Milwaukee, Wisconsin. His most recent books are *Democracy, Security and Development in India* (St. Martin's/Macmillan, 1996); editor, *The Nuclear Non-Proliferation Regime* (St. Martin's/Macmillan, 1998), and co-editor, *India's Nuclear Security* (Lynne Rienner, 2000).

Siddharth Varadarajan is a senior editor with the *Times of India*. He is the author of a major study on the Indian media and communalism, published as 'The Ink Link: Media, Communalism and the Evasion of Politics', in K.N. Pannikar, *The Concerned Indian's Guide to Communalism* (Viking, 1999), and is currently writing a book on Indian foreign policy.

William Woodger is a freelance researcher and computer consultant, and has conducted commissioned research on the wars in Yugoslavia for several freelance journalists. He currently works as a Research Assistant at South Bank University, London, and researches war reporting for the LIRE Media Group.

References

Aksoy, Asu and Kevin Robins (1991) 'Exterminating Angels: Technology in the Gulf', *Media Development*, October, pp. 26–9.

Andrew, Christopher (1995) *For the President's Eyes Only: Secret Intelligence and the American Presidency from Washington to Bush*. London: HarperCollins.

Aukofer, Frank and William P. Lawrence (1995) *America's Team, The Odd Couple: A Report on the Relationship Between the Media and the Military*. Nashville, TN: Vanderbilt University Freedom Forum First Amendment Center.

Baker, Chris (1991) 'The New Age of Imperialism', *Socialist Action*, Spring, pp. 3–8.

Baudrillard, Jean (1995) *The Gulf War*. London: Power Publishers.

Beigbeder, Yves (1999) *Judging War Criminals: The Politics of International Justice*. London: Macmillan.

Bell, Martin (1995) *In Harm's Way: Reflections of a War Zone Thug*. London: Hamish Hamilton.

Bildt, Carl (1998) *Peace Journey: The Struggle for Peace in Bosnia*. London: Weidenfield and Nicolson.

Bougarel, Xavier (1996) 'Bosnia and Hercegovina – State and Communitarianism', in David A. Dyker and Ivan Vejvoda (eds) *Yugoslavia and After: A Study in Fragmentation, Despair and Rebirth*. London: Longman.

Boutros-Ghali, Boutros (1999) *Unvanquished: A US–UN Saga*. London: I. B. Tauris.

Boyd, Charles G. (1995) 'Making Peace with the Guilty: The Truth about Bosnia', *Foreign Affairs*, Vol. 74, No .5, pp. 26–9.

Brock, Peter (1993–94) 'Dateline Yugoslavia: The Partisan Press: Coverage of the War in Bosnia-Herzegovina', *Foreign Policy*, No. 93, Winter, pp. 152–72.

Brzezinski, Zbigniew (1997) *The Grand Chessboard*. New York: Basic Books.

Carapico, Sheila (1998) 'Legalism and Realism in the Gulf', *Middle East Report*, No. 206, pp. 3–6.

Chandler, David (1999a) *Bosnia: Faking Democracy After Dayton*. London: Pluto Press.

—— (1999b) 'The Bosnian Protectorate and the Implications for Kosovo', *New Left Review*, No. 235, pp. 132–4.

Chomsky, Noam (1992) 'The Media and the War: What War?', in Hamid Mowlana, George Gerbner and Herbert I. Schiller (eds) *Triumph of the Image*. Boulder, CO: Westview Press.

—— (1999) *The New Military Humanism: Lessons from Kosovo*. Monroe, ME: Common Courage Press.

Chopra, Ashok (1998) 'Kosovo: Will Nato Intervene to Break Up Serbia?', *United Services Institution Journal*, Vol. 128, No. 533, July–September, pp. 475–84.

Chossudovsky, Michel (1998) *The Globalisation of Poverty: Impacts of IMF and World Bank Reforms*. London: Pluto Press.

Clement, Christopher (1997): 'Returning Aristide: The Contradictions of US Foreign Policy in Haiti', *Race and Class*, Vol. 39, No. 2, pp. 21–36.

Cohen, Lenard J. (1995) *Broken Bonds: Yugoslavia's Disintegration and Balkan Politics in Transition* (Second Edition). Boulder, CO: Westview Press.

Combs, James (1993) 'From the Great War to the Gulf War: Popular Entertainment and the Legitimation of Warfare', in Robert Denton (ed.) *The Media and the Persian Gulf War*. Westport, CT: Praeger, pp. 257–84.

Cordesman, Anthony H. (1999) *The Lessons and Non-Lessons of the Nato Air and Missile Campaign in Kosovo*. Washington, DC: Center for Strategic and International Studies, July.

Cox, Michael (1995) *US Foreign Policy After the Cold War: Superpower Without a Mission?* London: Pinter/Royal Institute of International Affairs.

Curtis, Mark (1995) *The Ambiguities of Power: British Foreign Policy Since 1945*. London: Zed Books.

Deacon, Bob and Paul Stubbs (1998) 'International Actors and Social Policy Development in Bosnia-Herzegovina: Globalism and the "New Feudalism"', *Journal of European Social Policy*, Vol. 8, No. 2, pp. 99–115.

Deichmann, Thomas (1999) 'Wie in Deutschland Demokratie sabotiert wird', *Novo*, No. 41, July–August, pp. 14–19. [http://www.novo-magazin.de]

Denitch, Bogdan (1996) *Ethnic Nationalism: The Tragic Death of Yugoslavia* (Second Edition). Minneapolis: University of Minnesota Press.

Derbyshire, J. Denis and Ian Derbyshire (1988) *Politics in Britain: From Callaghan to Thatcher*. London: Chambers.

Dickson, Sandra H. (1994) 'Understanding Media Bias: The Press and the US Invasion of Panama', *Journalism Quarterly*; Vol. 71, No. 4, pp. 809–19.

Dorril, Stephen (1993) *The Silent Conspiracy: Inside the Intelligence Services in the 1990s*. London: Heinemann.

Drucker, Peter F. (1993) *Post-capitalist Society*. Oxford: Butterworth-Heinemann.

Edgerton, David (1998) 'Tony Blair's Warfare State', *New Left Review*, No. 230, pp. 123–30.

Flournoy, Don M. and Robert K. Stewart (1997) *CNN: Making News in the Global Market*. Luton: University of Luton Press.

Füredi, Frank (1994) *The New Ideology of Imperialism*. London: Pluto Press.

Galtung, Johann and Mari Ruge (1973) 'Structuring and Selecting News', in Stanley Cohen and Jock Young (eds) *The Manufacture of News*. London: Constable, pp. 62–72.

Glasgow University Media Group (1985) *War and Peace News*. Milton Keynes: Open University Press.

Glass, Charles (1999) 'Hacks versus Flacks: Tales from the Depths', *Z Magazine*, 1 August. [http://www.zmag.org]

Glenny, Misha (1996) *The Fall of Yugoslavia: The Third Balkan War* (Third Edition). London: Penguin.

Gowan, Peter (1999) 'Making Sense of Nato's Balkan War', in Leo Panitch and Colin Leys (eds) *Socialist Register 2000: Necessary and Unnecessary Utopias*. London: Merlin Press.

Gowing, Nik (1997) *Media Coverage: Help or Hindrance in Conflict Prevention?* (Report to the Carnegie Commission on Preventing Deadly Conflict). New York: Carnegie Corporation.

Gray, Chris Hables (1997) *Post Modern War*. London: Routledge.

Greenberg, Susan and Graham Smith (1982) *Rejoice: Media Freedom and the Falklands*. London: Campaign for Press and Broadcasting Freedom.

Gunn, Simon (1989) *Revolution of the Right*. London: Pluto Press/Transnational Institute.

Gutman, Roy and David Rieff (eds) (1999) *Crimes of War: What the Public Should Know*. London: W. W. Norton & Co.

Halimi, Serge (1997) *Les Nouveaux Chiens de Garde*. Paris: Liber-Raisons d'agir.

Halliday, Fred (1986) *The Making of the Second Cold War*. London: Verso.

Halperin, Morton H. and David J. Scheffer, with Patricia L. Small (1992) *Self-Determination in the New World Order*. Washington, DC: Carnegie Endowment for International Peace.

Harris, Laurence (1984) 'State and Economy in the Second World War', in George McLennan, David Held and Stuart Hall (eds) *State and Society in Contemporary Britain: A Critical Introduction*. Cambridge: Polity Press, pp. 50–76.

Harris, Robert (1983) *Gotcha! The Media, the Government and the Falklands Crisis*. London: Faber.

Hartmann, Florence (1999) 'Bosnia', in Roy Gutman and David Reiff (eds) *Crimes of War: What the Public Should Know*. New York: W. W. Norton & Co., pp. 50–6.

Hellinger, Daniel and Dennis Judd (1991) *The Democratic Façade*. Pacific Grove, CA: Cole Publishing Company.

Herman, Edward (1998) 'Bombing a la Mode', *Z Magazine Online*, December. [www.zmag.org]

Hill, Stephen M. and Shahia P. Malik (1996) *Peacekeeping and the United Nations*. Aldershot: Dartmouth.

Hume, Mick (1997) *Whose War is it Anyway? The Dangers of the Journalism of Attachment*. London: Informinc.

Ignatieff, Michael (1998) *The Warrior's Honour: Ethnic War and the Modern Conscience*. London: Chatto and Windus.

International Commission on the Balkans (1996) *Unfinished Peace: Report of the International Commission on the Balkans*. Washington, DC: Carnegie Endowment for International Peace.

Jha, Prem Shankar (1999) 'Tragedy in the Balkans: Nato's Monumental Blunder', *World Affairs* (New Delhi and Geneva), Vol. 3, No. 2, April–June, pp. 98–117.

Johnstone, Diana (1999) 'Das Racak-Massaker als Auslöser des Krieges', in Klaus Bittermann and Thomas Deichmann (eds) *Wie Dr. Joseph Fischer lernte, die Bombe zu lieben. Die Grünen, die SPD, die Nato und der Krieg auf dem Balkan*. Berlin: Tiamat, pp. 52–68.

—— (2000) 'Making the Crime Fit the Punishment', in Tariq Ali (ed.) *Masters of the Universe? Nato's Humanitarian Crusade*. London: Verso.

Kaldor, Mary (1990) *The Imaginary War*. London: Verso.

Keeble, Richard (1997) *Secret State, Silent Press: New Militarism, the Gulf and the Modern Image of Warfare*. Luton: John Libbey.

—— (1998) 'The Myth of Saddam Hussein: New Militarism and the Propaganda Function of the Human Interest Story', in Matthew Kieran (ed.) *Media Ethics*. London: Routledge, pp. 66–81.

Kellner, Douglas (1992) *The Persian Gulf TV War*. Boulder, CO: Westview Press.

—— (1993) 'Gulf War II: The Media Offensive', *Lies of our Times*, May, pp. 17–19.

—— (1995) 'The US Media and the 1993 War Against Iraq', in Yahya R. Kamalipour (ed.) *The US media and the Middle East: Image and Perception*. Westport, CT: Greenwood Press, pp. 105–18.

King, Will (1999) [untitled] in Peter Goff (ed.) *The Kosovo News and Propaganda War*. Vienna: International Press Institute, pp. 121–3.

Klare, Michael (1998) 'The Rise and Fall of the "Rogue Doctrine". The Pentagon's Quest for a Post-Cold War Military Strategy', *Middle East Report*, No. 208, pp. 12–15 and 47.

Knightley, Phillip (1986) *The Second Oldest Profession: The Spy as Bureaucrat, Patriot, Fantasist and Whore*. London: Andre Deutsch.

—— (1989) *The First Casualty* (Second Edition). London: Pan.

Lévy, Bernard-Henri (1996) *Le Lys et la Cendre: Journal d'un Ecrivain au Temps de la Guerre de Bosnie*. Paris: Grasset.

Lewis, Peter and Corinne Pearlman (1986) *Media and Power*. London: Camden Press.

Little, David (1994) *Sri Lanka: The Invention of Enmity*. Washington, DC: US Institute of Peace.

Luckham, Robin (1983) 'Of Arms and Culture', *Current Research on Peace and Violence IV*; Tampere, Finland, pp. 1–63.

Maass, Peter (1996) *Love Thy Neighbour: A Story of War*. London: Papermac.

MacArthur, John R. (1993) *Second Front: Censorship and Propaganda in the Gulf War*. Berkeley, CA: University of California Press.

MacKenzie, John (1984) *Propaganda and empire: The manipulation of British public opinion 1880–1960*. Manchester: Manchester University Press.

McNair, Brian (1995) *An Introduction to Political Communication*. London: Routledge.

Michal, Wolfgang (1999) 'Orientalische Fragen. Deutschlands Rolle im Kosovo-Krieg', in Klaus Bittermann and Thomas Deichmann (eds) *Wie Dr. Joseph Fischer lernte, die Bombe zu lieben. Die Grünen, die SPD, die Nato und der Krieg auf dem Balkan*. Berlin: Tiamat, pp. 77–84.

Moilanen, Jon H. (1998–99) 'Building 21st-Century Leaders', *Military Review*, Vol. LXXVIII, No. 6, December–February, pp. 58–67.

Morrison, David and Howard Tumber (1988) *Journalists at War: The Dynamics of News Reporting in the Falklands Conflict*. London: Sage.

Nambiar, Satish (1999) 'Nato Celebrates its Fiftieth Anniversary by Destroying Yugoslavia', *Mediterranean Quarterly*, Vol. 10, No. 3, Summer, pp. 15–24.

Øberg, Jan (1999) *Preventing Peace. Sixty Examples of Conflict Mismanagement in Former Yugoslavia since 1991*. Lund: Transnational Foundation for Peace and Future Research.

Owen, David (1996) *Balkan Odyssey*. London: Indigo.

Pavkovic, Aleksandar (1997) *The Fragmentation of Yugoslavia*. New York: St. Martin's Press.

Paxman, Jeremy (1990) *Friends in High Places: Who Rules Britain?* London: Michael Joseph.

Peak, Steve (1982) 'Britain's Military Adventures', *Pacifist*, Vol. 20, No. 10.

Petras, James and Steve Vieux (1996) 'Bosnia and the Revival of US Hegemony', *New Left Review*, No. 218, pp. 16–17.

Prades, John (1986) *Presidents' Secret Wars: CIA and Pentagon Covert Operations from World War II through Iranscan*. New York: William Morrow.

Reginald, R. and Dr Jeffrey M. Elliot (1985) *Tempest in a Teacup*. San Bernardino, CA: Borgo Press.

Reul, Sabine (1999) 'Wir sind bereit! Vom Aufbruch in Bonn zum Aufbruch auf dem Balkan', in Klaus Bittermann and Thomas Deichmann (eds), *Wie Dr. Joseph Fischer lernte, die Bombe zu lieben. Die Grünen, die SPD, die Nato und der Krieg auf dem Balkan*. Berlin: Tiamat, pp. 185–93.

Rieff, David (1995) *Slaughterhouse: Bosnia and the Failure of the West*. London: Vintage.

Robertson, Geoffrey (1999) *Crimes Against Humanity: The Struggle for Global Justice*. London: Penguin.

Saighal, Vinod (1998) 'Subcontinental Realities at the Turn of the Century', *United Services Institution Journal*, Vol. 128, No. 533, July–September, pp. 456–74.

Schostak, John (1993) *Dirty Marks: The Education of Self, Media and Popular Culture*. London: Pluto Press.

Shaw, Martin (1987) 'Rise and Fall of the Military-democratic State 1940–1985', in Martin Shaw and Colin Creighton (eds) *The Sociology of War and Peace*. London: Pluto Press, pp. 143–58.

Silber, Laura and Allan Little (1996) *The Death of Yugoslavia* (Second Edition). London: Penguin.

Simpson, John (1998) *Strange Places, Questionable People*. London: Macmillan.

Sloyan, Patrick J. (1999) 'The Fog of War', *American Journalism Review*, June. [http://ajr.newslink.org/ajrsloyjune99.html]

Smith, Robert Freeman (1994) *The Caribbean World and the United States: Mixing Rum and Coca-Cola*. New York: Twayne Publishers.

Stech, Frank J. (1994) 'Winning CNN Wars', *Parameters*, Autumn, pp. 37–56.

Stephan, Cora (1999) 'Das Wissen um die Ungewißheit des Sieges', *Novo*, No. 42, September–October, pp. 23–5. [http://www.novo-magazin.de]

Swift, Richard (1999) 'Lies and the Laptop Bombardier' *New Internationalist*, No. 314, July, pp. 24–5.

Taylor, Philip M. (1992) *War and the Media: Propaganda and Persuasion in the Gulf War*. Manchester: Manchester University Press.

Thomas, Robert (1999) *Serbia Under Milosevic*. London: Hurst.

Thomson, Alex (1992) *Smokescreen: The Media, the Censors and the Gulf.* Tunbridge Wells: Laburnham Books.

Treverton, Gregory F. (1987) *Covert Action: The CIA and the Limits of American Intervention in the Post-war World.* London: I. B. Tauris.

Védrine, Hubert (1996) *Les Mondes de François Mitterrand: A l'Elysée 1981–1995.* Paris: Fayard.

Verdery, Katherine (1996) 'Nationalism, Postsocialism, and Space in Eastern Europe', *Social Research*, Vol. 63, No. 1, pp. 82–3.

Vickers, Miranda (1998) *Between Serb and Albanian: A History of Kosovo.* London: Hurst.

Wesley, Michael (1997) *Casualties of the New World Order: The Causes of Failure of UN Missions.* Basingstoke: Macmillan.

Willey, Barry E. (1998–99) 'The Military–Media Connection: For Better or For Worse', *Military Review*, Vol. LXXVIII, No. 6, December–February, pp. 14–20.

Woodward, Bob (1987) *Veil: The Secret Wars of the CIA.* London: Simon & Schuster.

Woodward, Susan (1995) *Balkan Tragedy: Chaos and Dissolution after the Cold War.* Washington, DC: Brookings Institution.

Zimmermann, Warren (1995) 'The Last Ambassador: A Memoir of the Collapse of Yugoslavia', *Foreign Affairs*, Vol. 74, No. 2, pp. 2–20.

Zumach, Andreas (1999) '80 Prozent unserer Vorstellungen werden durchgepeitscht', in Thomas Schmid (ed.) *Krieg im Kosovo.* Reinbek bei Hamburg: Rowohlt Taschenbuch Verlag, pp. 63–81.

Index